Made in Lancashire

Made in Lancashire

A Collective Biography of Assisted Migrants
from Lancashire to Victoria
1852–1853

Richard Turner

MONASH
UNIVERSITY
PUBLISHING

Made in Lancashire: A Collective Biography of Assisted Migrants from Lancashire to Victoria 1852–1853

© Copyright 2021 Richard Turner

All rights reserved. Apart from any uses permitted by Australia's Copyright Act 1968, no part of this book may be reproduced by any process without prior written permission from the copyright owners. Inquiries should be directed to the publisher.

Monash University Publishing
Matheson Library Annexe
40 Exhibition Walk
Monash University
Clayton, Victoria 3800, Australia
publishing.monash.edu

Monash University Publishing brings to the world publications which advance the best traditions of humane and enlightened thought.

Monash University Publishing titles pass through a rigorous process of independent peer review.

ISBN: 9781922464361 (paperback)
ISBN: 9781922464378 (pdf)
ISBN: 9781922464385 (epub)

Design: Les Thomas

Typesetter: Jo Mullins

Cover image: Emigrants embarking from Great Britain. Wood engraving published in *The Australasian Sketcher* (Melbourne: Alfred May and Alfred Martin Ebsworth). State Library of Victoria, A/S18/12/80/sup.

A catalogue record for this book is available from the National Library of Australia.

CONTENTS

List of Figures..vi
List of Illustrations...viii
Abbreviations..x
Acknowledgements: 'Bring Up the Bones'..........................xi

1 The Best of Our Population: An Introduction.................1
2 Populating the Biography: An Overview of the Primary
   Source Records...16
3 A Quite Unprecedented Achievement: The Colonial Land
   & Emigration Commission as Migration Agents................35
4 Made in Lancashire...57
5 Cooperatives and Building Society Shares: From Revolution
   to Reformation in the Greater Manchester Area..............77
6 Australy for Ever..89
7 The Golden Lands..108
8 Lives from the Diggings...................................129
9 Free Selection and Free Grass.............................147
10 An Advancing Civilisation.................................170
11 Marvellous Melbourne......................................190
12 We Did Not Come All This Way to Tug Forelocks:
   A Conclusion..209

Notes...214
Bibliography..232
Index...238
About the Author..244

LIST OF FIGURES

Fig. 1.1   Assisted migrants to Victoria, 1839–1871 5

Fig. 1.2   English and Welsh emigrants, 1821–1889 9

Fig. 2.1. Number of Lancashire cohort from *Register* identified and not identified in the 1851 English and Welsh Census 20

Fig. 2.2. Number of Lancashire migrants featured in collective biography in comparison to those listed in *Register* and "identified in 1851 English and Welsh Census 32

Fig. 3.1. Assisted and unassisted migration from UK, 1852–1854 40

Fig. 3.2. Migration from UK to Victoria, 1848–1854 40

Fig. 3.3. Payments towards passage required of government-assisted migrants 49

Fig. 3.4. Minimum prescribed clothing for migrants 49

Fig. 4.1. Total numbers by family status and nationality 60

Fig. 4.2. Familial makeup of Lancashire migrants recorded in *Register* . . 61

Fig. 4.3. Familial makeup of Lancashire migrants identified in 1851 Census 62

Fig. 4.4. Male occupations as recorded in *Register* 63

Fig. 4.5. Male occupations as identified in 1851 Census 63

Fig. 4.6. Married women recorded as employed in 1851 Census 69

Fig 6.1.   Where cohort went within 5–6 years of disembarkation 93

Fig. 7.1. Population on goldfields by gender and age 110

Fig. 7.2. Gold yield per annum 1851–1871 117

Fig. 7.3. Major occupations in mining districts from the 1854, 1857, 1861 and 1871 censuses 118

Fig. 7.4. Goldmining occupations as returned in the 1854, 1857, 1861 and 1871 censuses 118

Fig. 7.5. Population of mining districts by dwelling type in the 1857, 1861 and 1871 censuses. 127

LIST OF ILLUSTRATIONS

Bears Lagoon Hotel built by Joseph Doody and his sons 1

Richard Seddon. 4

Australian sketches, the Melbourne Immigrants' Home 16

Assisted migrants preparing to board a ship for Victoria 35

Birkenhead Emigration Depot 39

On the deck of an Australian emigrant ship. 54

19th Century Southern Lancashire Industrial Landscape circa 1850. . . . 57

Chartist Demonstration 1848. 59

'Heroic' young women power-loom weavers 68

Mellor Street, Ardwick 77

Boys employed in a Manchester textile factory circa 1847 82

Whitworth Street Cleaning Machine. 86

Canvas Town, Melbourne. 89

Great meeting of gold diggers, Mount Alexandria. 99

Graham Berry, Family Grocer, 1850 104

The reality of the gold diggers lives was not the romance of the
free-spirited digger 108

New Chum Line of Reef, Bendigo. 112

A remarkable experiment in democracy – a Mining Board election. . . . 121

The Great Western Company's quartz crushing and amalgamating
mill 129

Eldorado Gold Mine, a Wellington Company's quartz mine 133

List of Illustrations

Descendants of the Proctors believe this portrays Mary Butler and three of her children 144

The ideal of the yeoman farmer. 147

The reality – A selector's new home 152

Builders of a New Nation. Bears Lagoon women. 164

Bridge Street, looking east from Sturt Street, Ballarat, c. 1886-1887. . . . 170

Cobrico Cheese Factory, Terang, c 1900. 176

Central School, Bendigo. 182

Marvellous Melbourne. One of the great suburban land auctions of the 1880s. 190

Hoddle Street early 1860s. 195

Hoddle Street, 1886 195

Bluestone quarry where John Holt was to become foreman, c 1866 196

Berry's hard working sons of toil. Eight hour demonstration in Melbourne's Zoological Gardens in 1864. 209

ABBREVIATIONS

ADB	*Australian Dictionary of Biography*
BDM VIC	The Victorian Register of Births, Deaths and Marriages
BPP	British Parliamentary Papers
CLEC	Colonial Land and Emigration Commission
GRO	General Register Office of England and Wales
NLA	National Library of Australia
NSW	New South Wales
NZ	New Zealand
PRO	Public Records Office of England and Wales
PROV	Public Records Office of Victoria
SLV	State Library of Victoria
Register	*Register of Assisted British Immigrants 1839–1871*
UK	United Kingdom of Great Britain and Ireland
US	United States of America
VPP	Victorian Parliamentary Papers

ACKNOWLEDGEMENTS

'Bring Up the Bones'

In 2009, as my film career collapsed around me, I took up an offer of refuge in Bendigo from Tom Pender, a close friend and videographer on a couple of my film projects, and his father, Carl Pender, a Vietnam vet. It was an odd friendship but it was what got me back on my feet and energised again. Shortly after I settled in Bendigo, Tom took me out to the Bendigo campus of La Trobe University where he was studying for a fine arts degree in photography. While waiting for him to do whatever he needed to do that day, I went exploring.

At some point I ended up in the Humanities Building, known to all, I later discovered, as Fawlty Towers for its dodgy construction. Somehow I ended up walking out enrolled in a Humanities degree. Among the courses I took in my first semester was 'Out West & Down Under', a comparative history study of the rural Midwest of the United States and Victoria beyond the Great Dividing Range, run by Charles Fahey. It was my introduction to the Public Records Office of Victoria (PROV) and to the delights of the primary research material that could be found in archives such as the PROV. Thus began my journey to write this book.

This book would not have been possible without Charles Fahey's support, who, as one prominent historian said, knows where all the 'bodies are buried'. Nor would it have been possible without the support of two others who supervised me through the writing of my thesis on which this book is based: Emma Robinson, who was always ready to kick me if I didn't pay enough attention to women; and Jennifer Jones, who rather more kindly admonished me for not paying attention to religious belief. I also thank the La Trobe University History Department for providing valuable support. I'd like to thank my old and good friends: the author Martin Edmond, who read my manuscript and provided excellent advice through the publication process; and Larry Galbraith, who was always there to support me when I was working on my thesis.

Of course none of this would have been possible without the Archives. Archival institutions are always an endangered species, among the first to be deprived of funding by any government, state and local, seeking easy budgetary cuts. I'd especially like to acknowledge the contribution of the PROV, the State Library of Victoria (SLV), the Public Records Office (PRO) in Kew (UK), the Manchester City Library and Archives, the Maritime Museum on the Mersey side, and the British Library. The staff in all these institutions went beyond the call of duty to help me with my research.

My thanks to Monash University Publishing and their publishing team, Greg Bain, Sam van der Plank, Joanne Mullins and Les Thomas, who have been generous in their support. Finally, I would like to thank Julia Farrell who has been a diligent and exacting copy editor helping me greatly improve the final manuscript.

Chapter 1

THE BEST OF OUR POPULATION

An Introduction

Bears Lagoon Hotel built by Joseph Doody and his sons, who are portrayed in this photograph.
Courtesy of the East Loddon Historical Society.

> *I have continually been worried by the Messrs Ettershank ever since I first selected. Whether this may be a <u>ruse</u> on their part to cause me to lose my land altogether the land is even more preferable to us than the £5000 as it is taken up as a permanent home for my family. Moreover I may state that land is letting up here with right of purchase at £10 per acre and my father and I have 100 acres under crops and fallow and as I have nothing else to depend upon now it would be a matter of the most serious consequences if I should be deposed of the land after spending so much time and money in improving it to its present state of a working proposition.*
>
> William Doody, Bears Lagoon. Letter to the Minister of Lands, 28 October 1877[1]

William Doody was just 22 years old when he complained to the Minister of Lands for the Crown Colony of Victoria about his avaricious neighbour, John Ettershank. William, his father Joseph Doody, and neighbouring small farmers and cultivators (selectors) had been locked in conflict for the previous five years with pastoral interests (squatters) who grazed large herds of sheep across much of Victoria. In this David and Goliath struggle, the squatters were represented by John Ettershank, a member of the powerful Legislative Council (Upper House) in the self-governing colony.

It would be another three years before the conflict was decided in favour of the Doodys and their fellow selectors. By this time Joseph Doody was dying from mercury poisoning, or Mad Hatter's syndrome, contracted on the goldfields. William believed that his father had been worn out by the struggle. But the Doody family never regretted fighting for what they believed was the very reason for migrating to this brave new world.

William Doody was born in 1855 on the goldfields of Sandhurst, or Bendigo, as it later became known. His father, Joseph, and mother, Lucy, had arrived in Victoria two years earlier on the *Thames*, part of a shipload of assisted migrants from the British Isles. They were aged in their mid-20s at the time and had been born in Manchester, where both worked in skilled positions in the industries then expanding into the suburb of Ardwick. The new home the couple rented in Ardwick marked them out as being from the more prosperous sections of the Manchester working class. On the surface there seemed no compelling reason for them to choose to make the perilous voyage – they lost one child on the journey and another a year later – for an uncertain future in the newly formed Colony of Victoria. However, the discovery of gold must have been a powerful lure.

Between 1 July 1852 and 30 June 1853, 21,694 assisted migrants arrived in Victoria on 63 ships, representing an average of 5.25 ships per month. It was by far the biggest intake of assisted migrants in any single 12-month period until the post–World War II era, and coincided with the sudden surge in the number of unassisted migrants arriving and heading for the goldfields. Of those assisted migrants, 225 men, women and children were identified in the shipping records as being from Lancashire, among them Joseph, Lucy and their daughter (also Lucy), who disembarked in March 1853 in Melbourne. Almost all these Lancashire migrants were from the southern third of the old Lancashire County (pre-1972 borders). It is these Lancashire migrants whose collective biographical stories are explored in this book.

Joseph, while not striking it rich, prospered on the goldfields, and it was this hard-won prosperity that enabled him, his sons and others like them to fight their wars with the squatters, rich merchants and conservative politicians. Alfred Deakin, Australia's second Prime Minister and the son of a Victorian gold-digger, famously said:

> Why do you all but ignore the discovery of gold and its many consequences? You know perfectly well what it meant to us materially … but have not realised perhaps the extent to which it revolutionised our early politics… It gave us a large proportion of the best of our population, men with a far wider and more advanced liberalism.[2]

This book explores what Deakin meant by 'the best of our population' and 'men with a far wider and more advanced liberalism', and why the assisted migrants were left out of the story by Australian historians.

The impetus for this book on those South Lancashire migrants is drawn from the early biography of Richard Seddon. Seddon was, and remains, New Zealand's longest-serving Premier or Prime Minister (1893–1906), leading a government that, according to Keith Sinclair, 'made New Zealand for a time the most radical state in the world'.[3] Subsequent mythologising emphasised Seddon's individual exceptionalism by sidelining family and community. Yet Seddon is a product of a colonising process, which rendered kinship and community ties more prominent. Seddon's extraordinary political achievement can only really be understood by exploring in depth his origins in both entrepreneurial rural tenant farming and the industrial working classes at the very epicentre of the Industrial Revolution in South Lancashire. This book attempts to understand why certain members of his family, wider kinship groups and neighbourhood community networks chose to migrate to the new worlds, and to answer questions such as: How imbued were they by the Chartist ideals of small proprietorship, home ownership and respectability? How much were they lured by the prospect of rapid social mobility? Did they have visions of a new and better Britain?

Critical to any discussion of the migrants' views of a new and better Britain is the Chartist movement and what exactly it encompassed. Pickering believes that Australian historians' assessments of the influence of Chartism in Australia have been invariably based upon the 'Six Point Charter' for democratic reform.[4] In recent years, historians have rescued British Chartism from this narrowly defined program and demonstrated the breadth of its aspirations. Chartist schemes for collective self-improvement included education, health, rural resettlement and an informal economy based on the rituals of mutuality, family obligation and cooperative consumerism.[5] It is these aspirations that influence my discussion of Chartism and its export to Victoria with the migrant cohort.

Richard Seddon.
Photographer: Patricia Susan Fry.
Ref:1/2-058363-F, Alexander Turnbull Library, Wellington, N.Z.

Port Phillip Bay and Gold

A British Act of Parliament separating the territory previously known as the Port Phillip District from the Colony of New South Wales (NSW), and establishing the new Colony of Victoria, was proclaimed on 5 August 1850. It was to be another 11 months before a reluctant NSW Legislative Council passed the enabling legislation. Writs for the election of Victoria's first Legislative Council were issued on 1 July 1851.[6]

Remarkably, just six days later, on 7 July 1851, the *Geelong Advertiser* announced the discovery of gold at Clunes.[7] Within a few months, rich finds of gold were also discovered at Ballarat, Mount Alexander and Sandhurst (Bendigo), sparking one of history's greatest gold rushes. Between 1851 and 1860, one-third of the world's output of gold came from Victoria.[8]

It is hardly surprising to find that such quantities of gold transformed a colonial economy that had previously been largely dependent on wool and the pastoralists who ran large properties outside Melbourne. Indeed, Geoffrey Serle makes the point that, until the 'great blessing' of the discovery of gold in commercial quantities, the more thoughtful and responsible citizens of Victoria were gravely worried that 'the ironic consequences of separation were to be ruin and stagnation'.[9] It was perhaps a further irony that these same thoughtful and responsible citizens would later agree with the Reverend Mereweather's comment that gold so transformed society that 'we have here the French Revolution without the guillotine'.[10]

One of the greatest transformations was simply the huge influx of people into the colony, as Figure 1.1 below demonstrates.[11] Between 1837 and 1850, a total of 106,592 immigrants were recorded as arriving in NSW, including the Port Phillip District. Assisted immigration totalling 85,106 people far outweighed unassisted immigration, at only 26,942.[12]

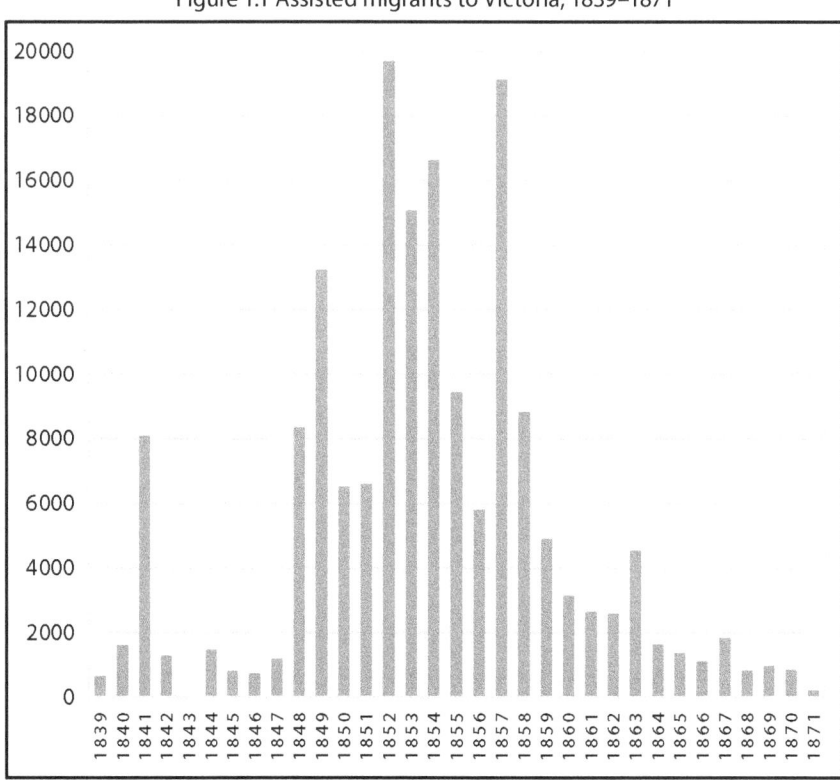

Figure 1.1 Assisted migrants to Victoria, 1839–1871

Source: PROV VPRS 7310

In the next 10-year period, between 1851 and 1860, more than five times that number arrived in Victoria, with the total of all immigrants being 584,000 men, women and children. Of these, 88,100 were assisted immigrants, with the balance of 495,900 being unassisted immigrants.[13]

It is noteworthy that, despite the huge influxes of unassisted immigrants, the Victorian Government substantially increased the amount of money it was willing to pay to bring assisted migrants over from Britain in the period 1852 to 1857. When studying the *Register of Assisted British Immigrants 1839–1871* (hereafter the *Register*) and much of the available contemporary newspaper commentary, it is not surprising that most historians of early colonial Victoria have followed Serle's lead in assuming that this sudden sharp increase in assisted migration, if they noticed it at all, was a response to the labour shortages faced by pastoralists caused by workers deserting their employ for the goldfields.[14]

For the year July 1852 to June 1853, the *Register* records that more than 60% of adult male occupations were rural labourers, while contemporaries regarded most of the single adult women as little better than doxies (prostitutes), the dregs of poorhouses.[15] In the eyes of 'free' colonists', the assisted migrants were no better than transported convicts. This explains why many Victorian historians such as Bate, Blainey and Broome have followed Serle's lead in dismissing the economic importance of assisted migration to Victoria after the discovery of gold.[16] Such historians have painted these migrants as the unskilled poor and not of the calibre of the better skilled working-class and middle-class unassisted migrants who were by then pouring into the colony.

This picture of the assisted migrant has been sharply challenged in recent works by historians such as Graeme Davison, David Fitzpatrick, Robin Haines and Eric Richards.[17] Haines's scholarship is particularly important as it examined a substantial cross-section of assisted migrants to emphatically conclude that assisted migrants were not 'third-rate free-loading immigrants' but on the whole shared similar socioeconomic origins with unassisted immigrants travelling steerage to Australia, Canada, New Zealand and the United States of America (US) during the same period.[18]

Eric Richards recently argued that in the history of British Imperialism 'emigration of the British people is normally relegated to a footnote … in the general life of the nation and in the history of British imperialism'.[19] In the case of assisted migrants, consigned to the dustbins of the Australian story is perhaps a more apt description. Yet a third of migrants from British ports arriving in Victoria in the years 1852 to 1857 were assisted migrants. For this reason it is worth examining more closely who they were and what we can ascertain about their motivations in migrating, and the substantial roles they played in the building of a nation, in both Victoria and Australia.

I have done this for the 225 Lancashire assisted migrants through the writing of a collective biography that explores their socioeconomic origins at a county, town and parish level in England, as well as their settlement patterns and the 'new planting of the ideas, aspirations and institutions they found meaningful in their homelands'.[20] This book demonstrates that, on the whole, these Lancashire migrants were from the semi-skilled and skilled industrial working classes who were prospering from the Industrial Revolution. They were of the same calibre of the unassisted migrant, who Davison describes as drawn from the:

> mobile, ambitious but 'uneasy' stratum of the British working class that congregated … in zones of insecure craft or semiskilled Labor on the inner perimeter of London and other large towns.[21]

As later chapters explore, they played a significant role in shaping the political, social and cultural development of Victoria and Australia, particularly in establishing themselves as a substantial proportion of the small-property-owning classes.

Funding for government-assisted immigrants during this period was provided from monies raised by the sale or lease of lands in the colonies. Well before the discovery of gold, and in the build-up to separation from NSW, Charles La Trobe, who would become the first Governor of Victoria, was flagging to the Colonial Office that he wanted to substantially increase the amount of land funds being used for assisted migration. Unlike NSW, the soon-to-be-independent Colony of Victoria had a large surplus in the land funds held by the Exchequer of the United Kingdom (UK).[22]

It was clear that, by the late 1840s, prior to the discovery of gold, skilled labour was already becoming scarce. Melbourne newspapers, throughout the second half of the 1840s, were filled with complaints about the quality of the available workforce and lack of skilled tradesmen, while in 'surviving letters of pastoralists there were many complaints about the scarcity and inefficiency of shepherds'. All wanted a better class of free migrant and urged La Trobe to act.[23] Act La Trobe did, as did the Colonial Office through the Colonial Land and Emigration Commission (CLEC). The discovery of gold, and the rather short-lived labour shortage caused by the gold rush, provided them with an excuse to pursue agendas other than that called for by established colonists in Victoria.

Gold was clearly a paramount factor in motivating the migration of James Seddon, his family and the eight other Lancastrian families, including the Doodys, who sailed on the *Thames* from Liverpool to Victoria in November 1852. However, it is important to consider what other underlying motives may have led to the Seddon family's decision to undertake the arduous four-month sea voyage to the new colony.[24] This involves exploring the usefulness of classic push-pull models of migration, and asking what other types of approaches may help us connect an individual's migration decision to patterns of migration within the societies of departure at a local, regional and national level to patterns of settlement in the receiving society.[25]

Leaving England

In the century between the end of the Napoleonic Wars in 1814 and the outbreak of the Great War in 1914, approximately 52 million migrants left Europe to make new homes in the Americas and other parts of the world, including the temperate anglophone colonies of Australia, New Zealand and South Africa. More than 10 million, or 20%, of these migrants were British, excluding the Irish who made up another 6 million.[26] Until well into the second half of the 20th century, historical explanations of this 'great migration' were dominated by neoclassical economic explanations of the motivation to migrate.[27]

It was through these hypotheses that push-pull models of migration were developed. The primary economic model, which Baines calls 'the international economy model', argues that the direction of migration flows is determined by the well-known factors of supply and demand.[28] In the 19th century, European countries had abundant supplies of capital and labour relative to available natural resources. However, there were overseas regions – mainly the Americas and the anglophone colonies – where natural resources were abundant but capital and labour scarce. This led to the redistribution of population and capital to those regions. This model has developed many variants as its initial deficiencies became apparent.

All these variants are usually presented by historians as aspects of the simple to understand 'push-pull', or 'rational choice', model perceived to account for the motivations of the individual migrant. The concept of push-pull assumes that potential migrants are in possession of sufficient information to make a rational judgement as to whether their lifetime 'welfare' – that is, all the benefits available to them including material and non-material – would be greater if they emigrated than if they stayed at home. As Baines notes, this is a huge assumption because:

the majority of emigrants – i.e. those who were not escaping from pogrom or famine – would have had great difficulty in explaining whether they had been 'pushed' out of Europe or 'pulled' towards their destination.[29]

If push-pull theories of 'motivations' dominated the European experience it would be expected that emigration rates from individual European countries would be inversely related to their degree or rate of economic development. Yet this was not the case; and it is with English migration that the inadequacy of classical economic theories of emigrant motivation are most strikingly revealed, as Figure 1.2 demonstrates.

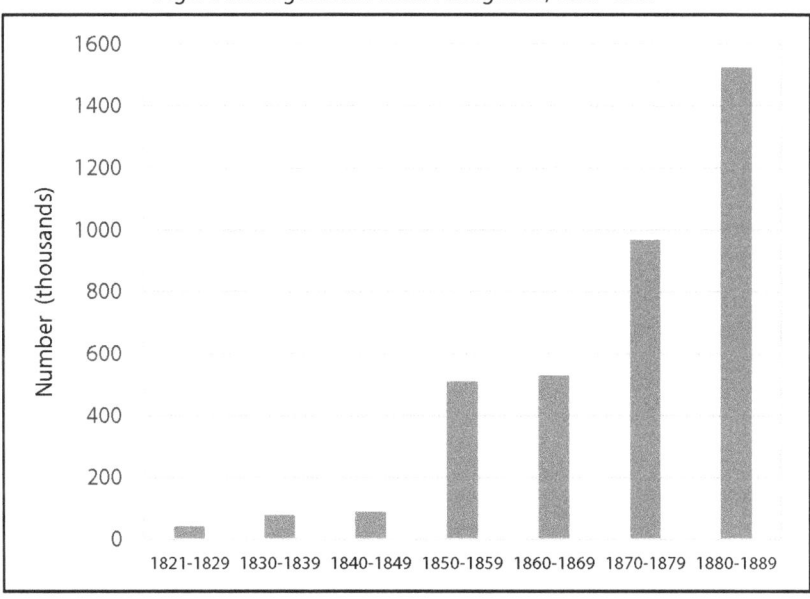

Figure 1.2 English and Welsh emigrants, 1821–1889

Source: Baines, Migration in a Mature Economy, *Appendices 2 & 4.*

In every decade of the 19th century emigration from England increased. Charlotte Erickson noted that, in the three decades between 1820 and 1850, when its town and industrial bases were growing at their peak rates for the entire century, England experienced an emigration boom.[30] In the 1850s, the departure rate was nearly five times that of the previous decade. In the 1870s and 1880s, departures literally doubled over the previous decades. England had the fourth-highest emigration rate (3.72 persons per 1000) of all European countries after Ireland (11.6), Norway (5.38) and Scotland (5.16).[31]

This explosion in emigration from England should never have happened according to conventional emigration theory. From 1849, England entered a prolonged economic boom that lasted into the 1880s. This saw a maturing of its industrial base, labour shortages in high-wage regions, and a steady decline in the rate of population growth.[32]

Prior to the work of Erickson and Baines, historians either tended to treat 19th-century English migration as 'an embarrassing subject, best ignored', or analysed it in accordance with a set of social, economic and demographic variables that treated British migration as a single stream.[33] Richards argues that 'in the annals of economic history emigrants feature primarily as labour, respondent to the dictates of the emerging global economy'.[34] Baines identifies this as the main gap in the scholarship on British, and particularly English, emigration, arguing:

> the shortfall in cross section studies is particularly important because they are likely to throw doubt on the results of studies which treat all British emigration as part of a single stream.[35]

Baines was one of the first historians to break down English and Welsh emigration at a local cross-sectional level, in this case at a county level, starting with the decade 1861–1870.[36]

The estimates from this decade provide the closest available data to the year 1852–1853 covered by this book. The total level of emigration from England and Wales in 1861–1870 was also similar to that of the previous decade of 1851–1860. Baines's estimates demonstrate that it is almost as futile to seek an explanation for English migration by attempting to group counties according to common sets of socioeconomic variables as it was to treat migration as a single national stream. An example of this is provided by Erickson, who attempted to analyse British emigration patterns by grouping counties into low-wage agricultural, high-wage agricultural, low-wage industrial and high-wage industrial economies, and ended up highlighting the contradictions raised by such analysis.[37]

Lancashire had one of the highest rates of emigration, second only to London in the total number of emigrants. As a percentage of the total population of the county, the Lancashire emigration rate of 5.8% was well above the average rate for England, at 4.6%. Yet Yorkshire, next door to Lancashire and a main rival in the industrialisation stakes, had an emigration rate of 2.9% – well below the national average. Two other northern adjacent counties, Durham and

Northumberland, classified as high-wage industrial by Erickson, and which also border each other, further demonstrate the lack of correlation between economic determinants and emigration. At 12.1%, Durham experienced the highest rate of English emigration after Cornwall, while Northumberland's rate was a miserly 3.2%. Agricultural labourers, seeking overseas opportunities or land denied to them in a rapidly industrialising England, were long believed to make up a substantial proportion of emigrants in the 1850s and 1860s.[38] However, the figures for predominantly agricultural counties such as Berkshire (5.1%), Norfolk (2.2%), Herefordshire (6.4%) and Cambridgeshire (1.5%) present an equally patchy picture of rural labourers' desire and/or ability to emigrate.[39]

We are fortunate to have some detailed data on Cambridgeshire as the county was the subject of a major study by La Trobe University postgraduate student, Colin Holt, in the late 1980s. This study was undertaken along lines recommended by both Baines and Erickson.[40] Holt, while not questioning the then-predominant economic theories of migration, concludes that 'many other factors are necessary to turn these … thoughts [of migration] into action'.[41] The most important finding of Holt's study, though not recognised as such in his thesis, is just how much variation exists in the rate of emigration across the parishes of Cambridgeshire. Again, there is no consistency across shared social, economic or demographic variables.

Paul Hudson and David Mills, who took Holt's data and delved further to examine the circumstances of 164 men, women and children who migrated from Melborn, Cambridgeshire to Melbourne, Victoria, conclude:

> All but two of the emigrating households which could be located in the 1841 census returns lay within nodes of no more than 75 yards of a central household… Crucially this propinquity of emigrants was not a product of the Melborn housing market in 1841 … it is also possible to point to several [neighbouring] rows of cottages which contained no emigrants at all.[42]

Baines argues that the one thing we can be sure about was that 'there were psychological barriers to emigration that had to be overcome'.[43] Holt, Hudson and Mills claim that the crucial psychological factor in the decision to emigrate was the 'kin groupings who were willing to emigrate, reinforced by networks of friends who were also willing to go abroad'.[44]

I am not fully convinced by their arguments because there is still the crucial factor of an individual or family group taking that first step. Why did one kinship grouping or friendship network, and not a neighbouring group or network sharing exactly the same economic and social demographics, choose to migrate? Moreover, these studies all endeavour to fathom the motive of the 'emigrant' and not those of the 'immigrant'. A more useful exploration is one of the 'migrant' as a person concerned with being 'received' as much as with 'leaving'. The Seddons represent a classic example of a growing circle of friends and family who were 'received' into a society in which friends and family were already establishing themselves.

The studies discussed above point to the challenges migration poses for contemporary scholarship. Since the beginning of this century, migration studies have tended to be subsumed into the wider fields of 'empire' or 'transnational' studies. Investigation or discussion of British migration, especially English migration, has taken place almost entirely inside wider empire studies.[45] In their discussion of migrant motivation and experience, these works often produce contradictory findings, as the discussion is shaped each author's particular thematic. The strength of all these works, however, is that they tie the places of destination and places of origin to each other. They also all recognise that each individual's migration decision involves complex agencies that are not readily explained simply by 'rational choice' theorising. On the whole, they do not divide migration into an emigration–immigration dichotomy, which Harzig, Hoerder and Gabaccia argue was one of the major deficiencies of earlier migration historical discussion.[46]

New Plantings

Collective biography or prosopography is a well-known historical tool. In an excellent essay published over 40 years ago, Lawrence Stone lays out the many possible pitfalls of applying a prosopography approach, but argues that it 'may be most useful in identifying revolutions of rising expectations' and any popular movements of social, cultural, political or economic change that result.[47]

Many of the studies of particular migrant streams, both national and regional, or of groups of migrants, have either explicitly or implicitly relied on the techniques of prosopography to develop their studies and draw their conclusions, including most recently Richard Reid's 2012 study of Irish assisted migration to NSW, *Farewell My Children*.[48] However, many studies, like Reid's, reveal little about the socioeconomic origins of the migrants beyond what is recorded in the shipping records kept by all the Australian colonies, and do not attempt to follow the migrants' settlement patterns once disembarked. This book proposes by way of example a far more comprehensive and productive approach to Australian and New Zealand migration research, of which much more still needs to be done.

The Australian records for assisted migrants are rich in comparison to those for unassisted migrants. The mass digitisation of British census and other records over the past decade makes the task of tracing the migrants' local residential, social and cultural origins relatively easy compared to that faced by earlier historians. The raw computing power available today gives a historian the ability to arrange, organise and investigate with far greater complexity and variety than was possible for earlier pioneers of migration history such as Charlotte Erickson. This access to much wider range and variety of records, when combined with local historical studies, allows for far more detailed and close-up cross-sectional analysis of the complexities of agency underpinning migrant trajectories between societies and communities.

A methodological model that Harzig, Hoerder and Gabaccia call a 'systems approach to migrant trajectories' has been developed with the intention of providing a comprehensive framework with which to explore these complexities. This is the model adopted here. The 'systems approach' connects migration patterns in the society of departure at the local, regional and state levels to the patterns of the migrants' settlement in the societies and cultures receiving them. In *Victorian Gold Rushes* Weston Bate frames this approach through the concept of cultural transmission:

> By that is meant the transfer to Australia of old world institutions and ideas as part of the life experience of the migrants. An unusual mix of people was deposited. They achieved a new planting (onto pastoral foundations) of the ideas, aspirations and institutions they found meaningful in their homelands.[49]

The systems approach looks very much like prosopography. However, its supporters argue that it is intended to avoid one of the great failings of prosopography.

Many of the surviving records available to historians are concerned with ownership and transmission of property. This results in an over-emphasis on economics in any collective biography. A systems approach theoretically allows for the inclusion of a multitude of other factors, at micro and macro levels, in both the sending and receiving societies, which provides a counter-weight to the 'rational choice' economic theories of migration. It should be noted, however, that the migrants who populate this collective biography, once in Victoria, demonstrated an overwhelming desire to acquire, maintain and transmit property to their children, as evidenced by the abundant surviving property records. Indeed, Bate claims that 'goldfield communities had easily the highest level of homeownership in the world'.[50] The extract from the letter written by William Doody to the Minister for Lands that opened this chapter provides a prime but far from unique example of this desire.

A major question that arises when undertaking migration research is whether a systems approach or any other theoretical modelling is helpful in illuminating the decisions made in the sending and receiving countries by those who, on the whole, were a very remarkable set of characters. Just how much did individual bravery, daring, opportunism or foolhardiness impel the 19th-century English migrant? What role did these exceptional characters' traits or flaws, depending on one's perspective, play in shaping the receiving societies and cultures?

The government officials, shipping agents and sea captains involved in shipping the lower-order migrants, assisted or unassisted, in crowded steerage conditions on the long voyages to Australia and New Zealand lived in perpetual fear of revolt by these people. Yet the migrants showed remarkable discipline, stoicism and ability in organising themselves to make the best of their conditions.[51] In Australia and New Zealand they went on to build societies and cultures that, no matter how imperfectly, argued for a greater democracy and humanitarianism than that found in their home counties.

This is what the qualitative aspect of this historical narrative attempts to shed some light upon. Richard Seddon, for instance, was following in the footsteps of many uncles and cousins. Among his first ports of call in the colonies was Castlemaine, where various Seddons worked substantial gold licences in cooperative partnership with many other diggers. These Seddons have been buried by history, yet the existence of a 'Seddon' suburb and 'Seddon House' on the outskirts of Castlemaine are mute testaments to the role of this family in turning the goldmining communities of Forest Creek into a thriving regional centre that outlasted gold. As miners, shopkeepers, builders and farmers, the Seddons played a vital role in building that community.

On board the *Thames* with the Seddons were Joseph and Lucy Doody, father and mother of William Doody. There is a remarkable and rich primary source material for the Doodys from the time of Joseph Doody's birth in the London Road district of Manchester, to his climb to skilled plumber living in Ardwick, through the goldfields and on to the land at Bears Lagoon. The Doody family story illustrates many of the themes we see emerge from the stories of other families and individuals told in this biography.

Drawing on these themes it is possible to come to an understanding of the significant role the migrant cohort played at the local level in the socioeconomic development of Victoria, and to give human face, from a bottom-up perspective, to the momentous historical movements that shaped the colony. This is not a history of 'great' men and women, but it is the same history that drove the ambitions, ideals and politics of Australia's and New Zealand's political heroes such as Graham Berry, James McPherson Grant, George Grey, Henry Parkes and Richard Seddon. This book puts the Lancashire assisted migrants at the centre of the national stage.

Chapter 2

POPULATING THE BIOGRAPHY

An Overview of the Primary Source Records

Australian sketches, the Melbourne Immigrants' Home.
Australian Sketches by W. Ralston.
National Library of Australia, nla.obj-nla.obj-135890912.

The 'Wanata' was a Ship of 1160 Tons – her decks were of the average height of about 7 feet. She left Liverpool on the 10th of June with 821 passengers on board and arrived in Hobsons Bay on the 17th of September. Fever had broken out on the voyage from which and from other causes 39 deaths had occurred either during the voyage or soon after arrival. Of these who died 30 were children.

Extract from an inquest by the CLEC into the
high death toll on this voyage[1]

In 'British emigrants and the making of the Anglosphere' Richards suggests that English migrants are frequently perceived as 'awkward historical characters'. He argues that they are usually omitted from the English story altogether, or if they are lucky enough to be included they are relegated to 'the sidelines as spearholders'. He also asserts that, despite their huge numbers and extraordinary spread across three continents, they are 'rarely treated as prime movers in their own right', but are perceived as pawns on a chessboard, to be moved by 'the drivers of the so-called Anglosphere'.[2] Baines calculated that over 10 million people emigrated from England in the 'long nineteenth century'.[3] How do you resurrect the stories of the 200-odd Lancashire migrants from among those 10 million, especially as they were among the shiploads of assisted migrants who were, on the whole, despised by colonial elites and, too frequently, by Australian historians as 'lumpen masses'?[4]

The Lancashire migrant cohort seem to have left no surviving letters to relatives or friends, and no diaries or journals – the sources used by Richards, Haines, Davison and Fitzpatrick to resurrect some of the bottom-upward stories in support of their claim that government-assisted migrants were not the illiterate dross often portrayed. I therefore had to develop an alternative approach. This chapter provides an overview of the British and Australian primary source resources accessed as part of my research, how they were used in this collective biography, and how, as a result, the migrant stories that feature in this book took shape.

The Shipping Records

The starting point for the research was the *Register of Assisted Immigrants from UK 1839–1871*, primarily the *Register* books kept between July 1852 and June 1853. Erickson has noted that these records, in comparison to many other British migration sources, are 'rich on questions such as origins, occupations, family, age and literacy', making them a very useful tool.[5]

The *Register* records the first and last name of every landed immigrant (including children), age on arrival, the occupation of all males and all single women aged 14 years or more, county of origin, professed religion and denomination, and whether they could read and write. The records exclude the occupations of married women, presumably due to the societal expectation that these women were solely homemakers. This information was provided by the CLEC agents to each ship's captain upon the embarkation of the migrants for the voyage to Australia.

The records given to the ship captains were duly crosschecked by the Victorian immigration clerks with the migrants on disembarkation and entered into the *Register*. The original records made in Britain by the CLEC prior to embarkation have not survived. However, we can presume they recorded some of the information provided in the original applications for assisted migration passage. There is a notable discrepancy between occupations recorded in the *Register* and the *Census Returns of England and Wales 1851*.[6] This raises substantive questions which are explored in later chapters.

The immigration clerks in Victoria recorded what happened to the migrants upon their immediate release from the immigration depot, or 'disposal' as it was termed. As the gold rush gathered momentum, a growing number of migrants, especially families, went off on what the *Register* described as their 'own account'. A sufficient number of the migrants, however, are recorded in the *Register* as going directly from the depots into contract employment, which provide us with a snapshot of occupations, wages and employers.

In comparison, the unassisted migrant shipping records are notable for their lack of information or inaccuracy of the records. An example of this can be found by examining the entry for Richard Hall and his family, who came from Bury, Lancashire, and travelled to Victoria as steerage passengers on the *Kate*, leaving Liverpool in December 1852. Richard Hall's voyage was recorded in a wonderfully evocative diary that details the mistreatment of steerage passengers on ships carrying unassisted migrants to Victoria during the gold rush years. His diary accounts present a stark contrast to the treatment of assisted migrants on ships contracted by the CLEC (see Chapter 3).

Hall and most of the adult males listed on the same page of the records are recorded as being from Ireland, with no county mentioned, and with the occupation of farmer.[7] Yet Australian and English records confirm that Hall and his family were natives of Bury, and that he he had been a leading hand in a textile factory.[8] The question of why Hall and the others were recorded as farmers from Ireland cannot be answered. I doubt it was the passengers misrepresenting themselves, and the state of the handwriting in the ship's list handed to the immigration agents suggests a last-minute write-up by a rum-soaked ship's captain.

It would have been of great historical benefit to compare the identified cohort of assisted migrants with a selection of unassisted migrants from Lancashire in the year covered by this book. However, the paucity or total inaccuracy of information within the records for unassisted migrants handed to the Victorian immigration agents by ship captains at the conclusion of these voyages makes it almost impossible to draw a sample except where rare cases, like Hall's, where a diary or similar documentation exists.

How 'rich' are the assisted migrant records? Erickson, Baines and others have argued that the *Register* can tell us a lot about agricultural labourers who were migrating, as more than two-thirds of the adult male migrants are recorded as agricultural labourers or in rural artisanal occupations in the *Register*. This might indicate that the records are of little use for a discussion of migration by those not from rural backgrounds. However, almost all of the adult male Lancashire immigrants recorded as being agricultural labourers were in fact engaged in industrial occupations in the industrial belt of South Lancashire. It is clear from these records that those applying for assisted migration were smart enough and had the referees to game the system. How complicit in this was the CLEC is less clear, although later chapters suggest the Commission understood full well where and from whom the applications were coming.

What the records do is provide a wealth of information that allows us to cross-reference them with other primary source material, and to test and engage with some of the assumptions made by Australian historians about migration to Victoria in the gold rush period. Families with at least one child provide the best entry point into such research. These families are thus the key focus of this book.

UK and Lancashire Records

The 1851 English Census, taken just a year prior to the cohort's departure for Australia, was the most significant of the English records. It was also the first of the digitised records to provide a function for the addition of 'spouse' and/or 'child' to the parameters of a search.[9] There were 32 families among the cohort and 21 of these families with children could be identified with certainty, while 11 families could not be identified in the 1851 Census. There are a number of possible reasons why these families cannot be cross-referenced: some of the folios and pages of the census are badly damaged or missing; some homes and families may well have been missed during the collection of returns; some families may have been away on the night of the census and therefore not included; and some families may have been living in another county despite nominating their native county as Lancashire in the *Register*.

Regarding this last possible reason, it is not clear from the *Register* what 'Native County' meant to some prospective applicants for assisted passage. For the greater majority it would appear to have been understood as birthplace, with most of those identified also actually resident in Lancaster. But for one Scottish-born family and a small handful of others this was clearly perceived as meaning their place of residence.

Among the cohort were 17 married couples with no children who proved difficult to match with any certainty to persons recorded in the 1851 Census. It was only possible to match six couples with certainty, and three others with a degree of probability. There were eight couples for whom no records could provide a possible match. One intriguing aspect of this search of couples was the number of men and women who shared the same given names and were close in age. A consistent finding of the research was how few were the given names commonly used in this period of Lancashire history. One example of this is a young couple, James and Elizabeth Wood, who landed in Geelong on 22 December 1852.[10] The 1851 English Census lists two other couples bearing exactly the same given names and with ages within a year of the couple who landed in Victoria. One of these couples migrated to the US a few years later, causing considerable confusion for those attempting to track these two particular migrating couples. They have been frequently conflated in genealogical family trees created by websites such as *Ancestry*.

The final two groups within the migrant cohort are single adult males and females aged 14 years or older. It was expected that these persons would be difficult to identify in the 1851 Census Returns. However, readily identifiable were three of the teenage males, aged between 14 and 15 years, and two teenage females, aged 14 and 17 years. Five of the other seven males were additionally identified in the Census Returns. While the females proved more challenging to locate in the records, it was exciting to identify 15 of the other 31 single young women.

Figure 2.1. Number of Lancashire cohort from *Register* identified and not identified in the 1851 English and Welsh Census

Makeup	No. from *Register*	No. Identified in Census	No. Unidentified in Census
Married couples with children	33	22 (67%)	11 (33%)
Married couples with no children	17	8 (47%)	9 (53%)
Single adult males (14 years and over)	10	8 (80%)	2 (20%)
Single adult females (14 years and over)	33	17 (51%)	16 (49%)

Sources: PROV, Register of Assisted British Immigrants VPRS 7310, bks 6–10; PRO, Census Returns of England and Wales 1851 HO107.

The English Census provides a wealth of information regarding not only an individual's residence, occupation and birthplace but also the general makeup of the communities in which they resided. By tracking backwards and forwards in the pages surrounding an entry on an identified migrant, it is possible to draw a detailed picture of their local residential and socioeconomic origins. In the cases of identified migrants from Manchester and Liverpool it was possible to compare this information to local rate books and some very good local histories.[11]

The rate books of Ardwick in Manchester, from the early 1840s through to 1852, and those covering the new residential developments that followed the Liverpool docks expansion northward along the Mersey, provide a detailed picture of a growing and increasingly confident segment of the working classes. Although admittedly still a minority, they were settling into newer, bigger and more comfortable housing, and able to afford the higher rental costs associated with these new housing developments.

The British National Archives at Kew has archived a massive *Registry of Friendly Societies* that contains the formation deeds and annual records of all registered friendly societies, building societies, mutual societies and cooperatives from early in the 19th century. These records, particularly those for the Greater Manchester area, tend to reinforce a picture of a better-off working class working alongside a reforming middle class to improve conditions for themselves. It is from this segment that the migrant cohort were mostly drawn.

It was not possible to connect all the migrants, particularly the families, to these movements as thoroughly as Joseph and Lucy Doody could be connected (see Chapter 5). But, as so many of the cohort lived in areas where movements such as Chartism, unionism, cooperativism and mutuality were most active, and which contained the better skilled labouring and artisanal classes, this tends to confirm a picture of the cohort as made up of confident and opportunistic working-class migrants. These were families and individuals highly capable of taking advantage of the offer for assisted passage to Victoria to better themselves in the same way they had taken advantage of the new avenues opened up on the docks of Liverpool or in the rapidly growing manufacturing base of Greater Manchester.

Manchester City Library and Archives Centre proved a valuable resource, with much of its archival material now digitised. Another important resource in Manchester was the People's History Museum with its Labour Archives and Study Centre. The museum has a remarkable collection of banners carried in working-class and labour movement demonstrations from the height of the Chartist movement through to the present day.

The banners on display included those from the building societies, cooperatives and mutuals that thrived in the 19th century. The intricate work that went into the creation of these banners, their colour and artistry, attest to these organisations' importance in Lancashire history. There is a strong focus in the museum's collection on the growth of the cooperative movement in Manchester from the post–Napoleonic War period to the beginnings of World War II, which reinforced the importance of mutuality and cooperativism in the lives of the Lancashire working class and thus the migrant cohort.

The Lancashire Archives in Preston, the Liverpool Maritime Museum Archives, and the Liverpool City Library and Archives all provided a quantity of valuable primary resources. The Preston Archives has the only complete collection of all the published Piggott's Lancashire trade directories, which proved essential in telling the Doody story.

Both the Liverpool Maritime Museum and Liverpool City Archives hold a small volume of correspondence relating to the period of research, including dealings between the CLEC and shipping lines contracted to transport the assisted migrants, and a small number of letters from first- or second-class passengers travelling on the same ships as some of the assisted migrants. Finally, the British Library's digitised newspaper collection provided a major reservoir of non-government primary source material that illuminated a valuable chronology of the growing interest in and increasing excitement generated by the discovery of gold in Australia.

Of the CLEC records, only the inward and outward correspondence books of the Commissioners have been preserved and are now lodged in the National Archives at Kew. Sadly, the correspondence books of S. Walcott, who was the permanent secretary for the CLEC and a prolific correspondent during his tenure as secretary, were not preserved. For instance, he wrote to 6000 parish priests across England and Wales in a three-month period to explain the emigration program and obtain their support for the program. Fragments of his correspondence did survive and can be found in other archives. These letters demonstrate his concerns for the emigration program and the difficulties facing the CLEC in implementing it. The correspondence books of the Commissioners mainly contain communications with the Colonial Office, Exchequer and Australian colonial governors. This correspondence rounds out a picture of an energetic branch of the Colonial Office actively pursuing a colony-building agenda.

British Parliamentary Papers that proved useful included the annual reports of the CLEC, the Poor Law Board and the colonial governors. Reports by various parliamentary select committees have also provided useful material for this book.

Victorian Records

A question frequently asked by American and British historians is why Australian and New Zealand historians and sociologists do not use gathered street-by-street, household-by-household census data, as has become common in North America and British historical and socioeconomic studies. The answer is that they simply do not exist. The census authorities in the colonies and then countries of Australia and New Zealand had policies to destroy these collected household returns once the required global data had been extracted from them. Australian historians are thus deprived of what is proving to be one of the most useful tools in historical research on communities outside those of the elites. We need to make up for this absence through the inventive use of other primary sources.

Birth, Death and Marriage Certificates

The most important primary source for tracing the trajectory of migrants once they arrived in Victoria is the Victorian Registry of Births, Deaths and Marriages (BDM). Victoria was one of the earliest British colonies to systematically and comprehensively record this information and to issue a certificate for every birth, death and marriage. While the BDM registers were still somewhat patchy in the year of the arrival of the cohort of migrants, between the years of 1854 and 1856 the issuing of certificates became thorough and comprehensive across all of Victoria, including on the goldfields.

Registry entries for births contained information as to the name of the child, their sex, and when and where they were born; the father's name, occupation and county of birth; the mother's name, maiden name and county of birth; and where the parents were married. This register proved invaluable in the crosschecking against the English data. It was also an essential tool for tracing, over time, the movement of families across Victoria. Those who went to the goldfields were often highly perambulatory and birth certificates evidenced this movement around the various goldfields.

Death certificates were equally informative. These entries in the BDM recorded the name and occupation of the deceased; when and where the person died; the cause of death; the given and family name of the deceased's father and mother, if known; where the deceased was born and how long they had lived in Australia; the spouse's name and where they were married; and, lastly, any offspring in order of birth. While there are a number of 'unknowns' for the father and mother of deceased migrants from the cohort, the majority of death certificates do record the names and birthplaces of at least one of the parents left behind in England. Even when the spouse was predeceased, the surviving children were, on the whole, remarkably well informed about grandparents whom they had never met or known.

As with the BDM's birth certificates, death certificates also provided a valuable tool for crosschecking against English sources and assisted with deeper exploration of the English origins of the migrants. The occupation recorded at death can at times indicate how well a migrant prospered in the colony. For instance, 'Gentleman', as recorded in Alexander Trickett's death certificate, suggests that the deceased prospered in Victoria. However, it is striking how many of the males in the cohort were still being described as labourers upon their death. This is noticeable among the Liverpudlians, which may be suggestive of the cultural significance the 'free' labourer had in Liverpool (see Chapter 4). Several of these migrants, such as Thomas Bailey in Terang, had become substantial property owners and played significant roles in creating local industry.

There were fewer marriage certificates used in the research for this book because they simply pertained to adults, male or female, who were single when they arrived in Victoria. Typically they contained much less information than was found in birth and death certificates. This made cross-referencing against English primary sources difficult. However, in a few cases, such as that of Emma Hugo, Hannah Ashcroft, Ann Foy and John Holt, marriage certificates contributed snippets of information that led to further biographical information that filled out their stories in intriguing ways.

Finally, it also became clear that not all the single adults needed to formalise their relationships by marriage. At least four of the young women featured in this collective biography felt no need to marry, but, in each case, settled down with lifetime partners.

Wills and Probate

Wills, Probate and Administration files were significant primary documents used in building this collective biography. In Chapter 1, I discussed the dangers of prosopography and collective biography, particularly as the surviving primary sources are almost entirely documents and legal records dealing with property. However, as the acquisition of property, whether an urban freehold home or business premises, or a rural and regional property, was the overwhelming product of the cohort's settling of Victoria, probate documents and wills came into their own. These records contained essential information as to what property had been acquired, the pathways to acquisition of the property, the maintenance of the property, income or sustenance derived from the property, and the all-important transmission of the property to the migrants' children.

Prior to the introduction of the Torrens land titles system to Victoria from 1862 on, property outside the major Victorian cities of Melbourne and Geelong was usually identified by parish and a unit or block number. Detailed parish and township survey maps exist and are part of the PROV's digitised map collection. By identifying the block on these maps, the original owner can be identified as well as the method by which they acquired the block, whether it be via mining lease or licence, through the various selection schemes, or by auction.

In the case of selections, the property identification file numbers on the parish maps lead directly to a huge archive of land files kept by the PROV. Selection and other land files were in some cases highly revealing, and not just the dry documents recording the administrative and financial steps that led to acquisition of freehold. The sentiment surrounding the acquisition of the properties is frequently displayed in these documents. In the absence of diaries, journals or letters to friends and relatives, it was often these land files that revealed something of the personalities of these people, and of their neighbours and communities. The Doody family's and John and Jane Proctor's land files stand out in this regard. Through them it was possible to build a rich historical narrative, not only of the struggle over the land between selectors and squatters but also about the huge emotional investment made by migrants in the ownership of land (see Chapter 9).

Surprisingly, considering the effort required to acquire property, several of the adult male migrants died intestate. In some cases, leaving no will may have been a result of dying before the potential testator expected. In others, it may have been based on a natural presumption that the spouse and/or children would inherit and equitably divide the property. The probate documents in these intestate cases did reveal some detail about the nature of the relationships in these families. Overall, the presumption that the spouse and/or children would fairly deal with each other seems to have been valid. There was no intestate case where the family argued or litigated over the estate and the division of assets, suggesting that, even if they did not remain close, they accepted the mandated legal division of property.

Deceased estates subject to a will tended to follow a pattern where there was an equal division of all the assets among the male and female surviving children. A surviving wife was usually provided for in her lifetime, with the estate then being passed on to surviving children of the testator. In a small number of cases, such as that of Ann Wheeler (née Proctor), the widow controlled all the assets and income during her lifetime, either through a trust or other arrangement, with the estate only passing to the children upon her death.

Ann Wheeler, in her own will, endeavoured to tie up her husband's estate in trust for another five years. Clearly, she did not trust her children to preserve the hard-won estate. In only one case, that of Mary Ann Morey (née Trickett), did a woman with significant property assets of her own die before her husband. She bequeathed all her estate to her spouse.

A few of the wills identified led to some intriguing revelations about personal and family dynamics that did not always match the CLEC's (or indeed the colonial administration's) belief in the enduring nature of marriage. In a handful of cases there is also a suggestion of estranged siblings and even estrangement between parents and some of their children, but they are rare. Finally, there were several men among the adult generation of the migrant cohort who left no will and for which there was no probate. On first encountering this, I assumed that the husband and wife, who had gone to the goldfields, had been unsuccessful but stayed on in the township and died without property. This is not necessarily an incorrect assumption but testing it against other sources is required.

The opposite proved true in some cases, with parents turning over substantial assets to their children well before their deaths. Mary Ann Morey's father, Alexander Trickett, is one example in this regard; another is that of Jane (née Wiseman) and her husband John Cornthwaite. In the case of James Guy, he ensured that all five of his children owned property before he died, even though, on the surface, he did not seem to have been very successful as a goldminer. One of his daughters, a spinster, on her death owned a substantial cottage in Kew that he had purchased for her.

Another common reason for there being no probate where there is no will was that the children did not know they had to seek it to inherit the property. This was the case with the children of James Woods, who, in the early 1940s, discovered that they needed to seek probate and have the title transferred to their names when they attempted to sell a property outside Stieglitz.

Electoral Rolls

The inaugural Victorian parliamentary election for the Legislative Assembly and the Legislative Council was conducted in 1857. The Electoral Roll compiled in 1855–1856 for that election is largely intact and now in a digitised searchable database. While suffrage was limited for that election, it was still sufficiently wide to capture a substantial portion of the adult males of the migrant cohort who were enrolled to vote because of mining rights, or because they had acquired property soon after their disembarkation. Enthusiasm for enrolment was such that, in at least one case, an underage male, John Holt, enrolled to vote.

To be eligible to enrol to vote for members of the Legislative Assembly, males needed to be aged 21 years or more; have resided in the colony for at least one year; be able to read and write; to own property worth £50, rent property for at least £10 per annum, lease Crown lands (which included mining leases or licences), or have a salary of at least £100 per annum. Identifying individuals was occasionally difficult where there were two or more men bearing the same name in the same electoral district.[12] In some cases they were the same person, as multiple enrolments did occur where individuals qualified under different criteria. There are, however, several ways to cross-reference individual identities against other primary sources.

As would be expected, considering the number who went to the goldfields, mining leases or licences were the primary avenue for males of the cohort to qualify for inclusion on the electoral roll. Property ownership was a substantial runner-up, confirming a picture of the cohort's adult male migrants moving quickly into property ownership. An intriguing aspect is the number of employees of merchants and tradespeople who qualified for the roll because they were earning a salary of exactly £100 per annum when the average wage for those positions was no more than £60. Young John Holt mentioned above is one of those qualifying because he was earning the princely sum of £100 as a carter for a grocer on Smith Street, Collingwood.[13]

In succeeding Lower House elections, suffrage was extended to all men 21 years or older, making Victoria the first British government to grant a key demand of Chartism to its male residents. Ironically, however, there may have been fewer men on later rolls than in 1856 because residential qualifications were subsequently placed on the right to enrol. Rolls were compiled from rate books, with non-householders having to apply and prove their residential status in the electorate. However, these later Victorian electoral rolls are incomplete as local electoral officers frequently destroyed them after an election.

It is not until the early 20th century, immediately after Federation, that the electoral rolls come back into their own as a useful primary resource. The first Australian federal electoral roll is for the election of 1903, the first election after Federation. Suffrage was granted to all adults, male and female, 21 years of age or older. The Australian Electoral Commission has preserved this and all subsequent rolls very well, and they exist in a digitised searchable database form. This proved useful in tracing the movements and occupations of child migrants and their Australian-born siblings within Victoria and to other states.

Land Files, Rate Books and Mining Records

There is a bewildering array of land files reflecting the different ways land could be acquired in the colony, and the variety of legislation enacted to make land, particularly rural land, accessible to a substantial portion of Victoria's residents. Acquisition could be by auction in town and country prior to 1863; the conversion of mining leases on Crown land to freehold; the acquisition of land through the various Land (Selection) Acts from 1860 onwards; and through the Closer Settlements Acts that eventually replaced the Selection Acts. The direct purchase of freehold and leasehold property, particularly by ex-miners from the 1870s on, became an important entry into property ownership.

There are also other land files that document legal disputes, particularly matters of conflict between squatters and selectors. Navigating this collection often revealed that the drive to acquire property involved complex motives that could be as much emotional as material. One young woman, in a letter to the Lands Department, described how selecting allowed her to escape from her controlling father (see Chapter 9). The Doodys' struggle to secure their selection at Bears Lagoon demonstrates the richness of the land files, not just from a legal and financial point of view, but through the various letters, notes and comments they contain, including the letter from William Doody that opened Chapter 1.

Rate books are the final important resource to add to the land files. Although the books are often still scattered across Victoria, held by town and county local authorities or local historical societies, and thus difficult to access as a consolidated resource, those that were consulted provided significant detailed information regarding the development of the cities and townships, and the development of industry and commerce in the emerging urban environments. Apart from Davison's work in *The Rise and Fall of Marvellous Melbourne*, there has been little investigation of early artisanal culture in Melbourne and other large cities such as Ballarat and Bendigo. The rate books confirm the central place in the industrial, commercial and suburban development of these urban centres of the artisanal culture that arose during the gold rush period and continued through to the early 20th century. The Melbourne rate books, combined with trade directories, such as the *Commercial and General Melbourne Directory* and the *Melbourne and Suburban Directory*, tracked in detail the pursuit by several of the migrant cohort of urban and suburban dreams from the time they landed in Victoria.

The mining records are much more fragmentary, particularly in relation to individuals, the cooperatives they formed to work the diggings and their mining efforts. Compiled and published on a six-monthly basis, the *Surveyors Reports for the Mining Department* provide a reliable picture of the quantity of gold extracted from the various goldfields, the total numbers working the fields, and the types of mining (alluvial, deep lead, quartz) that were productive.

The reports do provide excellent material on the evolution of gold-digging and mining from the earliest days of the single independent digger sifting for alluvial gold with pan and cradle, to the industrial-scale alluvial puddling operations, and the capital- and labour-intensive deep lead and quartz mining operations. For instance, the surveyors reports reveal that puddling, a form of industrial-scale alluvial mining, produced more gold on 'played out' Mount Alexander fields in the 1860s than the individual diggers collectively extracted during the area's gold rush heyday.[14] This explains why many of the cohort of migrants who went to the goldfields continued as working miners well into the second half of the 1860s, while making a steady transition into industrial, commercial and agricultural pursuits in the same goldfield districts.

Compiled from *Victoria Government Gazettes*, the *Mining Shareholders Index 1857–1886* by Marion McAdie, a local goldfields historian, is a useful database detailing the original registration and listing of mining companies and their initial shareholders. This index provides a range of information about who among the migrant cohort were still pursuing mining ventures and/or investment well into the 1880s. A surprising number of the cohort who had stayed on in the goldfields were indeed owner-operators or investors in substantial mining ventures.

However, precise information regarding the ultimate success of these listed companies, including whether the promoters actually raised the proposed capital subscription and became operating concerns, is much more difficult to find. Among those more readily assessed were such successful miners as Edward Morey and his wife, Mary Ann (née Trickett), Joseph Doody, John Cornthwaite, the Seddon family and the remarkable Proctor boys. For many of the others, success or otherwise is veiled in obscurity. Some of the other records discussed above, such as wills, probates and land ownership documents, suggest that those of the cohort who went to the goldfields made, at the very least, a living wage from digging.

Trove's Digitised Collections

An extremely important resource is Trove, the National Library of Australia's digitised collections, in particular its growing searchable database of Australian newspapers. The two Victoria-wide newspapers that covered what might be called the national topics of importance were the *Argus* (founded in 1848) and David Syme's the *Age* (founded in 1854 and still publishing today). The *Argus* was originally the home and mouthpiece of the reformers in the colony and was described by Serle as 'the bane of government' in its agitation for electoral reform.[15] By the end of the 1850s and into the 1860s, the *Age* emerged as a far more radical mouthpiece, and the *Argus* became associated with the more conservative-leaning establishment.

David Syme was a successful goldminer who had lived the rough, ready and hard-working lifestyle of the digger. He never forgot where his sympathies lay.[16] The newspapers provide an extremely important source of information about political priorities and controversies. They were vigorous in their editorial commentary on various reform activities, radical factions and progressive movements of the time, and were highly partisan participants in the various political factions emerging in Victoria. These publications also devoted a considerable proportion of their coverage to rural and regional affairs, running columns rounding up news from the regions and growing townships outside Melbourne.

An important source of the *Argus*'s and *Age*'s information came from the small regional newspapers that sprung up across Victoria. The first were goldfields papers including the *Mount Alexander Mail* (1854), the *Bendigo Advertiser* (1855) and the *Ovens & Murray Advertiser* (1856). Both the *Advertiser* newspapers remain in publication and are significant regional newspapers. As selectors and other small farmers occupied increasing amounts of rural land and the surrounding villages grew into townships, the number of local newspaper titles in circulation also grew. Often only published once or twice a week and no more than four to six pages in length, they provided an insight into the fascinating minutiae of local concerns and interests. Advertisements in these publications reveal as much as the articles do about the resources available to, the lifestyles being pursued by and the concerns of the growing communities.

Populating the Collective Biography

An essential aspect of this collective biography's historical narrative was the Lancashire origins of the migrant cohort, and the economic, political, social and cultural values of the communities from which they migrated. The personal stories of those Lancashire families and individuals who were unable to be identified in either the 1841 or 1851 English and Welsh censuses have, on the whole, not been included in this collective biography.

A further winnowing down of the migrants' stories occurred after the migrants' arrival had been recorded in the *Register* and they were discharged from the migrant depots in Melbourne or Geelong. Many of those excluded from this study were people who simply vanished from the records. This was a particularly prevalent for single women. Many of the single young women were quickly married and subsumed into society under their husband's name.

However, it was surprising how few of the married couples without children could be traced beyond the migrant depots. I would have expected to be able to follow them through the birth records of children as most of the childless couples were aged in their 20s, but I frequently came up with negative searches for these couples in the BDM. Were they more mobile and moved on quickly to other states or countries in search of better opportunities to achieve the goals that had motivated their decision to migrate in the first place?

Another factor excluding singles and even married couples without children was the number of shared names in similar age groups among those who had migrated in the years 1852–1853. It was too easy to be tracing what seemed to be absorbing stories only to discover that the person or couple being researched was not part of the migrant cohort. The three couples mentioned above bearing the same given and family names are examples of such.

Mobility is a big factor in these migrant stories. Many were highly mobile after disembarking in Victoria, even if only around the goldfields. Others from the cohort, or their children, moved on to other Australian colonies, New Zealand, South Africa or North America. Some returned to England either permanently or for visits, thus putting a stake into the heart of the prevalent myth that assisted migration was akin to transportation and a life sentence in exile.

As the central purpose of this research was to explore the migrants' settlement in Victoria, and their impact on Victorian society and culture and its impact on them, I have on the whole not followed those migrants who moved on to other colonies in Australia or to New Zealand. There are the occasional exceptions, such as a couple and their three children who were mining in Bendigo and ended up on the same New Zealand West Coast goldfields as Richard Seddon. As noted above, there were a few returnees to England, although remarkably only one family did so permanently, with the others returning to Victoria. The Mack family spent eight years in Melbourne, where they seem to have modestly prospered without going to the goldfields, and then returned, with three additional children, to Kirkdale in Liverpool, where they bought a terrace house. There are also indications that a few individuals and families moved on to the US, but my attempts to track these people did not meet with much success.

The number of people whose stories feature in this collective biography in comparison to the total number from Lancashire recorded in the *Register*, and the numbers who were identified in the 1851 English Census, is shown in Figure 2.2.

Figure 2.2. Number of Lancashire migrants featured in collective biography in comparison to those listed in *Register* and identified in 1851 English and Welsh Census

Makeup	No. from *Register*	No. identified in census	No. featured in this biography	As % of *Register* no.	As % of census no.
Married couples with children	33	22 (67%)	16	48%	73.0%
Married couples with no children	17	8 (47%)	8	47%	100.0%
Single adult males (14 years and over)	10	8 (80%)	7	70%	87.5%
Single adult females (14 years and over)	33	17 (51%)	10	30%	59.0%

Sources: PROV, Register of Assisted British Immigrants *VPRS 7310, bks 6–10*; PRO, *Census Returns of England and Wales 1851 HO107*.

A question does arise as to how representative the family groups and individuals featured in this book are of the Lancashire cohort as a whole. This cannot be tested definitively unless all those recorded in the *Register* as being from Lancashire were identified in the 1851 English Census, and could all be traced beyond disembarkation in Victoria. An average of 61% of the four groupings from the cohort recorded in the *Register* could be identified in the 1851 Census, while those featured in this biography make up 77% of those identified in the 1851 Census. This indicates that they form a good representative sample on which to base the conclusions and assumptions drawn in this book.

The great weakness of prosopography is its reliance on property and property transaction matters to write a collective biography and draw conclusions. This quite probably becomes less of a weakness the closer we are to the subjects of research. Here the separation is no more than 160 years and the societies and communities in which they settled are still recognisable and familiar to us. However, the one area where this weakness becomes clear is in any discussion of religion or religious belief in the lives of the migrant cohort. Except for two cases, those of Thomas Proctor and Thomas Rainford, it would be easy to come away convinced that the cohort were indifferent to religion or religious belief. And perhaps they were. In all the primary source material I have examined, including wills, God or mention of religious belief is missing; yet, when it comes to the education of their children or their health and wellbeing, there is plenty of comment.

In the *Register*, over 90% of the Lancashire migrant cohort identify as Anglican, but that is not an unusual feature of England of the time. The Church of England was woven tightly into every corner and niche of the fabric of English society and culture. It was a little over a hundred years since religious denominations other than Anglican had been tolerated. The CLEC, as discussed in the next chapter, leaned heavily on local parish priests, all Anglican, in their recruitment drives. In addition, as noted in Chapter 3, various nonconformist denominations, especially the Methodists, vigorously opposed working-class migration to the colonies.

Victoria and Australia were initially a predominantly Anglican society. Blainey argues that there was an explosive growth in nonconformism in the second half of the 19th century. Indeed, he says that nonconformist sects in Victoria had become so strong that they outnumbered Anglicans by the end of that century. Blainey also claims that in terms of church attendance these sects were 'far ahead of the Anglicans'.[17] This may well be true; however, the 1891 Victorian Census suggests that those identifying as Anglicans still easily outnumbered all the other nonconformist sects and remained the predominantly held religious identity in the colony.[18]

The Bears Lagoon community provides a typical example of regional or rural life centred around an Anglican church. There was no resident parish priest and other denominations could use the church. It largely operated as a town hall, and social and community centre. The sports grounds were next door to it – cricket in summer, footie in winter. Tea and lunches were prepared by the ladies of the village in the church. In his discussions on Methodism, Davison tends to credit the social and entertainment aspects, such as singing and dancing, over religious worship for his family's attendance of the church in Forest Creek.[19] I assume that in the case of the migrant cohort they observed certain rituals such as baptism and confirmation of their children, marriage and funeral rites in their local church, and certain important religious ceremonial days; but other than that they appeared to have little impetus to demonstrate their belief or otherwise, whether in Lancashire or Victoria.

There were no towering political, cultural or social success stories among the Lancashire migrant cohort, although in one case a family who migrated produced one of Australasia's greatest reforming premiers and prime ministers. Among this cohort we have a handful of people who were very successful financially, sometimes as a result of gold and sometimes from other businesses. The majority, however, were at best moderately prosperous. In this regard, though, how do we measure success for these migrants? In their own terms, a husband, wife and three children who ended up owning 12 acres on the edge of a growing regional town, on which they established a small but successful business, grew their own vegetables, ran chickens and pigs and built a substantial cottage, and with the husband able to vote by secret ballot, could well have perceived themselves as content in their pursuit of happiness.

Chapter 3

A QUITE UNPRECEDENTED ACHIEVEMENT

The Colonial Land & Emigration Commission as Migration Agents

Emigrants embarking from Great Britain.
Alfred May and Alfred Martin Ebsworth, Australasian Sketcher, *18 December, 1880.*
State Library of Victoria, a/n: A/S18/12/80/sup.

> *I am desired to acquaint you that Sir J P is aware of the difficulty of conducting well-regulated Govt. Emigration at the speed you propose, which is quite unprecedented & amounts to a rate of 36,000–40,000 persons per annum, but that under the extraordinary circumstances of the present case, he cordially approves of you making the attempt and will be very happy if your efforts are successful.*
>
> Herman Merrivale, Permanent Undersecretary for the Colonial Office, to the Land and Emigration Commissioners, dated 17 May 1852[1]

The extraordinary circumstances to which Merrivale was referring were the discoveries of gold in NSW and Victoria and the resulting gold rushes. Following a public announcement on 14 May 1851 of a major gold discovery, the first big gold rush was to Bathurst, NSW. Three days later, the *Bathurst Free Press* announced, 'A complete mental madness appears to have seized almost every member of the community. There has been a universal rush to the diggings'.[2] This madness was more than surpassed in Victoria when, on 5 September 1851, the *Argus* publicised the discovery of very rich alluvial goldfields at Mount Alexander and Forest Creek in present-day Castlemaine.[3]

The *Argus* report triggered a stampede to the diggings. In what seemingly portended social chaos and economic catastrophe to many people in authority, employees in the towns of Melbourne and Geelong and workers on the outlying great pastoral estates and small farms deserted their stations in droves. The following extract from an article in the *Geelong Advertiser* titled 'A Deserted City' evocatively captures the fears that the nascent colony was about to be rent asunder:

> The current of our male population has set steadily in the direction of the gold diggings ... The ordinary relations of social life appear to be suspended by general consent. Already there are whole streets where hardly a single head of a family is to be found at home – the softer sex have it all their own way; and like Penelope, in Ithaca, are piously employed in superintending the domestic economies, and waiting patiently for their lords laden with golden spoils ... Meantime business relations of the city are bordering on stagnation. Contractors cannot complete their old engagements, and of course cannot enter into new ones. Hence, there is not employment even for the few remaining artisans left ... Shopkeeping is at a standstill ... Lawyers are left clerkless.[4]

By early 1852, the alarm expressed by the colonial authorities had spread to British industry, especially textile businesses heavily dependent on the Australian wool clip. The Yorkshire woollen industry became particularly vocal, lobbying the British Government and the Colonial Office to take action to ensure the Australian wool clip was harvested and shipped to them.

Tasked with resolving the crisis were the Commissioners of the CLEC, who reported directly to the Colonial Secretary.[5] The CLEC's establishment had been a decisive step by the British Government in support of large-scale British emigration to the colonies, particularly the Australian colonies. The efforts of the CLEC in meeting the demands of the Victorian and NSW colonial governments during the 1850s were a triumph of administrative organisation, as the then Colonial Secretary, the Duke of Newcastle, acknowledged when he instructed Merrivale to write to the Commissioners:

> to state that he has had much satisfaction to taking this opportunity to place on record his sense of credit which he considers due to your Board for the success with which you met the difficulties and unprecedented demands of the past year.[6]

The Duke had every reason to be pleased. The CLEC had lifted enormous political pressure off him and his government. The Colonial Office had passed the buck to the Commissioners.

The Colonial Office afforded the CLEC unprecedented independence of action, and repeatedly refused to intervene in the Commission's conduct of this government-organised migration program on a scale never previously imagined or seen. It is quite extraordinary how little acknowledgement colonial or migration histories give to the scale of the program and how well thought out it was. The CLEC rapidly responded to the panicked calls of the colonial authorities for labour to replace workers who had flocked to the goldfields, resisted completely political pressure in the UK to empty the poorhouses and ship their inhabitants to Australia as indentured labour, and ignored the demands of the pastoralists of Victoria to provide them with cheap agricultural labour.

The CLEC as Emigration Agents

The Colonial Office and the CLEC were acutely aware of how thin the veneer of British authority was across its far-flung Empire. For the Colonial Office, the Eastern Australian colonies presented an opportunity to build self-sustaining and stable British outposts that would assist in securing its Eastern Empire. Edward Gibbon Wakefield provided the solution as to how large-scale emigration could be encouraged without drawing upon domestic public funds. Wakefield promoted the idea of using land sales in the Australasian temperate colonies as a basis for encouraging successful colonisation of these lands by British people.[7]

By passing the cost of emigration on to the colonies, Wakefield not only made government support for emigration palatable for British political leaders, but also provided a means of meeting the demands of an imperial policy increasingly focused on British India and the Crown's growing interests in South-East Asia and China.

It was with this perception that 'policy moved decisively beyond tentative beginnings' and the CLEC was established and 'charged to oversee and promote emigration'.[8] The CLEC's empirical methods, forceful assertion of its independence and applied expert knowledge provided a remarkable vision for this mid-19th-century migration program to Australia and the imperial strategic interests that drove it. What is also remarkable, considering the logistics involved in shipping such a huge number of free migrants around the world in wooden sailing ships, is just how minimally staffed the Commission was throughout its lifetime.

On 1 July 1852, besides the three full-time Commissioners, the London office had 6 staff members, with another 18 staff employed across 11 port cities in the UK: Liverpool, Plymouth, Glasgow and Greenock, Dublin, Belfast, Londonderry, Sligo, Galway, Limerick, Cork and Waterford. Of these ports, only Liverpool (with five staff members) had more than a single Emigration Officer.[9] Approximately 80% of CLEC staff were half-pay Naval Officers. The CLEC was also given a large degree of financial independence when the *Australian Colonies: Wastes Lands Act 1842* fixed minimum prices for the sale or lease of lands and required at least one-half of the proceeds to be used to promote emigration to the Australian colonies.

By the early 1850s, these land sales were generating substantial sums of money for the CLEC to invest in the promotion of migration to the newly independent Colony of Victoria. A stable, efficient and well-funded bureaucracy was in place when, in 1852 and 1853, a response was required by the CLEC to the urgent demands of the colonial administrations of the Australian colonies following the discovery of gold.

The Migration Program

The CLEC was thus well placed to respond to the urgent, even hysterical, pleas of the two governors of those colonies. Victorian Governor Charles La Trobe, for instance, was writing in heavily underlined words about the urgent need to secure new labour if Victoria was not to grind to a halt. La Trobe made a promise of a substantially increased sum of money for the immediate recruitment and passage of 'artizans & mechanics' and 'single young females' to Victoria.[10]

In response to La Trobe's plea, the Commissioners outlined a plan, in a letter to the Colonial Secretary dated 4 May 1852, to recruit and ship 11,000–12,000 people to Victoria over the following 12 months. They estimated that the funds available from Victoria would allow them to send the migrants at a rate of

1600 persons per month and calculated that six to eight ships would need to be contracted on a monthly basis as transport.[11]

In the end, the CLEC recruited and provided passage for more than 20,000 persons to Victoria in 1852, with another 30,000 following in the next two years. All told, over the three years 1852–1854, the CLEC recruited and transported over 100,000 men, women and children to NSW and Victoria in response to the gold rushes. It was, as Merrivale described, a 'quite unprecedented' government-organised movement of people.

Birkenhead Emigration Depot.
The Illustrated London News, *10 July 1852*.
National Library of Australia, nla.obj-135889210.

Greater numbers of migrants were being carried to North America from British ports every year, but that was a journey of 10 days. The voyage to Victoria took, on average, 100–120 days. Recruitment, as the Commissioners noted, was undertaken against a backdrop of rising real wages and labour shortages in Britain, strident opposition from Guilds and the nascent union movement, and the objections of some religious denominations such as the Methodists.[12]

Figure 3.1 shows migration, both government-assisted and unassisted (or what the CLEC classified as 'Spontaneous migration'), from the UK to Australia recorded by the CLEC in the years 1852–1854.

Figure 3.1. Assisted and unassisted migration from UK, 1852–1854

Year	Spontaneous (% of total)	Government (% of total)	Total
1852	53,527 (61.0%)	34,354 (39.0%)	87,881
1853	34,578 (55.5%)	27,723 (44.5%)	62,301
1854	42,172 (51.0%)	41,065 (49.0%)	83,237

Source: BPP, General Reports of the Colonial Land and Emigration Commissioners, 1853–1856.

Figure 3.2. Migration from UK to Victoria, 1848–1854

Year	Spontaneous (no. of persons)	%	Government (no. of persons)	%	Total
1848	1232	17%	5952	83%	7184
1849	3859	38%	6409	62%	10,268
1850	3075	73%	1140	27%	4215
1851	2020	35%	3724	65%	5744
1852	37,255	65%	20,313	35%	57,568
1853	29,698	69%	13,569	31%	43,267
1854	35,384	69%	15,907	31%	51,291
Total	112,523	63%	67,014	37%	179,537
Total 1852–54	102,337	67%	49,789	33%	152,126

Source: BPP, General Reports of the Colonial Land and Emigration Commissioners, 1849–1856.

Figure 3.2 presents the number of persons migrating to Victoria for the seven years spanning 1848–1854. The sheer size of the numbers migrating during the gold rush period is at its most obvious in this chart. Prior to the announcement in early May 1851 of the discovery of gold in Victoria, the population of the colony on the census date of 2 March 1851 was 77,345.[13]

What is remarkable about the data shown in Figures 3.1 and 3.2 is that most Australian historians have tended to follow Geoffrey Serle's lead, as expressed in *The Golden Age*, by downplaying the significance of government-assisted migration in the populating of Victoria after the discovery of gold.[14] Yet this migration program continued to play an extremely important role with one-third of all migrants to Victoria between 1852 and 1854 being government-assisted. Serle estimates that up to a third of the spontaneous (unassisted) migrants had moved on from Victoria by the end of the decade.[15] If this is correct, then the influence of the assisted migrants on the development of Victorian colonial society and culture is even more striking.

That assisted migrants were more likely to stay was predicted by the CLEC in a letter to the Colonial Secretary in April 1853. This letter outlined the steps the CLEC was taking to ensure that the 'greatest possible number of industrious, active and healthy colonists' were being selected for the government emigration program.[16] As various correspondence between the CLEC Commissioners and Merivale between May 1852 and June 1853 makes abundantly clear, their primary objective was to ensure that the individuals selected for the migration program were those who would stay on and contribute meaningfully to the building of self-sustaining communities in NSW and Victoria.[17] This was an objective shared most strongly by the Governor of Victoria, Charles La Trobe – after his initial panic at the loss of labour to the goldfields.

The assisted migrants of this period have unfortunately been characterised as 'pauper migrants'. In describing unassisted migrants, Serle contributed to this unfounded perception by arguing:

> It is beyond argument (despite the fact that no statistical proof can be advanced) that this group of unassisted migrants was magnificent economic material with education qualifications and professional and industrial skills superior to any other group of migrants to Australia, at least in the nineteenth century.[18]

It is not 'beyond argument'. Indeed, I argue that the government-assisted migrants were of similar magnificent economic material to the greater majority of the unassisted migrants travelling steerage to Victoria in those crucial years. There seem to be two major reasons for the belief that the assisted migrants were the poor leavenings of British society.

The first major reason underpinning this belief is that the English political and landed classes came to view migration programs as an opportunity to rid themselves of the poor and discontented. The Poor Law rates that all landowners had to pay were frequently seen as a burdensome tax, while many of this class had still not got over their fright in the 1840s when revolution seemed an ever-present threat. The Colonial Office and the CLEC were flooded with letters from florid country gentry proposing various schemes of indentured labour that amounted to slavery or transportation not of the criminal classes but simply the poor.

The most 'reasonable' of these schemes was proposed by 'a very influential deputation' representing English wool manufacturers who met with the CLEC Commissioners in early June 1852 and 'expressed their strong apprehension that the Emigrants sent out by this Board … will be unable on their arrival to resist the attraction of the goldfields'. The wool manufacturers' solution was a form of contract that bound the migrant to work in agriculture or pasturage for a minimum of two years and, if they had not found their own engagement within 14 days of arrival, to accept 'any master proposed to them by the Governor of the Colony'.[19]

As the CLEC could not refuse the demands such an influential delegation outright, the Commissioners sought the legal opinion of an eminent Queen's Counsel, Mr Robert Lowe, 'whose known ability and intimate knowledge of the Law of New South Wales would render his opinion conclusive'. It was Mr Lowe's written opinion that:

> No contract such as had been suggested could be legally formed to bring the Emigrant under the Master and Servants Act in the Colony – that it would not be possible to detain the Emigrant until he had formed an engagement as was proposed without exposing those who detained him to criminal proceedings – and that the suggested contract was not the most advisable mode of meeting the difficulty.[20]

This legal opinion effectively put an end to pressure to create some form of government-assisted emigration program based on indenture.[21]

The Poor Law Board, the authority overseeing the *Poor Law Act*, also effectively killed any hope of emptying the poorhouses when it wrote the following:

> As bearing upon this subject we think it right to observe we declined during the past year to sanction any expenditure from the Poor Rate in aid of emigration to the Australian Colonies (except in cases presenting special circumstances) on the ground that the condition of those colonies appears to us at present to be such as of itself to attract largely voluntary and independent emigration.[22]

Both Mr Lowe's legal opinion and the Poor Law Board's determination provided the cover the CLEC required to resist political pressure in the UK and to independently pursue its own agenda in the selection of candidates for assisted migration from those who chose to apply voluntarily and seemed the most fit to be colonists.

The second major reason underpinning the mischaracterisation of government-assisted migrants was the attitude of the colonists themselves, especially the pastoral and merchant elites. The problem with selecting energetic, self-motivated and skilled workers was, characteristically, that they were not interested in labouring away at dead-end jobs, especially those as difficult and lonely as shepherding.[23]

The goldfields and the economic opportunities on offer in burgeoning Melbourne were far more attractive, especially as they offered far more likely and, as later chapters demonstrate, rapid routes into property ownership. The colonial elites were inclined to lay the blame on the CLEC and accuse it of selecting migrants who were obviously worthless and shiftless for not wanting to work on large pastoral estates.

La Trobe unfortunately contributed to these perceptions when he initially panicked and insisted that he did not want farm labourers as they went straight to the goldfields, and instead asserted that 'the introduction of artizans and mechanics should be secured as far as possible'.[24]

As La Trobe was paying for the program (and at that point the CLEC thought it was going to have difficulties fulfilling the quotas it had set), the Commissioners obliged him by sending out several parties of weavers. In fact, several persons in the UK claiming expert colonial experience had suggested that 'weavers, flax dressers, and other persons' who were considered enfeebled by their labour in the textile industries might possess 'the all important qualification of unfitness for the goldfields'.

By the time La Trobe got back to the CLEC correcting himself, the Commissioners had already decided 'it best to discontinue this exceptional mode of selection'. However, with the encouragement of La Trobe, they continued to select substantial numbers of the better-skilled mechanics and artisans particularly if they were family men with more girls than boys in their families as female children became one important way to attempt to correct the imbalance between single young men and women.[25]

The CLEC was so concerned about whether it could meet its self-imposed quota that it had at one point recruited a large number of emigrants from the western islands of Scotland. These migrants were, in part, funded through a Scottish Highland Society established to promote the emigration of Highland crofters and which enjoyed the patronage of HRH Prince Albert. Although these Scottish migrants were 'wanting in the tidiness and activity of English migrants', the Commissioners hoped that they 'may prove useful for the purposes of the sheep farmer' and trusted 'that they will be acceptable in the colony'.[26]

They were not. Even the Scottish middle-class residents of the colony were outraged by the importation of those from the 'primitive', 'barbaric' Western Isles.[27] Other places the CLEC looked to sources included Germans, Swiss 'and (by a very respectable committee at Madras) the half-caste population of India'.[28]

To the relief of both the CLEC and the colonial authorities, however, they did not have to source migrants from these countries, because their concerns about attracting good-quality emigrants had evaporated overnight, as this statement reveals:

> The growing eagerness to reach Australia soon rendered it unnecessary for us to close with applications of this kind, or to relax our ordinary rules in regard to British emigrants. This eagerness soon became excessive – so much so that at one time our office contained no less than 18,000 applications for passage to Australia. The only difficulty was how to dispose of the mass of business which was thus forced on the office. The number of letters received in the month of June, which in 1850 was 1,564 and in 1851 2,884, amounted in 1852 to 18,910, being at an average rate, excluding Sundays, of 727 a day.[29]

Strikingly, this flood of applications was coming from the skilled English working classes, groups who had previously shown a remarkable reluctance to migrate.

This surge in applications came against a background of a dramatic decline in emigration to the US and the Canadian colonies, particularly by the Irish and the Scots.[30] It also accompanied a surge in 'spontaneous' (unassisted) migration by the English, but not the Scots or Irish, to Victoria and NSW. As these developments happened concurrently, it is easy to assume that the discovery of gold was the immediate cause of this sudden increase in interest by the English in migration to Victoria and NSW, making this surge, at least on the surface, one of the purest examples of pull migration ever seen.

However, to view the gold discoveries in NSW and Victoria as the exclusive reason for this surge may be simplistic. Why was there a dramatic rise in English migration to Australia, while Irish and Scottish migration to everywhere including the Australian colonies declined dramatically from 1851? Gold may have provided an immediate opportunity, but we need to investigate further and look for other underlying motivations for the decisions of both skilled and semi-skilled mainly industrial English workers to migrate to such distant lands at that point in time.

Careful examination of the promotion of migration to the Australian colonies during this period provides one entry point to that investigation. The CLEC was assiduous in its promotion of migration, both government-assisted and spontaneous, to the Australian colonies, and particularly Victoria, from 1851 onwards. In preparation for the split of the Port Phillip District from NSW to form the independent Colony of Victoria, La Trobe had committed more than £100,000 from the Lands Fund to provide for the passage of English assisted migrants to Victoria.[31] The CLEC was well advanced in planning a recruitment campaign, which took into account the marked reluctance of the English working classes to migrate, when the gold rush labour emergency became apparent.

In the preceding years, the CLEC had developed an elaborate operation and network by which it could promote migration. From 1849, the Commission published a circular, which anyone could purchase for thruppence detailing the prices of transport to all the British colonies together with possible wages on arrival and other opportunities, in particular the possibility to acquire land. The 1852 circular went through three reprints.

Within Britain, the CLEC also maintained an extensive network of contacts with local parish priests, local authorities and Poor Law guardians. The Commissioners wrote to 6000 parish priests between May and June 1852, promoting the opportunities that government-assisted migration could afford.[32] There was also by mid-1852 a dozen or more spruikers of migration to Victoria conducting lucrative lecture tours across England to increasingly larger and enthusiastic audiences of mostly working-class people.

Although ostensibly independent of the CLEC, these spruikers never strayed far from the CLEC line regarding the opportunities offered by emigration to Victoria. The goldfields were substantially played down as a motive for migrating, while the CLEC and independent promoters emphasised the opportunity to work for wages that were 40–50% higher than wages in England and to use those monies to acquire land.[33]

The CLEC and the independent migration spruikers endlessly promoted Victoria as a colony in which fertile land was available in abundance for all. They argued that anyone with a small amount of capital, or who was ready to work for the high wages on offer, could acquire and own a small landholding within a relatively short period of time. They promoted a Wakefieldian vision of colonising temperate lands by British people.

However, where Wakefield argued for a complex and fairly slow process of settlement, which would maintain what he viewed as a proper ratio between land sales and supply of labour, the CLEC and its spruikers seemed to have thrown caution out the door in promoting the ease of land acquisition in the Australian colonies. In reality, such land was not readily available to the small family farmer, and, as a result, the colony saw long years of political turmoil. This, in light of what subsequent chapters reveal, suggests that the possibility of acquiring real estate, and not just farms or the lure of gold, was a major consideration and motivating factor for the English migrants.

The rise in the number of English people being selected for the government-assisted migration program was dramatic. Over the 12-month period of July 1852 to June 1853, the *Register* shows that the English made up 48% of those landed, the Scots 38% and the Irish 14%.[34] In the last six months of this period, the English composed 62%, the Scots 21% and the Irish 17%. The increase in the number of English being landed is even more remarkable for families. Families made up at least 71% of the migrants landed in the 12-month period, and in the last six months more than two-thirds of these were English families.[35]

The Scots and Irish consisted mainly of single young women during this 12-month period.[36] The CLEC found that English single young women, unlike English families, were not attracted to the program, thus the continued dominance of the Scottish and Irish in this grouping.[37]

Despite repeatedly arguing that neither the CLEC nor the governors gave preference to the selection of English over Irish or Scots, or Anglicans over other denominations, the Commissioners demonstrate a remarkable defensiveness in their correspondence and their reports to Parliament when they are forced to select among the Scots and Irish. Notwithstanding its looking to Ireland and Scotland as sources for single females, the CLEC never met the 50% quota that La Trobe wished to see granted assisted passage. In fact, single females made up a meagre 20% of the numbers recruited in that year.[38]

One way in which the CLEC managed to ensure that females of all ages outnumbered males being granted assisted passage during this period, and that the English were prioritised, was to ensure that English families with predominantly female members (including females regarded as adults because they were 14 years of age or over) were selected ahead of other families from the applicant pool.

Prior to 1849, 'free' or 'assisted' migration to Port Phillip had taken various forms, but from 1849 all government-supported migration was merged into a single plan under the complete control of the CLEC. The Commissioners maintained a rigorous and centralised application process, personally approving all recommendations for assisted passage. They used a rating system that was dependent on selection criteria encompassing occupation, age, health, sex and marital status that could and was regularly adjusted by the CLEC. This gave the Commissioners considerable flexibility in rapidly responding to evolving circumstances and meeting oft-changing colonial demands, while fulfilling Colonial Office imperatives.

With the surge in applications from prospective English migrants, the CLEC became ever more rigorous in applying the selection criteria for assisted passage as 1852 and 1853 progressed. The application process required considerable agency on the part of the applicants, which of itself must have winnowed out many who were not wholeheartedly committed to migrating.

Each applicant had to attach to their application three character references: the first from a citizen of good standing – that is, a property owner or substantial employer; the second from the local parish priest; and the third from a doctor. The first two were required to attest that the applicant was 'sober, industrious, and of general good moral character … in all respects capable of labour and going out to work for wages … and not in habitual receipt of parish relief'. The doctor had to attest that they were 'in good health, free from all bodily or mental defects' and had been vaccinated against smallpox.[39]

Despite the flood of applications, and the CLEC's rigorous vetting and selection process, the Commission seemed adept at turning around applications in a fairly short timeframe of four to six weeks. This timeframe still caused much anxiety among the applicants about the long delays in receiving news of the outcome, as the following exchange of letters placed in the public notice section of the *Manchester Times* on Saturday 19 June 1852 attests:

> *To the Editor of the Examiner and Times*
>
> Having had many applications from persons desirous to emigrate to Australia, and who have also applied to the authority in London, without having received any answer, we addressed Mr. Walcott, the secretary, on the subject, and in reply to our inquiry have received the enclosed, which for the information of your readers, we will thank you to publish in your next number, and oblige, yours, &c.
>
> RICHMOND & CHANDLER
>
> Victoria Bridge, Salford, June 17, 1852.
>
> ---

Colonial Land & Emigration Office,

Park-street, Westminster, June 16, 1852.

Gentlemen – I am directed by the colonial land and emigration commissioners to acknowledge the receipt of your letter of the 14th instant, and in reply beg to state that persons having applied to this office will have their cases at once inquired into. I am to add, that all applications will be attended to, but that, from the very great number of people now applying, cases can only be taken in their turn, and some delay necessarily occurs before it comes to the turn of a recent candidate to be considered – I am, gentlemen, your obedient servant,

S. WALCOTT, Secretary,

To Messrs. Richmond and Chandler, Implement Works, Salford, Manchester.[40]

This is a most curious advertisement. Richmond and Chandler were inventors and manufacturers of mechanised agricultural implements and machinery.[41] They were part of a new breed of industrialists turning Manchester away from cotton cloth manufacturing and remaking the city as a global centre of precision engineering. They were neither emigration agents nor shipping agents, and certainly not accredited CLEC recruitment agents. Further, there is no record of them having an interest in any of the philanthropic migration societies that flourished during this period.

Except for this one advertisement there is no record of their involvement in the recruitment of government-assisted migrants. Richmond and Chandler may have been simply assisting the workforce that was surplus to local requirements to migrate by helping them with the application process; or they may have seen an opportunity to open new markets in Australia as a good reason to encourage workers from Manchester to migrate.

Assisted passages were neither free nor even necessarily cheap. While the CLEC contracted the ships and paid the passage money, the applicants had to contribute a 'goodly' amount towards their passage. The assisted migrants' contribution varied according to the desirability of the candidates. Figure 3.3 provides the contributions expected of successful applicants.

Candidates were also required to outfit themselves and their families with a minimum prescribed list of clothing, as shown in Figure 3.4.

Figure 3.3. Payments towards passage required of government-assisted migrants

Classes	Under 45 years	45 to 49 years	50 to 59 years
Married agricultural labourers, shepherds, herdsmen and their wives; per head.	£1	£5	£11
Single women of the working classes.	£1	£5	£11
Married journeymen, mechanics and artizans, such as blacksmiths, bricklayers, carpenters, masons, sawyers, wheelwrights, and gardeners, &c, and their wives, per head.	£2	£6	£14
Single men (14 years and over) if accompanying their parents.	£2		
Single men if not accompanying their parents (when they can be taken).	£3		
Children under 14, per head	10s.		

Source: CLEC, Colonization Circular, 1852, 23.

Figure 3.4. Minimum prescribed clothing for migrants (including children)

For Males	For Females
Six shirts	Six shifts
Six pairs of stockings	Six pairs of stockings
Two pairs of shoes	Two pairs of shoes
Two complete suits of exterior clothing	Two gowns

Source: CLEC, Colonization Circular, 1852, 24.

In addition, applicants were required to bring 'three sheets for each berth, four towels and 2lbs. of soap per person', and were advised that 'the larger the stock of clothing the better for health and comfort during the voyage'.[42]

Keith Pescod follows the lead of earlier historians in arguing that this cost was beyond the financial capacity of most applicants and that 'frequently private donors, charitable organisations or the Poor Law guardians provided the money'.[43] It may well be that in the Richmond and Chandler advertisement we see a case of private donors helping the working class to cover this cost. However, Messrs Richmond and Chandler were at the beginning of their industrial career, so it is unlikely that they would have had the extra financial capacity to assist even a small number of migrants.

Robin Haines is much more cautious about whether there was ever a great deal of private subsidy of government-assisted migrants, suggesting that this is 'inestimable'.[44] In July 1853, in a letter to Merrivale reviewing the first year of the greatly enlarged program, the CLEC noted that there was little enthusiasm among private individuals or philanthropic organisations to subsidise migrants receiving government assistance. Further, the Commissioners made clear that they disapproved of private or charitable contributions towards the cost the migrant must bear as this could undermine the CLEC's intention to ensure that at least the family migrants were highly economically self-motivated.[45]

As for the Poor Law guardians, Haines notes that local guardians' attempts to subsidise emigration to any destination were frustrated by the tight scrutiny and control the Poor Law Board maintained over emigration matters and even the smallest expenditure to subsidise emigration.[46] The Board's annual reports show that it was extremely parsimonious in approving subsidies for emigration during this period. In the year July 1852 to June 1853, the Board approved just 384 applications for payment of assistance to emigrants to the Australian colonies, although the reports do not tell us for which colony.[47] I am inclined to take the view that, at least in the case of English families, migrants bore their financial contribution themselves, and were drawn from those working classes who were in steady semi-skilled or skilled employment and therefore had the wherewithal to meet that cost.

Shipping of the Migrants

The emphasis on 'health and comfort during the voyage' is an indicator of the final important task the CLEC had, which was to get the selected migrants to Australia safely and in good health. In the age of sail this meant ensuring a migrant's health and safety while in transit, particularly through the proper victualling of voyages that lasted on average 110 days. Overall, the CLEC was strikingly successful at this, providing the government-assisted migrants with a trouble-free embarkation, departure and passage to Australia. The intention was to land in the colonies fit and healthy migrants ready to work and contribute to colonial society. An important aspect of this was to minimise the trauma experienced by the migrants and impart a sense of wellbeing on the long voyage to Australia.[48]

The CLEC achieved this by regulating in minute detail all aspects of the performance of the ships it chartered, from carefully regulated food supplies through to strictly enforced ship hygiene. Life on board the ships for the migrants was also rigorously regulated from sun-up to lamps out. The officers of the CLEC absolutely understood the link between too much free time and boredom and disruption, as well as the link between poor hygiene and ventilation, on the one hand, and disease and ill-health, on the other.

As noted earlier, 80% of the staff of the CLEC were half-pay naval officers. The great naval victories of Nelson and other British naval commanders in the Napoleonic Wars are well known, but it is frequently overlooked that the British Navy maintained an effective blockade of Continental Europe for nearly a quarter of a century. This involved keeping properly supplied fleets of ships, and healthy crews, at sea for months and years on end. The Royal Navy was a triumph of administrative and logistical skill, and it is not surprising that the Colonial Office drew on this expertise to ensure that the dispatch of migrants to Australia went as smoothly as it did, given the precarious nature of the voyage and the wooden ships that carried the migrants.

The CLEC's job was difficult enough when it was dispatching one or two ships per month, to transport between 2000 and 4000 persons a year to the Australian colonies. But, in 1852–1853, this became a herculean task as the numbers of migrants being shipped soared to above 20,000 in a single year.

The shipping problems were compounded by the difficulty in securing suitable ships as a result of the gold rush:

> But while the colonies were thus furnishing funds, and the new attractions of Australia removed all difficulties in obtaining emigrants, a fresh obstacle arose to their despatch from this country. The number of vessels which were every week fitting with passengers was alone sufficient to cause a rise in the general rate of freight. But this rise was extraordinarily increased in regard to the Australian voyage, because when a ship once arrived at its destination the immediate desertion of the seamen followed as a matter of course, and rendered it wholly impossible to predict when the ship might get away. In August last 74 vessels were lying in Hobson's Bay – the sailors scarcely consenting to remain on board till the cargo was discharged.[49]

Richard Preston, an 18-year-old second-class passenger travelling on to Sydney, was deeply disturbed by what he saw when the ship he was sailing on put into Melbourne for three days in August 1852 to discharge a shipload of assisted migrants. Preston declared in a letter home, 'I should not like on no account to remain there'. He relates vividly the difficulty the ship's captain had in retaining its crew:

> While staying at Melbourne we had a meeting on board between the officers and the sailors, the reason for it was that the sailors got tipsy and wanted to make their escape so the officers were well armed and told them they would shoot the man that attempted so the sailors began to pitch into the officers and the officers began to use the butts of their pistols and some of them were severely bruised and several handcuffed and seven men deserted.[50]

Even facing these obstacles, the CLEC on the whole continued to maintain a good record for providing well-organised and competently captained ships for the transport of assisted migrants to the Australian colonies by paying only for passengers delivered alive and in a healthy condition.

Government agents in Victoria were also zealous in their inspection of chartered ships, frequently interviewing in confidence the assisted migrants to check that they were treated well. These agents could and did recommend that the full charter price be withheld if they were dissatisfied with the performance of a ship's captain and officers. Captains and officers on well-run ships earned bonuses – another incentive for them to act in accordance with the CLEC's exacting standards.

These standards and performance requirements stood in stark contrast to that of the unregulated passenger ships carrying full-fare-paying passengers, particularly during this gold rush period, as evidenced by the litany of complaints found in letters and diaries from men and women sailing to Australia. Although the various Passenger Acts applied and theoretically regulated the carriage of unassisted full-fare-paying migrants, when freed from the supervision of the CLEC officers and government agents in the colonies, ship captains and shipping agents frequently demonstrated rapacious and fraudulent behaviour, short-changing their passengers on rations and other essential supplies.

This entry dated 12 December 1852, in a voyage diary kept by Richard Hall, a full-fare-paying steerage passenger from Bury, Lancashire, is typical:

> Doyle, the clerk to the agent, is most exceedingly unpopular among all classes of passengers having on many occasions been shouted to scorn in the third cabin. The whole system of fitting out passengers appears to be carried out with a view to get the greatest possible amount of money from them without regard to keeping promises made or reference to

honour in transactions. A very unpleasant state of things on board the ship, especially considering the day is the Sabbath.[51]

A common practice was for a ship's captain to find an excuse to extract a second fare mid-voyage, when the passengers were at his mercy:

> Friday 21st January: An examination of the passengers' tickets having taken place. It was found some had lost them, and that in others there was mistakes. Those who have no tickets to show have been threatened with being made to work, and also being put ashore should we call at the Cape. It seems all advantages are taken and shows the necessity in dealing with such persons to have everything in writing, there being evidently no sense of honour in their transactions.[52]

Many captains showed little regard for the hygiene of their ships or the health of their passengers, as this journal entry by a second-class passenger, Edward Dash, documents:

> July 7 – Obtained from Mr. Ramsden an imperial pint measure and found that our water was more than 4 Quarts short of its quantity 12 Quarts as given out to us only measuring 9 Quarts and rather over 1 1/2 pints present Dash [the writer], Potts, T. Richardson Kirk A. Lyal.
>
> 10 a.m. we then apply'd to the Captain in reference to the measure used in serving out water it being as we endeavoured to prove to him far short of its proper quantity and as we were now much in want owing to the increasing warm weather he denied that the measure was short but at the same time refused to test it in any way telling us we might do our best finding we could get no redress from him.[53]

Dash went on to become a Receiver and Paymaster in the Victorian Treasury Department and was a devout Baptist known for his rectitude.

Dash and Hall, and many others, also chronicled the violent behaviour drunken officers and crew often displayed towards passengers. This was a problem infrequently found on CLEC-chartered ships because the quantity and quality of alcohol they could carry was rigorously audited, in both ports of departure and ports of arrival. It quickly became known among those seeking first- and second-class cabin passage to the Australian colonies that it was preferable to book one's passage on a ship chartered by the CLEC.

Although great attention was paid to providing the best care for passengers, there were at times some horrific losses of life on a few CLEC ships. Despite its grave concerns, the CLEC reluctantly gave in to the colonial authorities' demands that it include large families with children aged under seven years among its assisted migrants. The colonial authorities believed that the heads of such families would be more likely to remain in stable positions of employment, rather than head for the goldfields because they had a young family to look after. However, children aged under seven years were not suited to the harsh conditions and poor diet that these long ship-bound voyages entailed, and often died. While the overall death toll remained below 5% over the 12-month period, on three ships carrying a total of 1000 or more passengers the death toll was over 15%.

On the deck of an Australian emigrant ship.
W.G. Mason & J.S. Prout, The Illustrated London News, *20 Jan, 1849*.
National Library of Australia, nla.obj-135905815.

These deaths at sea were early in the period of the surge, but they caused considerable political agitation in Victoria and several questions were asked in the House of Commons. A subsequent investigation in both Victoria and Britain cleared the CLEC and the ships' captains of any dereliction of duty. In the case of the three ships with the high death toll, the ships had been carrying substantial numbers of Scottish Highlanders who had departed through Liverpool and had probably been exposed to infectious diseases that were lethal to children already weakened by the shipboard diet.

This was made clear in the inquest conducted into the high rate of mortality among children on the *Araminta*.

> 7. The provisions and water and greater part of the fittings appear to have been good – the Surgeons Officers and emigrants to have behaved well and the matron though wanting in energy to have done her best. But measles broke out very early on the voyage. 20 children died of this disease and several more of the diseases which it left behind. And the result was that among the 940 persons placed on board or born during the voyage 52 deaths occurred. Of these only 2 were adults and 46 below 4 years of age.
>
> 8. They state that the measles was brought on board by a child who had slept in a bed which some children sick with measles had occupied the night before there being no hospital.[54]

'They' refers to the CLEC depot at Birkenhead, where all Northern English, Irish and Scottish assisted migrants transited before embarkation.

This Merseyside depot had only opened in January 1852 and was considered the very model of a modern and well-run facility.[55] The placing of a child in a bed that had been occupied by infected children the night before seemed a rare lapse in precautions by the depot staff. Perhaps this facility was just too overcrowded and/or staff had failed to recognise how measles could be easily spread between children in stressful and overcrowded conditions.

Turning to maritime losses, between 1852 and 1857, the CLEC lost only one ship. It was wrecked as it entered Port Phillip Bay, but miraculously not a life was lost.

The CLEC was just one of several administrative units established both within and without the Colonial Office in the first half of the 19th century. Each unit was tasked with achieving certain objectives, all centred around one primary objective – the securing and maintenance of Empire. We can indeed see in the workings of the Colonial Office and all its tentacles the emergence of the modern administrative state, but perhaps not, as MacDonagh perceived it, 'innocent of doctrinaire intention'.[56]

The CLEC acted according to the drumbeats of the political imperatives of a Colonial Office determined to secure the future of Britain's expanding Eastern Empire. In Victoria, for a time these imperatives happily coincided with the needs and desires of its governing administration. Serle's view on the 'magnificent economic material' migrating into Victoria during the gold rush can be equally applied to the CLEC-selected migrants. These migrants were to become some of Victoria's most productive citizens and the British Empire's most loyal subjects.

Chapter 4

MADE IN LANCASHIRE

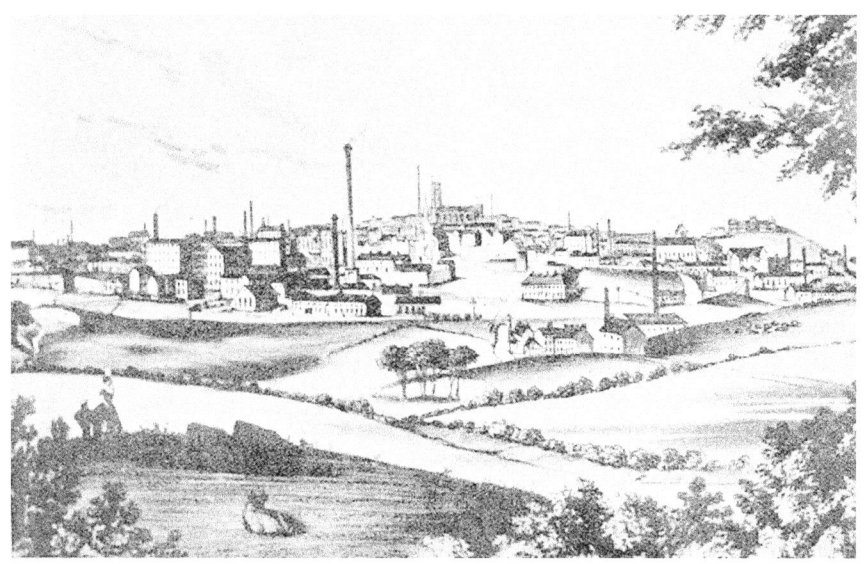

19th Century Southern Lancashire Industrial Landscape circa 1850.
Anthony Reach, Morning Chronicle, London, 28 Dec, 1849.
British Newspaper Archive, British Library.

They understood that it was their duty to work out their destinies for the good and advantage of mankind, and the promotion of that happiness and that contentment which should be placed within reach of all.

Richard Seddon, Prime Minister of New Zealand,
in an address in Bendigo, Victoria, in 1906
regarding his Lancashire migrant predecessors[1]

Richard Seddon was one of Australasia's most successful colonial liberal premiers and New Zealand's longest-serving Prime Minister (1893–1906). Tom Brooking, in his masterful biography *King of God's Own*, thoroughly catalogues Seddon's reform program and achievements in New Zealand.[2] Earlier biographers built a myth of individual exceptionalism around Seddon.

His great achievements were made greater by his family and community being sidelined from his biography. Yet it is only through appreciating his southern Lancashire inheritance, kinship bonds and community ties as first transplanted to Victoria that his achievements and great reform program can really be understood.

Among the first of these Seddons were James, Ruth and their five children aged between 1 and 12 years.[3] On 3 November 1852, they sailed from Liverpool on a barque named the *Thames*, which was carrying 397 government-assisted migrants. On board were another 44 passengers whose county of origin was Lancashire. This was one of the highest numbers of government-assisted migrants from Lancashire on any of the ships carrying assisted migrants in the 1852–1853 period.

The Seddons, like their fellow Lancashire passengers, and all but one family of five, came from the southern Lancashire heartlands of the British industrial and commercial revolution. They were, in the main, a strikingly entrepreneurial and opportunistic group of migrants who were to thrive in Victoria. They were not skilled in the traditional sense of having served an apprenticeship in what were regarded as the traditional artisanal crafts. They were essentially members of the urban working classes who had gained new industrial skillsets in the growing industrial and commercial economies of southern Lancashire.

As mentioned above, only one family of five resided north of Preston. This family came from a district in the very north of Lancashire that was home to a heavily industrialised strip of railway and shipbuilding industries supported by local coal and iron mines. It is not obvious why people from the more northern and less industrialised regions of Lancashire were generally not interested in migrating. Although it is probable that as industrialisation bypassed them they felt little need to uproot their lives, which had served them well for generations; whereas Southern Lancastrians exposed to the disruptive effects of industrialisation, and to Chartist and other radical movements and philosophies, would come to view the risk-taking of migration as an acceptable choice to make.

The migrant cohort were not, on the whole, comprised of internal migrants from outside of southern Lancashire. The vast majority of those who were identified in the 1851 Census Return, and in some cases in the 1841 Census, were born in the developing industrial and commercial centres such as Liverpool, Manchester, Bolton and Oldham. It is evident that the Lancastrian government-assisted migrants who migrated during this period were well equipped to develop and exploit opportunities arising in the new colony with the discovery of gold.

Chartist Demonstration 1848.
Robert Wilson, The Life and Times of Queen Victoria, Volume II *(1886).*
State Library of NSW, MMS ID 991015936059702626.

Indeed, Weston Bate has argued that those who 'came from Europe to Australia in the 1850s seem to have been equipped to play a very important role in the commercial, industrial and agricultural development' of Victoria. He noted:

> Historians have given us a picture of Ballarat in 1854 as an extensive mining camp, not an emerging urban community. They have stressed the relative complexity of mining, but have neglected the specialization of trade and have often completely overlooked the complicated interdependence.[4]

By digging down into the socioeconomic and cultural origins of the migrant cohort and then following their settling of Victoria, we can observe the colony's transformation from a pastoral economy dominated by a squatter/mercantile oligarchy to a vibrant and thriving social democracy with abundant opportunity for economic and social mobility.

The Lancashire Migrants

The 225 individuals identified in this study form a small portion of the total migrant intake to Victoria during 1852-1853 period, making up just 1% of the 21,343 government-assisted migrants from England, Wales, Ireland

and Scotland collectively and just 2.2% of the 10,140 migrants originating from England.[5] Over the 12 months between 1 July 1852 and 30 June 1853, the English made up 48% of the total number of migrants landed, but in the last six months of this period migrants from England composed two-thirds of the total number (66%). This rise was even more marked among family groups. Families made up at least 71% of the migrants landed in the 12-month period, and in the second half of this period nearly 80% of these were English families.[6]

Figure 4.1. Total numbers by family status and nationality

Makeup	Total number	Percentage (%)
Families including children aged under 14 years	15,250	71
Single adult males 14+	1929	9
Single adult females 14+	4162	20
Total number	21,341	100
English	10,140	47.5
Scottish	8134	38.1
Irish	3067	14.4
Total number	21,341	100

Source: PROV, VPRS 7310, bk 610.

Performing a complete break-down by occupation of all the males who arrived as assisted migrants in the year under study was beyond the scope and resources of this book. However, a sample of six ships with sizeable numbers of migrants was taken and all the English assisted male passengers were broken down by occupation. Between 50 and 60% of the males were recorded in the *Register* as being agricultural labourers. Another 25% were recorded as traditional village artisans such as blacksmiths, masons and carpenters.

The Lancashire cohort, as recorded in the *Register*, reflects a mirror image of the percentages above, both in familial make-up and male occupation. There is also a similar pattern of growth in numbers. In the three months from July to September 1852, only 27 of the individuals who landed in

Victoria were recorded as being from Lancashire; yet in the following three months, this figure more than doubled to 70 individuals. The final 128 assisted migrants, or 56% of the total, from Lancashire disembarked in the first six months of 1853.

Over the study period, married couples without children and married couples with children under the age of 14 years made up 81% of the Lancashire migrant cohort. This is 10% above the overall percentage of family groups originating from Britain for the study period. However, it matches the percentage of English family migrants in the last six months of the period. The increase in the prevalence of families among the assisted migrants was very much in line with the desire of colonial elites to prioritise migrant families in their misplaced belief that families with young children were less likely to rush to the goldfields upon landing and would seek secure jobs in the major cities of Melbourne and Geelong or on pastoral properties.

The CLEC had expressed considerable reluctance to comply with this desire because of the vulnerability of children aged six years or under on the long sea voyage. However, this was the one issue when the Commissioners were overruled by the permanent under-secretary.[7] There were three teenage males and two teenage females in the subject cohort migrating with their parents – Charles Bennett (aged 14 years), John Holt (aged 15 years), Smith Mercer (aged 15 years), Mary Lancaster (aged 14 years) and Mary Ann Trickett (aged 17 years) – who are included in the single adult categories because they were 14 years and over on embarkation. When we turn to the familial makeup of those identified in the 1851 English Census (Figure 4.3), we find that it is not markedly different from that recorded in the *Register* (Figure 4.2).

Figure 4.2. Familial makeup of Lancashire migrants recorded in *Register*

Makeup	Couple numbers	Individual numbers	Percentage (%)
Married couples without children	17	34	15
Married couples with children	33	66	29
Children under 14 years		82	37
Single adult males 14+		10	4
Single adult females 14+		34	15

Figure 4.3. Familial makeup of Lancashire migrants identified in 1851 Census

Makeup	Couple numbers	Individual numbers	Percentage (%)
Married couples without children	13	26	19
Married couples with children	18	36	26
Children under 14 years		52	38
Single adult males 14+		8	6
Single adult females 14+		16	11

It is within the categories of male occupations that we can best observe the CLEC actively charting its own course in the selection of migrants. Figure 4.4 below shows the percentages for occupations of all males, aged 14 years and above, within the Lancashire cohort as recorded in the *Register*. As would be expected considering the Victorian colonial authorities' insistence that the highest priority was sourcing agricultural labour, this category was predominant.

Listed under agricultural labour are one shepherd, one groom, and one forester who also lived and worked on his father's tenant farm. For reasons explained below, gardeners have been listed as a separate category; however, the reasonable expectation of the colonial authorities was that these persons would have the skills to market garden on the edge of the burgeoning cities. If gardeners are grouped with agricultural labourers, 50% of the males in the cohort can be said to have arrived with agricultural skills. 'Traditional artizans and mechanics' were also a priority, though precisely what defined 'traditional' would, at times, seem to be somewhat confused in colonial minds. This term certainly included those drawn from the ranks of village blacksmiths, masons and probably, at least in the first six months, carpenters and joiners.

The 50% of the Lancashire migrant cohort with agricultural skills, and the 23% with traditional rural-based artisanal skills, accords with the figures for the sample drawn from all assisted male migrants in the study year. What this demonstrates is that the colonial authorities in Victoria thought that the colony was receiving individuals and families who could best service its existing pastoral-based agricultural industry, which many thought would once again dominate the colony's economy once the gold rush had run its course.

Figure 4.4. Male occupations as recorded in *Register*

Occupation type	Percentage (%)
Agricultural labourers	43
Joiners/carpenters	19
Blacksmiths/masons	13
Brickmakers/bricklayers/plasterers	13
Gardeners	7
Other	5

Source: PROV, VPRS 7310, bk 6–9.

Figure 4.5. Male occupations as identified in 1851 Census

Occupation type	Percentage (%)
Carpenters/joiners	21
Urban labourers	21
Textile industry	15.5
Brickmakers/bricklayers/plasterers	10
Agricultural labourers	7.5
Scholars	7.5
Gardeners	5
Smiths/masons	5
Other	7.5

Source: PRO, Census Returns of England 1851.

As the year progressed the occupational mix changed somewhat, with men from building trades, such as brickmakers, bricklayers, plasterers, plumbers, glaziers, carpenters and joiners, becoming a larger proportion of the cohort. As noted in Chapter 1, there was a growing shortage of skilled building workers in Melbourne as early as 1848. By 1852–1853, the shortage had become acute as Melbourne's population exploded, triggering a massive gold-fuelled construction boom. Although government-assisted migrants who were skilled building workers had to contribute a passage fee (see Chapter 3) at least double that required of agricultural labourers, there seem to have been enough applicants from the building trades to enable the CLEC to increasingly favour these workers in the selection process.

The data in the *Register* seems to demonstrate that Governor La Trobe and the CLEC were responding in a timely and flexible manner to the labour requirements of the colony and its non-gold economy through the assisted migration program. However, when tracking the men's occupations back to the 1851 English Census Return, and in some cases the 1841 Census, glaring divergences arise between the occupations recorded in the Census and those listed in the *Register*. This was particularly marked among those described as 'agricultural labourers', as can be seen in Figure 4.5.

A Skilled Labour Force?

The accepted definition of 'skilled' in this period encompassed males who had served regularised apprenticeships in traditional crafts. The data in Figure 4.5 suggests that roughly 30% of the males in the migrant cohort fitted this profile of skilled. Occupations and occupational status, however, were in a state of considerable flux during the first half of the 19th century. The emerging industrial cities created new opportunities in skilled and semi-skilled industrial and commercial occupations. Most of the men and a significant proportion of the women in the cohort, whether single or married, had learned or gained skillsets in this changing and rapidly industrialising environment of southern Lancashire that advantaged them over the general urban proletariat of the time. It was this type of new worker – whether servicing the Liverpool docks, working on the railways, employed in the factories of Manchester or satellite cities such as Bury and Oldham, or engaged in the urban building trades – which overwhelmingly predominated among the migrant cohort, as recorded in the 1851 English Census.

Of those migrants in the cohort with occupations that were perceived as traditionally skilled, the vast majority were overwhelmingly employed in industrial situations. Two of the blacksmiths, Thomas Reynolds, aged 28 years, and James Sowcroft, aged 27 years, were recorded as employed as journeymen/smiths in textile factories in Oldham. Their addresses also denoted the industrial nature of their lives, with Reynolds residing in Soho Forge Square, a square full of foundry and textile workers, and Sowcroft living in the centre of Oldham's cotton mill district.[8]

All but one of the masons were residing in close proximity to the Liverpool docks. A substantial number of the carpenters and joiners also had strong connections with the Liverpool docks or with building works in greater Manchester. Two of the married men, James Woods and James Butler, were recorded in the 1841 English Census as children (aged 14 and 15 years, respectively) living in agricultural communities with their fathers who were agricultural labourers.[9]

Woods was still living in Bootle cum Linacre in 1851, but the village had transformed in 10 years from a primarily rural district into an urbanised locale servicing the expanding Liverpool docks. Butler had left the farming village of Pilling sometime prior to his 16th birthday to find employment as a railway labourer. A single young man, William Ashworth, aged 21 years, lived on his father's tenant farm but worked as a warper in the expanding textile district of Accrington in 1851.[10]

The three 14- and 15-year-old boys travelling with their parents – Smith Mercer, John Holt and Charles Bennett – listed in the *Register* as agricultural workers were recorded in the 1851 Census as scholars. Yet this does not mean that they were not working in a part-time capacity alongside their fathers. Changes in English child labour laws during the 1830s and 1840s restricting the number of hours children under the age of 14 years could work meant that many parents preferred not to report that their children were working even part-time. Two of the fathers of the boys mentioned above, however, were city gardeners and had been born respectively in Manchester and Liverpool, while the father of the third, John Holt, was a dockworker.[11] John's transition into employment as a carter soon after his arrival in Melbourne suggests that he had indeed gained experience with horses and carts back in Liverpool, but in an urban industrial or commercial setting rather than a rural one.

Of the other male migrants, only James Massey, aged 40 years, and William Atkinson, aged 21 years, worked as agricultural labourers on their fathers' tenant farms prior to migration. William Lancaster, aged 40 years, was listed as a 'waller' (that is, a dry-stone wall builder) living in Broughton; and Robert Holden, aged 33 years, was a logger, supplying timber for shipment to the Liverpool docks for construction and boatbuilding.[12] All four were located on the outskirts of cities that were undergoing dramatic expansions and were in a state of incomplete transition from rural districts to industrial or urban locales. Broughton, where Atkinson and Lancaster were born and raised, is now a sprawling dormitory suburb of Preston surrounded by and sometimes intermingled with farmland. Evidence of its mixed farming, mining and industrial past survives, such as a large quarry and an old factory building that once housed a machinery and engineering works.

Broughton was considered an important part of Preston's industrial landscape in the 1840s and 1850s, but an old stone pub dating from the early 19th century, several stone houses and a school provide heritage examples of the type of stone construction William may have worked on. Indeed, Broughton and its migrants are classic examples of economic historian Michael Winstanley's argument that a symbiosis developed between farming, urbanisation and industrialisation in southern Lancashire.[13] Although there is little evidence that the other adult males in the cohort had much, if any, direct experience in agriculture, the data on the migrants who came from townships such as Bootle, Broughton, Garstang and Haslingden reveals that, for some in the cohort, a rural environment was a not-too-distant experience.

For the women in the cohort, the *Register* only records the occupations of single adult females (14 years and older) but not those of wives. Single adult females had to be confirmed as being in steady employment and not from poorhouses to be eligible for assisted migration. This was strictly enforced not only by the CLEC but also by the Poor Law Board, who rejected repeated attempts by the local Poor Law guardians to submit lists of women they considered suitable candidates for assisted migration from the poorhouses.[14]

It is not surprising that the *Register* records 79% of the single women in the cohort as being in domestic service of one type or another. As discussed below, this was the primary occupation for young women in the cities. A further 12% were engaged in clothing trades, and included dressmakers, milliners and, in one case, a leatherworker. One woman, Sarah Foley, declared that she was 'never in service', and her sister, Mary, was recorded as a 'shopmaid'. There were two teenage girls classified as single adult females because they were aged over 14 years and travelling with their parents. Mary A. Lancaster, aged 14 years, was recorded as a domestic servant, while the indomitable Mary Ann Trickett, aged 16 years, was the only female recorded as engaged in factory work.[15]

The self declaration of Mary Ann as a 'factory girl' is remarkably bold as Lancashire factory girls had gained a reputation as 'a fallen creature disposed to indecency'.[16] The morality of Lancashire women who were working in factories had come under increasing scrutiny from the 1820s onwards as women entered the textile industry in large numbers. It was increasingly argued, particularly from the mid-century onwards, that factory work 'degraded and contaminated' female workers, and observations were made that the 'character and conduct' of females in Lancashire cotton mills were 'disgusting and appalling'.[17] This rising demonisation of the 'factory girl' was not just a product of middle-class morality separating the masculine sphere of work from the feminine one of home and domesticity. It was also a reflection of the rising status of tradesmen, shopkeepers and master craftsmen, who wished to set themselves apart from more lowly factory workers, while unions and guilds increasingly saw the influx of female factory workers as depressing male work opportunities and wages in the factories.

Importing single young women to Victoria was an attempt to correct the substantial imbalance between the male and female population that existed in the colony. The intention was for these women to marry and provide a stable domestic and civilising home life for their husbands and offspring who would naturally eventuate. Those trained and stably employed in domestic service were considered to have the necessary qualities required to make good wives for working-class men. Dressmakers, milliners and those engaged in similar occupations, which were viewed as giving them domestic skills, were considered the next best thing.

Thus, when turning to the data on women in the 1851 English Census, there is not the same glaring discrepancy between occupations recorded in the Census and those recorded in the *Register* that we find among the male occupations in those records. Domestic service was by far the single-biggest employer of single young women, even in the heart of industrial Lancashire, and thus this was by far the largest pool from which employed unmarried young women could be drawn.[18] But there were still enough differences in the records to warrant comment. Of the single young women authoritatively identified in the 1851 English Census, only 53% were engaged in domestic service, including the above-mentioned Sarah Foley. Factory workers accounted for 18% of the listed female occupations.

These young women, including Mary Ann Trickett, were not cheap and expendable unskilled workers but undertook skilled roles in cotton and woollen mills. Elizabeth Smith, for instance, was a power-loom weaver. Historian Anna Clark describes single young women in the cotton-weaving towns of southern Lancashire in the first half of the 19th century as 'heroic' in establishing a measure of financial independence as textile workers.[19]

The shop maid, Mary Foley, operated her own business in the markets of Liverpool as a 'dealer in poultry', while another young woman who may have been a friend of Foley, Margaret Kearney, was a 'dealer in fish' in the same markets. This bending of the truth in regard actual occupation or type of economic activity suggests that young women were equal to the menfolk in gaming the process to win assisted passage, and that they were well aware of those occupations that the authorities considered desirable and those deemed unacceptable.

According to the *Register*, married women did not have occupations. This refusal to acknowledge the occupational status of working-class women reflects the profound shift in middle-class attitudes towards working women that occurred in the first half of the 19th century. The evangelical Christian ideal of the 'angel in the house' increasingly dominated attitudes regarding the proper role married women were to play, not only in middle-class families but also increasingly within working-class households. The notion of separate spheres of living (being the private domestic and the public work domains, with a woman's proper role confined exclusively to the former sphere) paid little heed to the economics of working-class daily life. But, with a societal emphasis on 'religious and domestic virtues' and 'the moral regeneration of the nation', this notion was clearly a powerful motivator both in England and for the middle-class elites in the anglophone colonies. It is therefore not surprising to find that in the *Register* wives were never recorded as having an occupation.[20] Yet, of the married women from the cohort identified in the 1851 English Census, 41% were recorded as employed or engaged in economic activity.

'Heroic' young women power-loom weavers.
T. Allom, illustrator, Edward Baines, History of the cotton manufacture in Great Britain *(1835)*.
State Library of NSW, MMS ID 991016453789702626.

Data extracted by John McKay from the 1851 English Census on married women recorded as participating in economic occupations show 14% overall in England and Wales and 20% for the county of Lancashire. Figure 4.6 lists the percentage of married women recorded as economically occupied in those townships and parishes from which the migrant cohort was drawn.

Figure 4.6. Married women recorded as employed in 1851 Census

Township or borough	% employed
Blackburn	33.80
Oldham	33.42
Ashton under Lyne	31.14
Burnley	29.00
Manchester and Salford	22.65
Bury	23.05
Rochdale	22.68
Bolton	20.97
Liverpool	8.85
West Derby	6.31

Source: BPP 1852-3, LXXXVIII, 1851 Census of Great Britain, Population tables, II, vol. 1, cxl–cxlix

The percentage of married women recorded as being in employment in what are frequently referred to as the 'cotton towns' averaged 27% in the 1851 Census. By comparison, for Liverpool, the recorded percentage of employed married women, at less than 10%, was well below the Lancashire average. The figures for the married women from the cohort identified in the 1851 Census as living in Liverpool or West Derby show that 41% were economically employed, the same rate as that for all married women in the migrant cohort.

Caution needs to be observed in comparing and interpreting these figures. Townships such as Blackburn and Oldham were likely to have a greater percentage of married women in work than would a port city like Liverpool, where there was a much larger commercial merchant class. However, there are some conclusions that can be drawn regarding married women in the cohort, the work undertaken by them and the communities from which they were recruited.

Working women formed an important economic, social and cultural component of the cohort and of the communities from which they were drawn. What is striking is just what those occupations were. There were two power-loom weavers, several weavers, fettlers and carders, all considered skilled jobs in the factory hierarchy.[21] Bythell's contention that Lancashire women dominated skilled and semi-skilled factory work in the first half of the 19th century and were being paid similar rates as men for the same jobs is borne out by the examples from the migrant cohort.[22] Women making up the Lancashire cohort migrating to Victoria had diverse work and business experiences, including in newly created factory work, which provided them with skillsets and the entrepreneurial drive to play a significant role in the development of a diverse economy in the new Colony of Victoria.

The Southern Lancashire Beltway

Of all the people recorded in the *Register* as coming from Lancashire in the period of this study, only one family of five, the Butler family, are recorded in the 1851 Census as living north of Preston (which was then considered the northern boundary of industrial southern Lancashire).[23] The Butler family were living in Ulverstone in the far north of what was then still Lancashire, but is now part of Cumberland County. It was a heavily industrialised centre of mining, shipbuilding and steam engine construction for railways, and somewhat of an outlier when compared to other northern districts of the county. Of the rest of the cohort identified in the 1851 Census, 120 individuals (87%) were living or working in industrial or commercial urban areas connected to either the Greater Liverpool or Greater Manchester regions.[24]

A map of Lancashire drawn by Ian Hall in 1852 illustrates the dense web of rail, roads and canals spreading out from Manchester and interconnecting this southern beltway of industrial and commercial landscapes.

When Hall was drafting the map, 40–55% of Lancastrians lived either in Manchester or in industrial urban areas along this web of rail, roads and canals. Most men, and many of the women, were engaged in semi-skilled or skilled work in the textile mills, or employed in newly developing technological industries that were beginning to challenge cotton's dominance. In the 1840s and early 1850s, a quite dramatic political and socioeconomic transformation was occurring in this greater Manchester region, which reshaped Chartism and working-class democratic action in the region. This transformation is essential to understanding the migrant cohort's settlement of Victoria and the colony's political, socioeconomic and cultural development.

Merseyside

Sixty-five individuals (47%) from the Lancashire migrant cohort were identified as residing in Greater Liverpool, particularly the newer dockland suburbs marching north along the River Mersey. The majority of the adult males in the Greater Liverpool subset were associated with the docks in some form or another, and few in this subset, including the women, would have been unaffected by the vast maritime trade entering and leaving the heaving Port of Liverpool. According to the maritime historian Michael Stammers, in 1850:

> Liverpool was the second city of the British Empire and its ship owners and merchants controlled millions of pounds of assets and millions of tons of shipping … It was a great crossroads of sea and land; distributing goods was its business, not manufacturing.[25]

Few Liverpudlians would have believed in the myth that migration to Australia was akin to a life sentence in a distant land. But when the first shipment of gold from Victoria landed in Liverpool in December 1851, accompanied by two returning miners, any question that Australia might be an undesirable destination was put to bed.

Essential to understanding the difference between the migrants from the industrial Greater Manchester area and the Liverpudlian migrants is that commerce and the distribution of goods, not manufacturing, was Liverpool's main business. From the 1830s, the docklands underwent a massive expansion both north and south along the Mersey from their original central Liverpool location. David Williams argues that the major impetus for this expansion was the growth of bulk cargo trades: 'It was the growing volume, not value, of goods in overseas trade which largely accounted for … the rise of the port of Liverpool in the first half of the nineteenth century'.[26] This bulk cargo trade involved the import of primary commodities such as cotton, timber and grain, and included massive quantities of wool from Victoria, to fuel the industrialising northern centres such as Manchester and its hinterland, as well as the export of manufactured goods from those same centres. To handle this rapid growth in trade the acreage of the Liverpool enclosed docks grew by 470% between the 1830s and 1850s.[27]

This growth was at its most expansive to the north, where sand dunes and agricultural areas such as West Everton, Kirkdale and Bootle cum Linacre were engulfed by the construction of the new dockyards; of rows of terrace houses to accommodate the growing army of clerical workers, dock keepers, construction workers and labourers employed by the docklands; and of the warehouses of the stevedores and merchants.[28]

Earlier this chapter identified James Woods living as a young boy in 1841 with his family in Bootle, where his father was an agricultural labourer in an area dominated by agricultural labourers and tenant farmers.[29] By 1851, the agricultural labourer and the tenant farmer had vanished from Bootle to be replaced by workers employed directly or indirectly by the dockyards. James was one of these workers living in a street that had become home to better-skilled and better-paid workers choosing to avoid the low-status, mainly Irish areas of central Liverpool in favour of these newer more spacious terrace housing developments.[30] A substantial proportion of the migrant cohort identified in the 1851 Census as living in the Merseyside region were living in terrace housing in these newer areas, suggesting that, like the rest of the assisted migrants from Lancashire, the CLEC was actively recruiting migrants or favouring applications from better-off working-class areas.

There are some distinct social and cultural contrasts between these Liverpudlian workers and the workers from the industrialising areas of southeast Lancashire. In its early modern history, Liverpool conformed to the national norm for industrialising, but from 1800 onwards, 'as England industrialized … Liverpool de-industrialized'.[31] Belchem argues that this can be traced to the 'exaggerated pride' Liverpool took in its commercial image, a pride shared by its independent workers for whom the traditional casualism of the commercial labouring force 'was a cherished symbol of independence, the best guarantee of the freedom from … the tyranny of the factory bell'.[32] We get a sense of this when exploring the contrast between the occupations listed in the *Register* and those recorded the 1851 English Census.

Those males in the migrant cohort recorded in the *Register* as agricultural labourers who could identified in the 1851 Census as coming from Liverpool occupations were usually recorded as 'labourer' in the Census. Sometimes an entry was qualified using 'dock labourer' or similar. The streets on which they resided housed men who were working in occupations connected to the docklands. The labour mix found in these streets was predominantly of dockyard employees, railway workers, carters, porters, labourers, masons, carpenters and journeymen. The balance of the male migrants from Liverpool were either construction workers or artisans, with masons and carpenters predominating.

These were occupations in huge demand during the 1840s and 1850s, as the Liverpool docklands spread up and down the Mersey estuary.

It is difficult to get a clear picture of how well these people were doing financially, as much of Liverpool's documented labour history has focused on the Irish poor. Stammers claims that 'although dock work was on a casual basis, it called for a wide range of skills in slinging the cargo, [and] loading and packing it in ship holds to ensure that it was safe and stable on the voyage'.[33] Belchem furthers this argument, by saying that the Liverpool labourer was 'neither undifferentiated nor unskilled'. He proffers that there was a premium on proficiency and specialist know-how and that 'those with the knack were the first to find employment' and generally received higher wages than other unskilled workers who formed the rest of a work gang.[34] This may explain why many of these labourers from the Merseyside seemed content to hang on to the occupational label of labourer long after they had migrated and even once they had prospered.

Edward Holt and his son John provide a vivid example of this propensity to cling on to the labourer identity. Edward, his wife Harriet and their five sons aged from one to 14 years lived in Bootle at 190 Mersey Street North (now called Derby Road), which ran from central Liverpool through Kirkdale to Bootle. The Holt family were clearly part of the internal migration from old central Liverpool to the new housing areas developing alongside the expanding dockyards. Edward and Harriet had a five-year-old boy named David, born in Liverpool, and a one year old, Samuel, born in Kirkdale. Edward was a labourer while his oldest son, John, was recorded as a scholar. However, in the *Register*, John's occupation was recorded as groom. John may well have gained experience in handling horses for carters in Liverpool because, by 1856, he was working as a carter in Melbourne. There is no occupation noted for Harriet, although this does not mean that she did not do some sort of work. Many of the wives and single women on this street had occupations. Several were stall operators in markets dealing in fish, poultry, rabbits and dairy products. Others plied trades alongside their husbands, or worked as dressmakers or laundry women. At least three wives from the migrant cohort were skilled craftspeople in their own right.

Of the Merseysiders from the cohort, 54% were born in Liverpool metropolitan districts. Single adult females were exclusively born in the city, while a very high proportion of adult males were also born in Liverpool. It is the wives, presumably moving to Liverpool for economic opportunity, who predominate among the outsiders. Fewer than 30% of the Liverpool members of the cohort originated from outside the southern Lancashire region – predominantly from the surrounding English counties of Cheshire, Cumberland and Yorkshire. There were two families from Scotland and a handful of men and women from northern Wales who moved to and married in Liverpool. Despite the flood of the Irish into Liverpool during the 1840s, there were no Irish-born government-assisted migrants in the Liverpool subset of the cohort. If there is a pattern to internal migration among the Lancashire cohort, it was within the already close-knit industrial communities attached to the growing metropolitan areas of Liverpool and Manchester. This pattern of internal immigration was best personified by James and Ruth Seddon.

The Seddon family provide a quite remarkable portrait of migration from their origins in the mid-16th century with tenant farmer, William Seddon, the first recorded person to bear the name in Prescott, Lancashire. James Seddon's father was among an increasing number of Seddon family members who seized opportunity and migrated to Liverpool to work as a carpenter in the rapidly growing dockland workforce. Ruth, James's wife, is an example of a married woman who, prior to marriage, had moved to Liverpool in search of work as a seamstress or dressmaker.[35] She was from Cumberland across the county border. By the time of the 1851 English Census, James and his family were living in the Morpeth Docks area, across the Mersey at Birkenhead, where he was employed as a joiner. All his neighbours were employed in some capacity within the dockyards.[36] When in 1852 James (aged 35 years), Ruth (aged 34 years) and their five children, William (aged 12 years), James (aged 10 years), Robert (aged 9 years), Ruth (aged 5 years) and 1-year-old Agnes migrated, they were spearheading what was to become a flood of Seddons and their wider kinship and community groups migrating to the northeast of the US, Australia, Canada and New Zealand.[37]

What should be made of the preponderance of migrants originating from the urban industrialised and commercial areas of southern Lancashire? The argument that those identified through the 1851 English Census are unrepresentative can be dismissed as 61% of the cohort were identified in that census. This percentage was uniform across all ships that disembarked migrants from the Lancashire cohort. There are three common factors within this cohort. First, except for the one family mentioned above, all the cohort was drawn from urban industrial and commercial southern Lancashire. The tiny percentage that still lived rural lives were from fringe areas adjacent to rapidly expanding cities. Second, all the men occupied skilled or semi-skilled positions in the hierarchy of the working-class labour force, including those from Liverpool who were described as 'labourer' in the 1851 Census. Third, the women, whether married or unmarried, who were economically occupied outside domestic service were often working in positions alongside men. Their earnings were most probably above the average for women engaged in industrial or commercial work in England. Domestic servants could also arguably be included in the semi-skilled working-class category.

Although not as thorough as this interrogation, the casual review I have undertaken of the CLEC migration program in the four years subsequent to the study period, before it was wound down, suggests that the mix of occupation and location did not change substantially for Lancashire assisted migrants. So, why were central and northern Lancastrians not migrating while southern Lancastrians were migrating in increasing numbers? Workers associated with the expansion of the Liverpool docks, whether as labourers, masons, or carpenters and joiners, make up a good third of the adult male migrant cohort. Often they had seamen as neighbours, and in two cases as lodgers. The idea of the journey to Australia being a life sentence was an enduring myth, but, at least for Liverpudlians, an easily punctured one.

There is some evidence to suggest that a small proportion of the cohort were already mobile and ready to move in pursuit of economic opportunity. Despite the shipping records declaring that county was supposed to mean county of birth, a small number of the cohort were born elsewhere, in other English counties, Wales or Scotland. Except for the families and men mentioned as living in rural Lancashire, but close to the cities, there were very few native Lancastrians who were born outside the major urban cities, whether that be Liverpool, Manchester, Oldham, Bolton or similar urban centres. A few of the cohort had moved, but from one city to the next. The often-discussed pattern of migration – of rural to urban internal migration, and then emigration to one of the colonies or ex-colonies – does not apply to the greater majority of the Lancashire cohort. Although there is little written documentary evidence from these migrants, there are indications in their stories of tendencies towards upward mobility. Property ownership for these migrants, no matter how upwardly mobile they might be, was an increasingly unlikely proposition in the UK. The pursuit of property ownership via migration appears influential in shaping the individual decisions to take the ultimate risk and migrate to Australia.

The explosive surge in applications by English families from June and July of 1852, which was more than reflected in the surge of migrants from Lancashire, arguably suggests that the allure of gold was the most immediate pull factor. However, the determination to own property is the most influential driver to emerge in the later chapters of this collective biography. The migrant cohort determinedly set about, along with many of their neighbours and allies, to build a small-property-owning society. While it is difficult to define precisely what they meant by 'small', it usually encompassed the twin characteristics of being something that they were able to freely enter and being no larger than what an individual or group of individuals could reasonably work. In some industries, particularly mining from 1870s onwards, the capital requirements became such that this type of property ownership was not possible. However, a small-property-owning society became the prevailing ideology behind the political, socioeconomic and cultural development of Victoria.

Chapter 5

COOPERATIVES AND BUILDING SOCIETY SHARES

From Revolution to Reformation in the Greater Manchester Area

Mellor Street, Ardwick.
The house Joseph and Lucy moved into is the third door from the left.
Courtesy of the Doody family descendants.

With 1870 I returned to my inquiry ... again to Lancashire ... my sorrowful impressions were confirmed. In our old Chartist time, it is true, Lancashire working men were in rags by thousands, and many of them often lacked food. But their intelligence was demonstrated wherever you went. You would see them in groups discussing the great doctrine of political justice ... Now, you will seen no such group in Lancashire. But you will hear well-dressed working men talking, as they walk with their hands in their pockets, of 'Co-ops' (Co-operative Stores), and their shares in them, or in building societies.

Thomas Cooper, *The Life of Thomas Cooper: Written by Himself*[1]

From the Napoleonic Wars onwards, Manchester was viewed by many as the aggressive bastion of working-class militancy. It was the city to which adherents of the People's Charter (Chartists), together with other working-class radicals across the nation, looked for inspiration and leadership, and where the establishment morbidly feared violent revolution would be kindled. In the summer of 1848, when a significant section of the Chartist movement lost patience with Hector Berlioz's 'decent revolutionaries' and embarked on a conspiracy to engineer a national uprising, the signal for the uprising was to come out of Manchester.[2]

It never came, and historians ever since have debated the reasons for this 'dramatic watershed' in which Manchester made a 'swift transition from the militant working-class radicalism of the 1830s and 1840s to the relative quiescence of the age of equipoise'.[3] Historians of the 'Manchester School', led by Alan Kidd, have challenged the idea of a 'dramatic watershed' moment, arguing that it was neither swift nor a repudiation of working-class radicalism, and suggesting instead 'that popular politics was adapting to the industrial system'.[4] This school contends that Manchester's post-Chartist working class 'retained a strong sense of their working-class identity and value system' and at the core of this value system was a deeply held and enduring belief in the great worth of egalitarianism.[5]

Adherents of the Manchester School argue that a reassessment by the better-off working classes of the changing social, economic and political conditions in Manchester throughout the 1840s led to a practical change in tactics and strategies. They reject the arguments of Silver and Hobsbawm that an elite of union leaders was bought off by the middle class while the various instruments of oppression, such as a newly created police force, were used to contain and tame the working-class masses. The Manchester School believes, despite the angry rhetoric of class warfare that dominated Manchester's political dialogue during the 1840s, that middle-class liberals and working-class radicals and trade unionists were moving towards a political accommodation of each other's economic self-interests.

This led to the Liberal–Labour alliance that came to dominate the political landscape of Northern England during the second half of the 19th century. The most significant working-class contribution towards the development of this two-way street were the institutions of mutuality – cooperatives, building societies, provident funds and friendly societies – which all found their fullest flowering in Northern England. These institutions would provide impetus for a working-class political movement that increasingly realised that collectively it could implement Chartism at the local political level.[6]

An examination of primary source material in Manchester – rate books, trade directories, and building society, cooperative and local body records – found numerous connections between many of the migrants from the cohort and these developments. The most intriguing link was an accounting firm, Duffield, Lofthouse, Whitfield. This business first appeared in the *Manchester Rate Books* in connection with the Doody family. Searching for this firm in Manchester's secondary histories draws a blank. Yet the primary sources suggest that the firm of Duffield, Lofthouse, Whitfield was deeply involved in the developments that transformed Manchester's economic, political and social landscape from the late 1830s to the end of the 1860s. This firm of accountants were vital to my comprehension of the socioeconomic forces impacting on the migrants drawn from Manchester, and in understanding the communities and societies that the migrant cohort went on to help shape in Victoria. By exploring the origins of Joseph and Lucy Doody in Manchester, their pre-migration story and their connections to Duffield, Lofthouse and Whitfield, it is possible to gain an appreciation of what the migrant cohort planted in Victoria.

The Doodys of Manchester

Joseph and Lucy Doody were government-assisted migrants from Manchester who disembarked in Melbourne in March 1853.[7] Their subsequent settlement journey took them to the Bendigo goldfields, where they had four sons. The next leg was on to Bears Lagoon, where Joseph and his sons selected land and became involved with other selectors in a titanic battle with John Ettershank, a local pastoralist, or squatter. The Doody story in Victoria is remarkably well-documented, and reveals from a bottom-up perspective many of the major political, economic and cultural developments shaping the colony in the second half of the 19th century.

The Doodys, like so many of the gold-digger generation and the artisans, tradesmen and shopkeepers of Melbourne, were adherents of the particular brand of colonial liberalism that emerged in Victoria under the leadership of Graham Berry, three-time Premier of Victoria and a small shopkeeper from much the same background as the migrant cohort. The Doodys' Manchester story reveals much about the growing convergence of middle-class liberalism and working-class radical politics in Manchester, and thus the deep attraction and intense loyalty to the colonial liberal politics that emerged in Victoria.

Joseph Doody first comes to light in the 1841 English Census. Aged 13 years, he was residing at Granby Place in the London Road district with his mother, Mary, and four siblings, the youngest of whom, John, was 10 years old. All the family were recorded as having occupations in the textile industries. Joseph and John were employed in a fabric print works. Mary was a carder.[8] They were living in a one-up, one-down, back-to-back house typical of this district, for which Mary was paying a gross rent of £5 5s per week.[9] Joseph was born circa 1828 in Manchester. His parents were Irish, possibly from the northern counties, who had migrated to Manchester sometime between 1822 and 1824. This can be ascertained from the 1841 English Census as his oldest sister Ann (aged 19) was born in Ireland, but his other siblings – from Denis (aged 17) to the youngest John (aged 10) – were born in Manchester.[10]

Throughout his life, Joseph regarded himself as a Manchester Lancastrian rather than Irish and would continue to associate with other Lancastrians long after his migration to Australia. This may have been an essential survival tactic as anti-Irish prejudice peaked during the 1840s, particularly in the wake of the great famine of 1846, when Irish migration to Manchester became a flood and inflamed existing tensions over unskilled Irish workers driving down wages.[11]

Joseph's father, John, did not appear in the census data. Doody family trees suggest that John senior had died by the time of the 1841 Census. This may not be the case; but he was clearly not merely absent for the night. A search of the *Manchester Rate Books* shows that it was Joseph's mother, Mary, who was the registered tenant for a series of three-roomed tenements in and around Granby Row between 1839 and 1856, after which she moved into the home of her second daughter, Catherine.[12]

Granby Row was in the heart of the London Road district, Manchester's oldest industrial area. Engels called the street 'Manchester's oldest and thus its worst'.[13] H. K. McKeand, the district's Poor Law medical officer who actually lived in the area, vividly describes living conditions following the cholera epidemics of 1848 and 1849:

> Cholera principally localized itself in the centre of my district; a large square knot of old buildings, which is bound by the Medlock upon one side, and by Granby-row on the other, with its burial-ground, overflowing to repletion, and constantly exhaling the most fetid smells … The houses are all old, principally having cellars to them, full of courts without yards, and all built back to back with out, without any passage, and ventilation of course deficient; the neighbourhood has its due share of manure heaps, piggeries, bone-dealers, cinder accumulations, &c. &c. The drainage is very bad, as it is always is about the old dwellings; the privies are crowded with too many applicants, one sufficing in general a bundle of houses; the poor in these places, I find, make use of chamberpots, in preference, and empty them on the cinder heaps.[14]

About the time Joseph was preparing to migrate, his older brother, Dennis, who was still living in the Granby Row area, died of typhus, which, like cholera, was endemic to the area.[15] It is a reminder that, while Joseph and a significant minority of the working classes were to benefit from rising living standards throughout the second half of the 1840s, the majority of Joseph's family did not. In the decade between 1841 and 1851, Joseph acquired the skills to enable his escape from this impoverished and squalid district. There is no record of him serving an apprenticeship, so it is likely that he acquired his skills on the job.

The population of the London Road district consisted chiefly of unskilled millhands and hand-loom weavers.[16] These were the occupations most adversely affected by the economic turmoil and escalating mechanisation of the 1840s. Like many of her contemporary Lancashire female workers, Mary would have been earning a 'better wage than any other female worker' in the UK, but it is unlikely to have been sufficient for a single mother with four children.[17] This is probably why even her youngest child was in paid work.

Although the *Factory Act 1833* regulated child working conditions in the textile industry, Joseph would have been exposed to the concerted campaign for additional reforms to those child labour laws. There was an active Children's Factory Committee made up of children working in the same factories as Joseph. In 1836, they petitioned the House of Commons:

> We respect our masters, and are willing to work for our support, and that of our parents, but we want time for more rest, a little play, and to learn to read and write. We do not think it right that we should know nothing but work and suffering, from Monday morning to Saturday

night, to make others rich. Do, good gentlemen, inquire carefully into our concern.[18]

After massive agitation including one meeting in Manchester that attracted well over 100,000 people, additional legislation further limiting the number of hours children could work and requiring that they receive a regulated education was finally passed in 1847. The success of this campaign saw the Children's Factory Committee morph into a very active Manchester youth branch of the Chartist movement.[19]

Boys employed in a Manchester textile factory circa 1847.
Joseph Ashton, A Picture of Manchester *(new ed: 1969).*
State Library of NSW, MMS ID 991016453789702626.

The campaigns for safer and better working conditions for children would not have been the only industrial disturbances influencing Joseph. The Plug Strikes of August 1842 effectively shut down all the textile industry, including related industries such as the textile print works and dye factories. Although these strikes began as spontaneous protests triggered by the general economic distress of this period (including high unemployment, wage reductions and the surging cost of food staples), the collective withdrawal of labour led to a resurgence in Chartism in Manchester and surrounding textile towns. There is no direct evidence that Joseph was involved in or affected by the Chartist movement. However, throughout the 1840s he was acquiring the necessary skills to gain entry into the new industrial occupations known to have been among the most active in the Chartist movement and trade union politics generally. So Joseph was unlikely to have been unaffected by this radical activity.[20]

At the age of 21 years Joseph married Lucy Bowden (aged 23 years) on 12 August 1849. On the marriage certificate James Bowden, Lucy's father, was recorded as being a 'maker-up' (a garment-maker).[21] In the 1851 English Census, Lucy is listed as having the occupation of 'milliner'.[22] Over time, milliner has come to mean a hat designer and/or maker; but historically milliners, predominantly female, produced a range of garments for men, women and children, including hats, shirts, cloaks, shifts, caps, neckerchiefs and undergarments. All the Bowden family were engaged in outwork for the textile industry. Nigel Goose argues that the mechanisation of the textile industries in Lancashire resulted in a substantial growth of home-based production work.[23]

Meanwhile, Joseph Doody had moved from menial work as a child labourer in a print and dye business to being engaged as a plumber and glazier.[24] Moreover, the just-married couple moved into a brand new two-up, two-down terrace house located within one of Ardwick's new subdivisions, for which they were paying a gross rental of £8 15s per week. This was nearly twice as much as Mary Doody was paying for the tenement Joseph was leaving. The home and its neighbourhood were a far cry from the grimness of Granby Row, and Joseph and Lucy's willingness to embrace the new opportunities presented by industrialisation places them within an emerging working class seeking to leverage entrepreneurial prospects for the betterment of their families.

Initially, Ardwick was Manchester's first garden suburb for emerging industrialists and merchants desiring to escape the cramped and disease-prone old city to airy, light-filled houses with large gardens. However, by the mid-1840s, the suburb had commenced another transformation – into a powerhouse for the newer innovative engineering and chemical industries. In response to this industrial and commercial development, rows of terrace houses sprung up to accommodate the workers in these new industries and their families.

Mellor Street, which consisted of 20 houses, was the last in an expansive development around a main street called Chapelfield Road, which commenced in 1844 and was completed in 1849–1850 by the builders, Mellor

& Greenhalgh. Mellor & Greenhalgh were 'speculative builders with little capital recently risen from the working class themselves'.[25] In the 1833 edition of *Pigot's Manchester & Salford Directory*, Mellor was listed as a joiner living and working in the same London Road district as the Doody family.[26] By 1838, he resided at a sawmill and timber yard on Chapelfield Road that he owned and operated in partnership with Thomas Greenhalgh.[27] The 1842 *Manchester Rate Book* listed them as owning and operating a brickworks in the same area.[28] The 1842 records also noted them as the owners of a row of six newly constructed but empty houses on River Street and Chapelfield Road.[29]

In 1844 and 1845, Mellor & Geenhalgh engaged in an explosive burst of building activity, possibly because the business found an investor, the accountancy firm Duffield, Lofthouse, Whitfield.[30] The firm is notable for being the accountants for Richard Cobden and auditors for the Anti-Corn Law League (ACLL).[31] George Whitfield was also a cousin of Joseph Whitfield, one of the leading innovative precision engineers in Ardwick's emerging industrial undertakings, who developed the standardised screw thread and the first mechanised streetsweeper. Kidd describes builders such as Mellor as 'jerry builders', who 'usually did not work to any standard and were desperately inefficient'; but he may have been describing builders from earlier decades in suburbs like Ancoats, because clearly something a great deal more ambitious brought the builders and accountants together.[32]

During his 1920s childhood, Les Sutton, a local Ardwick historian and archivist, grew up in one of the houses built by Mellor & Greenhalgh, and offers this description of his parents' home:

> Our house is a two-up and two-down terraced, the rooms on the ground floor consisting of a parlour, kitchen (living room) and a tiny lean-to scullery. There are two bedrooms, stairs leading to these separating the parlour from the kitchen. The parlour window which fronts the house has hinged double wooden shutters which can be closed and barred but I have never seen these closed … Windows are glazed variously with two large or six small panes to each. Little more is done to break the monotonous frontage of terraced property, but the impression per street is not at all unpleasant … A small stone-paved backyard containing a wash-boiler, and a water closet abutting the scullery wall complete the permanent features.[33]

Sutton adds that, when built, these terrace houses were considered the height of improved living with their modern amenities, and even 70 or 80 years after construction they were enviously eyed by those living across the river in Ancoats.

Ardwick was part of the Borough of Manchester and governed by the Manchester Municipal Council. However, Ardwick had independent responsibility for 'Lighting, Cleansing, Watching, and Improving' its own neighbourhood. These responsibilities became a significant feature of Manchester's local government development. However, Manchester City did not enjoy independent status as a borough until 1838. It was not until 1843 that the town council, dominated by a commerce-based middle-class elite, managed to wrest political control from the Police Commissioners, the most important arm of the medieval rural-based manorial court leet that had previously run Manchester.

The Manchester Municipal Council set about reorganising Manchester's town and parish structures, and instituted several locally elected boards to manage municipal functions such as sanitation, drainage and garbage collection. The council had difficulty in attracting middle-class representatives to serve on these boards. But many of the Chartist and trade union leaders realised the benefits that could be derived from participation in this sort of activity. As one election leaflet of the period stated, they were:

> the men who would look after the courts and alleys in which the poor resided … the gentlemen part of such bodies did not do the work, and would not do the work. No, the work can and must be done by plain practical hardworking men like ourselves.[34]

This vigorous and practical engagement in municipal affairs by ordinary workers seemed to somewhat alleviate the middle class's morbid fear of trade unionism.[35]

Conversely, new inventions like Joseph Whitworth's Automation Street Sweeping Machine scared many of the older radicals, who saw industrialisation as the 'great evil' and Whitworth's machine as a demon personified – each machine commissioned by local authorities put 50 streetsweepers out of work.[36] However, for the working-class men increasingly dominating the local municipal boards such as Ardwick's, the machine was to be embraced for the benefits it brought to the health and wellbeing of their neighbours, lending support to Kidd's argument that popular politics was adapting to the industrial system.[37]

Hewitt argues that the promise of immediate if gradual improvement, in contrast to the less certain gains of Chartist political action, became increasingly important among substantial swathes of Manchester's working class.

Whitworth Street Cleaning Machine.
Manchester Courier, *14 September, 1844*.
British Newspaper Archives, British Library.

He suggests that this explains the growing popularity and importance of the mutuality movement, as exemplified by cooperatives and building societies, because 'by appealing to the individual action in co-operation for the common good, they helped bridge individual aspirations for improvement and working-class mutuality'.[38] The building societies that emerged out of working-class communities – Ardwick had its own building society – are a prime example of an individual's aspiration for ownership of freehold land finding an outlet through mutuality.

Chase argues that if O'Connor's great Chartist land scheme had been organised along the lines of the Mancunian Bowkett structures, it might not have been the disaster it became.[39] Charles Duffield, James Lofthouse and George Whitfield were among the trustees of several mutual organisations, and Duffield and Lofthouse were respectively the founding Secretary and the Treasurer of the South Lancashire Permanent Building Society, which acted as an umbrella for the many smaller neighbourhood- or industry-based societies. The aim of the South Lancashire Permanent Building Society was 'to enable the industrious classes to acquire with ease small independent freeholds of their own'.[40]

Duffield, Lofthouse and Whitfield's involvement in the development and promotion of mutual organisations could be seen as part of the effort by the middle class to control and tame the working class, as postulated by earlier historians. The Manchester School, however, is adamant that building societies were very much an affirmation of working-class identity, with values driven from within the movement rather than instituted and enforced from above. Participation in cooperative effort and engagement with mutual entities were to be significant contributing factors for migrant families succeeding in their dream of betterment via the goldfields and property ownership.

There is an intriguing connection between the ACLL and Duffield, Lofthouse and Whitfield's involvement with the building society movement. During 1845–1846, a House of Commons Select Committee on Votes for Electors explored allegations of vote-buying by the ACLL. Specifically, the ACLL was accused of providing sums of money to working-class individuals to invest in building society shares and thus gain the required property qualifications to vote. Witnesses to the inquiry alleged that this money was funnelled through Duffield, Lofthouse and Whitfield. The accountants were called before the Committee for questioning, but the allegations were never sustained. However, it is clear that the accountants were financing a number of individuals from 'the industrious working-classes' into property ownership, who thereby gained the right to vote through the pre-purchase of building society shares.[41]

The articles of association for the South Lancashire Permanent Building Society allowed for members to purchase shares on mortgage using the same shares as collateral, and documents reveal that Duffield, Lofthouse and Whitfield were acting as brokers for this finance. Amounts of between £50 and £500 were being loaned to purchase shares. Both Kidd and Hewitt confirm that, during the period 1840 to 1859, an increasing number of working-class individuals were admitted to the electoral roll in Manchester. Kidd and Hewitt suggest that this was due to the rising value of real estate in these decades.[42] Yet could the rise in the number of working-class individuals being admitted to the electoral roll be due as much to those newly entering property ownership or gaining the property qualifications through share schemes run by societies such as the South Lancashire Permanent Building Society?

It is tempting to speculate about how far Joseph and Lucy Doody may have advanced themselves if they had remained in Ardwick. By 1850, Joseph's boss, George Mellor, had lifted himself out of the working classes and was living in a substantial house on Ardwick Green.[43] However, therein may lie the nub of the matter. Whereas Mellor's story was not an uncommon one for a Manchester working man in the early years of the city's growth, as the 1840s progressed, so opportunities for advancement lessened as the increased complexity of mechanisation demanded ever greater capital resources, raising both property prices and building costs. Joseph and Lucy Doody may well have hit the ceiling for self-betterment in Manchester and saw assisted migration as a real opportunity to further themselves.

In refuting longstanding historical scholarship that treats Manchester in dichotomous terms, the work of the Manchester School has revealed a picture of Greater Manchester that is extraordinary in its heterogeneous nature. However, some themes do emerge that seem to be common to the region and to the migrant cohort. The most important was an aspiration, even hunger, for self-betterment in determinedly economic and utilitarian terms, often expressed through property ownership. These were people who had witnessed how the practical aspects of cooperation and gradualist improvement rather than revolutionary political action delivered the goods.

The Doody family doggedly, and often successfully, pursued these aspirations in Victoria, both on the goldfields and in creating industries, and then finally asserted their rights to property ownership as selectors in the face of aggressive rearguard actions by a defiant already-propertied pastoral and merchant elite. The Doodys did so by asserting themselves within a socioeconomic environment that enforced democratic social conditions on the colony. They were not alone, for, as Bate states, they were part of a mass experience not rivalled until World War I.[44]

Chapter 6

AUSTRALY FOR EVER

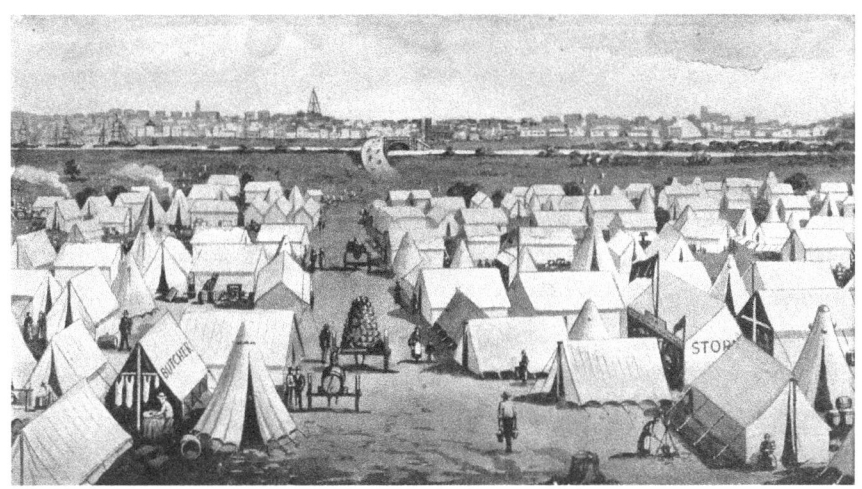

Canvas Town, Melbourne.
First home for many assisted migrant families in the 1850s.
Edmund Thomas. State Library of Victoria, a/n: H25127.

Weep not, dear mother, that I leave my home,
To seek my fortune on a foreign shore;
Yet give thy blessing ere my footsteps roam
Far from the land I may behold no more.

'The Emigrant Boy To His Mother', E.S. Walters 1852[1]

'Australy for Ever' is the title of a song that government-assisted migrants were said to have sung while sailing down the Mersey at the commencement of the first leg of their voyage to Australia.[2] The idea of the song and its universality of singing, whether lustily or mournfully, is probably as much myth as was the enduring belief that transportation to the colonies as either a convict or an assisted migrant was a life sentence. The line in the poem above 'far from the land I may behold no more' reflects that enduring myth. However, it is the prior line – 'yet give thy blessing ere my footsteps roam' – that best captures the spirit of the migrant cohort from the day they embarked on their ship to sail to Australia.

Disembarking in the New Land

Despite claims of an administration in complete chaos and near collapse as a result of the discovery of gold and the rushes that ensued, there is clear evidence that certain government services continued to function reasonably well in Victoria. One of those was the Victorian government agency responsible for receiving government-assisted migrants. The department employed a number of locally based migrant receiving agents who were responsible for checking the health and welfare of assisted migrants on arrival, and for making their swift disembarkation and dispersal into colonial society as comfortable as possible. This duty of care was built upon the chain of responsibility established by the CLEC for ensuring the welfare of the migrants during their long passage across the oceans.

There were well-established procedures for the reception of assisted migrants and all evidence suggests that these mandated processes were diligently discharged throughout the early gold rush years. Before a captain was permitted to disembark passengers, agents boarded the arriving ship to receive and check the records of both the ship's doctor and captain, and to ensure that there were no infectious diseases among the passengers. As part of the disembarkation procedure, the agents provided the migrants with an opportunity to confidentially raise any complaints about their treatment during their passage, which the migrants frequently took up. There were at least three occasions on which ships (the *Borneuf*, *Marco Polo* and *Ticonderoga*) had death rates on the voyage considered unacceptable by both the agents and, as the word was spread by the local press, the general public (refer to Chapter 3). It is perhaps easy to see the agents as treating the assisted migrants as expensive cargo, but humanitarian concerns do emerge strongly strongly in the agents' reports.

The assisted migrants were then discharged into depots prepared for them in Geelong and Melbourne to await, in the words of the *Register*, 'disposal'. As discussed in Chapter 2, meticulous records of both the discharge and disposal were kept. On setting sail from England, each ship's captain was provided with a comprehensive document listing every assisted migrant passenger boarded, with pertinent details transcribed from their original applications. Prior to Victoria's separation from NSW, the lists supplied to the ships' captains by the

CLEC were transcribed to the *Register* and checked off against disembarkation records made by the local agents. From 1852, the original information in the lists provided by the CLEC was no longer kept or recorded in the books.

This is a pity because every so often there seem to be anomalies in the records that suggest a migrant either tried to correct a record or to expunge something from the record that may have caused them embarrassment. For instance, Sarah Foley (aged 29 years), who arrived on the *British Queen* in May 1853, is recorded as 'never in service'.[3] Yet Foley was located in the 1851 English Census as a live-in housekeeper in Liverpool, and it is very unlikely that the CLEC would have accepted a single female applicant who was not employed.[4] Did Foley migrate to escape a lifetime of domestic service in England? It would have been exciting to discover what happened to her and whether she achieved some greater ambition after migrating, but unfortunately she is one of the individuals who disappear from the records after release from the migrant depots. Foley's other distinguishing feature is that she is one of only two single young female adults not travelling with family to be released on their 'own account'.

All the other single young females travelling alone were immediately released into some sort of employment situation, in marked contrast to family groups, couples or single adult young men. A few of these young women were given one-month contracts as domestic servants by the same two women, a Mrs Stevens of Franklin Street, Melbourne, and a Mrs Evans of Bourke Street, Melbourne.[5] A search of the records suggests that these two women regularly offered similar one-month contracts to newly arriving English, but not Irish or Scottish, single young women disembarking in either Geelong or Melbourne. These contracts stand out as unusual as the norm was for a period of between 3 and 12 months. It is most likely that Stevens and Evans were wives of emigration agents who would facilitate the release of certain young women from the depots.[6] All the other young women, except for a handful who had listed their occupations as dressmakers, milliners or other skilled occupations, were released into employ as domestic servants for £20–25 per annum. Young women with skills beyond domestic service were rapidly engaged by men and women with businesses in the trades and received a higher rate of pay. A couple of these women will return to this collective biography after having established themselves successfully in their own businesses or trades.

We do not see such restraints on the discharge or release of single young adult males, couples or families. As the year under study progressed, a growing number of the assisted migrants went off on their 'own account', presumably to join the gold rushes. One of the reasons for recruiting large young families was the belief that they would prefer reliable employment in rural occupations rather than undertake the risky trek to the goldfields. But this was not the case. Among the migrant cohort only three families initially entered contracts with employers in rural-based locations. In two cases, it is not clear whether the employer was a pastoralist or farmer, shopkeeper, tradesperson or publican. Regardless, these two families moved on to the goldfields very quickly.

The third, the Bailey family from Prescott, represent one of the exceptions – migrants who did not go to the diggings, but established themselves in a non-goldfield township, Terang. The father, Thomas Bailey, made an astute purchase of land adjacent to land reserved for the Terang Railway Station, and his sons and daughters played substantial roles in pioneering a factory-based dairy industry that developed with the expansion of the railways across Victoria. What we do see in the detail of the personal stories of the migrant cohort's settlement in Victoria is a pattern outlined in much broader brushstrokes by Victorian historians such as Bate, Blainey, Davison, Fahey, Grimshaw and Serle.

Settling into the New Land

Where members of the cohort went in the first five to six years after disembarkation in Victoria is shown in Figure 6.1. As can be seen, the majority headed for the goldfields. It is important, however, to remember that these goldfields that were in flux. As explained in the next two chapters, there was a rapid industrial and agricultural evolution, if not an industrial revolution, occurring on the goldfields. This momentous change encompassed a political revolution that was far-reaching, in that the males of the cohort who met certain criteria gained the right to vote. How they wielded that franchise was significant to the development of Victoria.

It is difficult to ascertain how quickly people, particularly married couples and families who went off on their 'own account', travelled to the diggings. However, there is some evidence that it was the exception rather than the norm to rush to the goldfields directly on disembarkation. Birth and death records for children suggest that there was a period of consolidation of between six months and a year (and in some cases two to six years) spent in Melbourne or Geelong, before those migrants who went to the goldfields did so. James Woods and his family went to the diggings at Steiglitz sometime in 1859 or 1860. Prior to that time, the Woods family were operating what was a relatively successful market garden in Geelong. This sober movement among the migrant cohort that went to the diggings suggests that they were, on the whole, well aware that life as a digger required capital, even if small, and commitment, which was huge; and that there were no easy pickings on the diggings. As discussed in Chapters 7 and 8, their experiences with Lancashire cooperatives and mutual societies would prove invaluable when they reached the diggings.

Fig 6.1. Where cohort went within 5–6 years of disembarkation

Destination	Families (child numbers)	Couples	Single adult females	Single adult males
To the goldfields	10 (23)	7	5	3
Stayed in Melbourne or Geelong	5 (15)	3	9	1
Settled in non-goldfields towns	1 (4)	-	-	-
Took up farming	1 (1)	-	-	-
TOTAL	17 (43)	10	14	4

Source: Author.

It was among those of the cohort who landed in Melbourne that a picture emerges of the type of labour the male heads of family accepted on disembarkation as they accumulated an initial financial stake. A little over a third of the male heads of family accepted contractual employment prior to discharge from the depots. The wages recorded for those contracted from out of the Melbourne depot were appreciably higher than the men could have earned in comparable positions in Lancashire. However, it should be noted that inflation was rampant in Victoria between 1851 and 1855: bread doubled in price, butter trebled, and the cost of eggs increased by a factor of six.[7]

As there were only three families in which the male head initially accepted contractual employment in Melbourne and never went to the goldfields, it can be assumed that many of those who accepted employment were interested in gathering a stake to enable them to move on, or later found reasons to move to the goldfields. Almost all those from the migrant cohort who made their way to the goldfields over the six-year period after disembarkation stayed on in the cities and townships that developed on the diggings or took up adjacent agricultural lands. These individuals were instrumental in the development of regional Victoria's industrial, commercial and agricultural infrastructure that the extraction of gold was able to finance. Unlike the Californian gold rush towns, the major Victorian mining towns did not wither and die with the end of the rushes.[8]

The most fascinating migratory journeys were often those of the children aged under 14 years at disembarkation, and later chapters explore several of their stories in more depth. One general observation that can be made is that male children seemed to cope with the uprooting far less successfully than female children. A significant number of these males later died alone, often from various diseases associated with alcoholism. However, with every hard-luck story, there are others that demonstrate remarkable fortitude in overcoming the worst odds. The three Butler children, who later took their mother's maiden name Proctor, survived the early death of their mother, Mary, on the goldfields and abandonment by their father, James Butler. They not only survived but thrived. All three were hugely successful in their own right. In particular, only-daughter Anne, who was five years of age on disembarkation, went on to build a successful business empire as a young adult.[9]

There are many questions that cannot be answered about how the mammoth upheaval of the migratory journey to Victoria affected the lives of the 82 children from the cohort, but we do get occasional glimpses that it was often traumatic. This is particularly noticeable for the children from the ships that had high mortality rates among the other child passengers.

Single young men, despite their small numbers in the cohort, also raise some fascinating insights and questions in relation to what was happening in Victoria during the years after their landing. Despite the prevalent belief that single young men would immediately decamp to the goldfields on landing, John Francis, described as a teacher in the *Register*, is the only one who can authoritatively be said to have done so. Francis was on the goldfields just two months after his arrival in Victoria. The primary sources that trace Francis's story reveal much about the diggings. The *Teachers Record Books* for teachers employed in the Victorian public education system were supposedly not commenced until 1863. Yet the first 500-odd records list teachers employed earlier than that date, including John Francis. Francis was employed at the Forest Creek National School (Mount Alexander) from 23 May 1853 to 23 June 1855.[10] He also had a mining claim.[11] Francis was not unusual in combining secure paid work with speculative mining on his own claim.

Schooling among the goldfields generation was highly prized, and also functioned as a form of childcare. Yet it is notable how often it is discussed as being run in an ad-hoc fashion, often out of tents by women. Government-run non-denominational schools are supposed to have followed more slowly, generally from 1856 onwards.[12] Yet here is evidence of a government run children's education facility on the goldfields in 1853. The teacher records are again evidence of a functioning bureaucracy that sought to provide educational opportunities for children on the goldfields and maintained detailed records of its schools and employees.

The *Castlemaine Rate Book* of 1856–57 also provides a comprehensive survey of every mining licence and property in the borough. It vividly captures the ephemeral experience of many who went to the goldfields in the first few years. The *Rate Book* entry for John Francis's rateable property recorded him simply as 'gone away'. The dwelling house on the land was noted to be a tent. It would seem Francis simply walked away, not even bothering to strike the tent.

Almost all the properties in the Forest Creek, Campbells Creek and Barkers Creek areas had structures on them that were described as tents or canvas enclosures. Such structures included stores, stables, taverns and, in one case, a hotel. A third of the properties had been abandoned by the time the collection of the rates became due.[13] The period 1855–1856 probably marks the distinct point when the nature of working shallow alluvial diggings was changing and gold extraction had become an industrial occupation best worked by large cooperatives with some capital (see Chapter 7).

Did John Francis, a scrivener, or clerk, from Liverpool, find working the diggings much too hard, or had he dug out his claim and left when it no longer produced a good return? Francis's more than two years at the diggings suggest the latter, though these are questions that cannot be answered because he vanished from the records after leaving Castlemaine. His story does pose other questions. In particular, if the colonial government was capable of providing public education for the colony's children and extended this opportunity to the goldfields as early as 1853, was the government really in such a state of complete breakdown as was generally postulated?[14]

Of the other single young adult males who could be traced, three were regarded as adult because they were over 14 years of age at embarkation but were under 16 years old and travelling with their families. The youngest of these males, Charles Bennett (aged 14 years at embarkation), died within a year of arriving in Geelong from a 'seizure of the heart'.[15] His family's grief is a clear reminder that just because death was much more common then, people did not feel it any less than we do these days.

Another of the three was John Holt, who managed to get himself on the *1856 Victorian Electoral Roll* despite being underage. Holt never left Melbourne and became the foreman of a bluestone quarry in North Fitzroy, now a football ground, which produced much of the stone for the monumental 19th-century buildings that adorn Melbourne.

The third young adult male, Smith Mercer, went with his family to the goldfields, where they prospered. Mercer eventually became a farmer in an adjacent agricultural area. Two good friends, Thomas Dickinson and William Atkinson from Broughton, took nearly four years to reach the goldfields at Creswick, where they settled and remained until their respective deaths. Their journey can be traced through the birth of Thomas's children (see Chapter 9).

The seventh of these young adult male migrants demonstrated that not all young men's eyes were glazed over by gold. John Booth was a 27-year-old brickmaker who landed at Geelong on 5 January 1853 and went off on his 'own account'.[16] He was a late selection as a single male migrant, and his application was probably approved by the CLEC because of his trade. Prior to mechanisation and big kiln production, brickmaking was considered a highly skilled occupation and in short supply in comparison to bricklayers. John did not head to the diggings, but shortly after his arrival went the other way, to Tasmania. In 1857, he married Jane Fraser who, with her family, were assisted migrants to Tasmania. John and Jane settled in Tea Tree, just outside Hobart, where he plied his trade of brickmaking and as a builder. He died in 1903 and is buried alongside his wife in the St Thomas Anglican Church cemetery in Tea Tree. The church was built of bricks he had made.[17]

Bate observes that 'historians who speak only of diggers neglect the role of shop keepers, tradesmen, lawyers, publicans, doctors and newspaper men'. He argues that appreciating these neglected roles is essential to understanding the 'much overlooked' transition from mining camps to permanent industrial and commercial regional centres such as Ballarat, Bendigo and Castlemaine.[18] This argument is also relevant to the development of the Victorian goldfields' two feeder ports, Melbourne and Geelong, where many of the migrant cohort remained. As will be seen in the subsequent chapters, the southern Lancashire assisted migrants, both male and female, with their industrial skillsets, expertise and entrepreneurial flair, were well-equipped to exploit and develop the many opportunities that gold would underwrite for the new colony.

The 'new plantings' by urbanised industrial and commercial working and lower-middle classes of their own 'ideas, aspirations and institutions' onto Victoria's pastoral foundations were explosive in their transformation of the colony's economy.[19] However, it is difficult to see this economic transformation being as successful as it was if it had not been accompanied by the revolutionary democratic transformation that took place in the first decade after the migrant cohort disembarked. This democratic transformation was fostered by the egalitarian social conditions on the goldfields, but quickly became an essential socioeconomic thread in the migrant cohort's settlement and development of Victoria.

The Victorian Ballot

When the first ship in this study, the *London*, disembarked its passengers in Melbourne on 25 July 1852, the Colony of Victoria had just celebrated the first anniversary of its separation from NSW and establishment as an independent British colony. Victoria was then a pastoral economy dominated by the squatters, holders of substantial pastoral leases frequently amounting to hundreds of thousands of acres. Together with the merchants from the big mercantile houses who 'sat like spiders at the centre of the pastoral web', and enabled by a small civil elite of colonial officials and lawyers drawn mainly from the British educated middle classes, the squatters dominated all aspects of the colonial government in Victoria.[20]

The first governor, Charles La Trobe, ruled with an Executive Council appointed by the Crown, on his own recommendation. However, La Trobe's ability to govern was fettered by a powerful Legislative Council of 30 members, of which only one-third was appointed by the governor. The majority two-thirds were elected from within a very narrow propertied franchise, both of the members and their electorate. Thus, the pastoralists and the mercantile elite dominated the Legislative Council. The majority of those serving on the Executive Council also had substantial property interests.

The head of the Executive Council was Colonial Secretary John Foster, and his cousin, William Stawell, was the Attorney-General. Between them, these two men controlled over 100,000 acres in pastoral leases.[21] This propertied elite correctly saw the uncontrolled flood of people into the colony prospecting for gold as a threat to their socioeconomic control of the fledging colony, but they were wrong in believing that the gold rushes were short-lived transient affairs that could be controlled and contained. Far from being ephemeral and transitory as this propertied elite desperately hoped, goldmining would dominate the Victorian political economy and social discourse for the next 20 years, and remained a major influence on Victoria's socioeconomic development well into the 20th century.

The assisted migrants on the *London* arrived in a Victoria which, on first appearance, seemed to be woefully unprepared for the discovery of gold in such vast quantities. In attempting to contain and control the inevitable gold rush frenzy, La Trobe had followed the NSW Governor's lead and imposed a stiff licence fee that all miners were expected to pay in advance for their right to stake out a claim and dig it. Each claim was restricted to 8 square feet and licence holders had to demonstrate that they had not deserted their employment without proper authorisation. These licences were widely seen at the time, and are still seen by modern historians, as an ineffectual attempt to curb the flood of people rushing to the diggings. Blainey called it 'administration by the tape measure rather than the brain'.[22] The NSW Government quickly adopted a more flexible approach in issuing mining licences, but La Trobe, who viewed the Victorian measures as temporary, ran into obdurate resistance to any policy change within both the Executive and Legislative councils.

While the Colonial Office was determined that Victoria would pay for the urgent demands it was making on the British Government, including those for troops and naval ships to be stationed in the colony, it instructed La Trobe that all new revenue-raising measures had to be approved by the Legislative Council. La Trobe proposed to replace the hated goldfields licence fees with an export tariff on gold, which was likely to increase government revenue substantially.

The members of the Legislative Council vetoed the proposed tariff and other measures designed to relieve the burdens placed on diggers. Specifically, the Council's members were afraid that the proposed measures could lead to a tariff on wool exports, substantial increases in the peppercorn rents the squatters were paying for their leaseholds, and, ultimately, the breaking-up of these landholdings. The result was bitter clashes between the governors (La Trobe and then his successor Sir Charles Hotham), the pastoral and mercantile interests, and the mining communities. This collision of interests led to widespread unrest on the diggings, with mass demonstrations on major goldfields like Mount Alexander, Bendigo and Ballarat, and ultimately to the conflict at Eureka Stockade in Ballarat.

Just prior to Christmas 1852, La Trobe received a dispatch from the British Government's Secretary of State, Sir John Pakington, encouraging the colony to draft a bill and constitution for self-government. Similar proposals were proffered to the colonies of NSW, South Australia and New Zealand. The Colonial Office proposed that there be a bicameral legislature with an elected lower house, the Legislative Assembly; and an upper house, the Legislative Council, appointed by the Crown.[23] The Victorian Colonial Secretary, John Foster, and his cousin, Attorney-General William Stawell, promptly took charge of drawing up a constitution for Victoria.

Great meeting of gold diggers, Mount Alexandria.
D. Tulloch & Thomas Ham. State Library of Victoria, a/n: H7800.

While their initial drafts did not go as far as that proposed for NSW, where William Wentworth zealously promoted the creation of what became widely derided as a 'Bunyip Aristocracy', it was clear that Foster and Stawell's intent was the maintenance of a narrow and propertied oligarchical control of Victoria. They dismissed the idea of an appointed Legislative Council, recognising that future governors could stack this body at will, instead proposing an elected upper house with a property qualification required of both its members and its electors to prevent all but the wealthiest squatters, merchants and civil elite from participating in its elective and deliberative processes. The property qualifications proposed for the Legislative Assembly, or lower house, were slightly less onerous, but still managed to make the British *1832 Reform Act* look generous.[24]

Surprisingly, substantial opposition to Foster and Stawell's proposals developed within the existing Legislative Council, led by John Pascoe Fawkner, himself a prominent landholder, but whose origins were as the son of a transported convict, or Van Diemenian. Fawkner himself had been sentenced to three years' hard labour and 500 lashes for attempting to help convicts escape from the penal colony. After his release, Fawkner became one of the first settlers in the new Port Phillip District and joined John Batman in establishing the settlement of Melbourne. He published a newspaper, the *Port Phillip Patriot and Melbourne Advertiser*. Despite his substantial landholdings, he became known as the 'tribune of the people' through his ardent opposition to the pastoralists, who were, he considered, 'grinding the bulk of the people to the very dust'.[25]

Less surprising was the vehement opposition from the mining or digging communities to the proposed constitution, including several members of the migrant cohort. The cohort were moving onto the goldfields at the very time that the easier pickings from shallow alluvial gold deposits were being exhausted, and an upfront licence fee had become an onerous burden on diggers, who were increasingly having to invest long months digging deep into clay or basalt to reach the 'lead' (see Chapter 7). Bate claims that what is often overlooked in historical discussion regarding the opposition to the licence fee that developed on the goldfields is that the diggers were not opposed to the fee per se. Nor was the dissent based solely around the oft-quoted 'no taxation without representation'. The most aggressive anger was directed towards the colonial government for failing to put the taxes raised back into development and infrastructure on the goldfields.[26] The miners or diggers, including those from the migrant cohort, were not just concerned with short-term personal gains; they were developing agendas and ideas about turning their mining camps into permanent homes.

Frustrated and humiliated at every turn, and harassed by a series of advertisements appearing in the *Argus* that read, 'Wanted, a Governor. Apply to the People of Victoria', La Trobe essentially gave up and submitted his resignation.[27] His replacement was Sir Charles Hotham, a naval flag officer, who had a very successful career as a naval officer, diplomat and financial administrator. Hotham was a reluctant appointee, but the new Colonial Secretary, the Duke of Norfolk, insisted that Hotham take up the appointment, believing he was 'a first rate man' who had all the qualifications to take the unruly Colony of Victoria into hand, and to find a compromise to bridge the 'divisions of the community'.[28]

Norfolk and the Colonial Office had three urgent priorities for Hotham. Paramount was to balance the budget and make sure the colony was paying for the escalating cost of its security. Despite the supposed riches flowing from gold, the Victorian deficit was over £1 million and rapidly growing. The annual police budget had grown from £25,000 to £300,000.[29] The second priority was to manage the transition to self-government and rein in the power of the Executive and Legislative councils. Third, Hotham was to head off any threat of rebellion in Victoria. The Colonial Office had reason to be concerned about rebellion. The rebellions in the Canadian Lower Provinces were still a recent memory, and the American Lone Star militias' involvement in those uprisings and the Texan War of Independence agitated the Colonial Office.

The British Ambassador to the US was among those who alerted Norfolk to the possibility that certain US individuals and factions were fomenting revolution in Victoria.[30]

How much validity there was in these concerns is, in hindsight, debatable. That Norfolk, however, expected Hotham to use force if rebellion came to Victoria is not. He provided Hotham with a second regiment, the 12th, to join the 40th already stationed in Victoria. Further, Norfolk ordered the military Commander-in-Chief in Australia, Sir Robert Nickle, to transfer his command from Sydney to Melbourne. Nickle previously had a highly distinguished military career suppressing rebellions in Ireland, Canada and Jamaica, while the 40th and 12th regiments were deployed in Lancaster in the 1830s when the Chartist movement reached its peak.[31]

William Craig, who was a digger at Ballarat and wrote *My Adventures on the Goldfields*, claimed that Hotham said, 'A little blood-letting would not do the unruly gold-miners any harm'.[32] As Craig was nowhere near the scene when this remark was supposed to have been made, it can be considered scuttlebutt, but it does reveal the tensions existing within the colony on Hotham's arrival. It is clear from correspondence and official dispatches that 'a little blood-letting' was the last thing the Colonial Office and Hotham wanted to see. Hotham's view was that:

> the tendencies to serious outbreaks amongst the masses of the population are usually a signal that the Government is at fault as well as the people ... It is not by the bayonet that these tendencies are to be eradicated, as this may leave behind it the seeds of a new or worse outbreak.[33]

Hotham's arrival in Melbourne and his quickly mounted tour through the goldfields were greeted with an enthusiasm that can only be described as rapturous or delirious. The rapture quickly wore off.

According to Blainey and Serle, Hotham's great failing was his inability to delegate or to include Foster and Stawell in the decision-making process.[34] According to Rusden and the *Sydney Morning Herald*, both writing shortly after Hotham's death, Foster, and Stawell bitterly resented the governor asserting his authority and countermanded or disregarded instructions he had issued.[35] William Bramwell Withers, who as a digger witnessed the events surrounding Eureka, and as a scholar published his *History of Ballarat* in 1870, was highly critical of Hotham:

> He was not a great politician nor politic, and his military instincts knew nothing of concession or compromise with people clamouring against

both law and administration. This must be remembered, as well as the equally obvious fact that his Excellency had difficulties of many kind to overcome.[36]

However, Withers admits Hotham did propose 'special deliverances' to avoid the 'Eureka collision'.[37]

The succeeding chapter delves more deeply into the protests on the goldfields over licence fees. But for now it is worth noting that Hotham, faced with recalcitrant Executive and Legislative councils, and mounting protests and rebellions on the diggings, chose to cut the Gordian knot by appointing a Royal Commission. If there were any doubts about Hotham's commitment to his statement that 'all power proceeds from the people', they were dispelled by his appointment of Fawkner as chairman of the Commission.

Many people refer to *The Commission Appointed To Enquire Into The Condition of the Goldfields Of Victoria* as the 'Eureka Commission'; however, it was established by Hotham several months before the Eureka Stockade Massacre. In fact, several leaders of the Eureka rebellion had, prior to the rebellion, been invited by Hotham to a personal meeting to put their cases to the Commission; but all refused his invitation.[38] What Eureka did was focus the attention of the Executive and Legislative councils on the urgency of the situation and led these bodies to accept completely the recommendations of the Commission.

The Commission's most important recommendations were for: the licence fee to be replaced by an export tariff; the autocratic Goldfields Commissioners to be replaced by district mining courts consisting of local miners elected by their own mining community; the Legislative Council to be expanded by 12 members, with four members appointed by the governor and the other eight elected by miners from the mining districts; and, finally, as was reluctantly agreed to by Foster and his allies, the property qualifications for lower house members to be removed and the franchise for this chamber to be widened to one of near universal male suffrage.[39] The period from La Trobe to Hotham and then to elected self-government in 1857 is critical to appreciating the transformation of Victoria's political and socioeconomic environment, as the migrant cohort moved out into the new communities that reshaped the colony's economy from one reliant on pastoral activities to an industrial and commercial powerhouse.

The Mining Courts, which are dealt with in greater depth in the following chapter, provided what was an extraordinary early experiment in democracy that was fervently embraced by miners. Hotham said of the courts:

> To the institutions of the local courts I have always given my warmest support. No one can be as cognizant of the wants of the miner, or more competent to decide in what relates to his business than the miner himself … instead of a restless discontented body, the miners have shown themselves attached to local authorities and indisposed to violate the law … on one or two occasions, when a temporary excitement has required that the police should be increased in a particular locality, a large body of the population have offered its service to the government.[40]

As Hotham predicted, the miners proved, in contradiction to the then prevalent belief that only men of great property could govern, that they were perfectly capable of governing for themselves, both reasonably and rationally.

An Imperfect Democracy

Joseph Doody is prominent in this narrative in part because his story exhibits how a Manchester boy born in the London Road district played a bottom-up role in Victoria's political, social and cultural development. None of the migrant cohort ever went on to be leading political players in the colony, although a few saw husbands, fathers-in-law or other relatives become important political figures.

Mary Ann Trickett married a gold-digger, Edward Morey, who went on to become Mayor of Ballarat and a Member of the Legislative Council. William Mercer married the daughter of James Henry Wheeler, who was a Member of the Legislative Assembly for 15 years and a government minister. Richard Seddon, a nephew of James Seddon, after a period on the Mount Alexander and Bendigo goldfields, moved to New Zealand and became Premier of the colony in 1893.

What is striking about these three men is the similarity of their English origins to that of the migrant cohort. They were not unusual. The majority of the new politicians, whether at a local borough level or in the Victorian Parliament, were of similar origins. William Nicholson, a self-educated grocer originally from Cumberland, became Melbourne's mayor in 1852, and, as a member of Victoria's Legislative Council, energetically and successfully campaigned for the secret ballot when the constitution was being debated.[41]

Graham Berry, three-time Premier of Victoria between 1875 and 1881, and Treasurer in seven Victorian governments between 1870 and 1893, became the unchallenged champion of people Davison refers to as:

the goldfields generation ... the free, skilled immigrants of the 1850s, often imbued by Chartist ideals of small proprietorship and respectability, and lured by the prospect of rapid social mobility.[42]

Berry, the son of a Twickenham tradesman, who established his own general store in South Yarra after he migrated to Melbourne in 1852.

Graham Berry, Family Grocer, 1850.
State Library of Victoria, a/n: H32520.

Berry's radical political program was summed up in his own words: making Victoria a 'fine country for the working man'. Geoffrey Bartlett in the *Australian Dictionary of Biography* (ADB) says of him:

> His lack of education and his emotional nature showed not only in his speech but also in his lack of originality or of interest in theory. He never questioned the fundamentals of politics or society, only the concentration of power and wealth ... in the Victoria of his vision, all honest, industrious men would prosper, no class would dominate and no economic or political theories should stand in his pragmatic way.[43]

Similar charges about a 'lack of education', dropping his aitches and having no 'interest in theory' were raised against Richard Seddon, perhaps the most successful of the colonial radical liberals, as well as many of the other prominent colonial liberal reformers. These criticisms were not only advanced by conservatives of the period, but also by the university-educated middle-class elites from the traditional British-orientated liberal factions, and often echoed by later academic historians.[44]

There was a widely held assumption that only university-educated elites were capable of developing the intellectual underpinnings of the humanitarian and radical political beliefs that emerged in Victoria in the second half of the 19th century, and which Berry, various other Victorian government ministers, and Richard Seddon, a Bendigo miner, attempted to put in place in Victoria and New Zealand. The intellectual underpinnings for the reforms were coming from the bottom up and driven by a migrant community well versed in Chartism, other radical political belief systems and programs, and utilitarian economics generally. In *The Golden Age*, Serle argues that the diggers developed a camaraderie similar to that shared by the veterans of long wars, and they held little respect for those who had not shared their experiences or demonstrated that they could perform the necessary hard labour.[45]

The Colonial Office's determination that Hotham should balance the colony's budget in the build-up to self-rule probably did much to discredit classic liberal economic thought in the colony. While much attention has been given to Hotham's response to the massive protests by the diggers and to the Eureka crisis, little attention has been paid to the economic crisis that Hotham was forced to engineer in late 1854 and over the course of 1855.

Yet, for the migrant cohort, as they were settling into Victoria, and for the emerging new breed of politician, this financial crisis was more profoundly disturbing than the Eureka Massacre. Hotham laid off three-quarters of Victoria's civil service and suspended all public works programs commenced, planned or proposed. There was a sharp rise in unemployment, exasperating the problems already caused by unsuccessful diggers streaming away from the shallow alluvial goldfields. This crisis ushered in an extended deflationary period across the colony, accompanied by significant drops in wages. It would take nearly 10 years for Victoria to fully recover from this bout of deflation brought on by an injudicious application of classic 19th-century liberal economic theory.[46]

Building a Better Britain

In their introduction to *Gold Tailings: Forgotten Histories of Family and Community on the Central Victorian Goldfields*, Fahey and Mayne argue:

> In the popular histories of this golden decade the early rush years take pride of place. These were the years of independent, free spirited diggers … yet for all their romance the early rushes were ephemeral affairs …

> Both deep lead mining and quartz reefing promoted the growth of towns and cities … Ongoing migration and subsequent family formation sustained the growth of these urban communities.[47]

Fahey and Mayne go on to contend that in the historical analysis of the goldfields experience, examination of family formation and community building during the industrial stage of the goldfield economy has been much overlooked. For these authors, family formation and community building are the tangible achievements of Serle's 'abstract hyperbole about a demographic revolution' that reshaped the nation.[48]

A similar argument was made by Richard Seddon in a speech during a visit to Bendigo in 1906, which began: 'A mining community moved in a sphere that sometimes appeared uninteresting to larger centres.' He went on to assert that the miners' efforts at family formation and community building 'promote[d] and improve[d] the conditions of their fellow men' and were the 'very bedrock of the Empire'.[49] Today we may find the connection between family formation and community building in Bendigo and empire building more than a little hyperbolic, but for Seddon and much of his audience, this was a fundamental truth. Seddon's rhetoric, however, was not about conjuring up some soaring baroque vision of empire; instead, it is surprisingly dull and utilitarian. Yet it resonated with the good burghers of Bendigo as it would have with the vast majority of those from the migrant cohort who settled permanently in the Australasian colonies.

One of the most important themes to emerge from this collective biography is the migrants' overriding determination to become freeholders. This would take many forms, whether it be as a storekeeper or business proprietor, the owner of a quarter-acre section in the emerging suburbs, or the purchaser of farmland. The migrant cohort set about determinedly, along with many of their neighbours and allies, to build a capitalist society, albeit one that was based on the concept of small-property ownership and that they could freely enter. In some areas of the economy, particularly mining from the 1870s onwards, this was not always possible. Yet in much of Victoria's developing socioeconomic culture, this vision would form the bedrock of the migrants' belief in building a better Britain.

These people were not socialist, but they did believe that government had a responsibility to build an infrastructure that would deliver better outcomes in health, education and public transport. They understood that the delivery of infrastructure by the government was vital to achieving equality of opportunity. This meant applying substantial public monies to the creation of public infrastructure such as hospitals and schools, the expansion of the railways across Victoria, and the development of facilities, such as those delivering clean fresh water to inland cities and towns. The building of a publicly funded railway network across Victoria was essential in transforming the Victorian migrants into 'a population of smallholders that constituted a social environment in which science and technology could be best applied'.[50] The migrant cohort became part of a population of small freeholders exploring how their industrial and entrepreneurial skills could be best applied for their own personal betterment and for the greater good of the communities in which they settled.

Chapter 7

THE GOLDEN LANDS

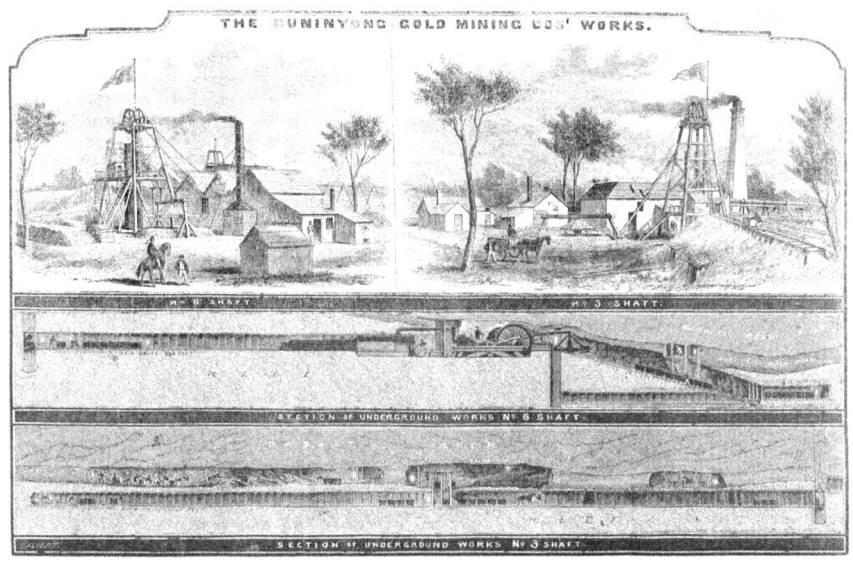

The reality of the gold diggers lives was not the romance of the free-spirited digger.
Samuel Calvert, Illustrated Melbourne Post, *24 June, 1865.*
State Library of Victoria, a/n: !MP24/06/65/84.

[the first] was the messy old period of tub and cradle, calico tents, hop beer, Police Magistrates, pickled onions, Gold Commissioners, sides of mutton, Coroners, and grilled chops. Next came the epoch of the puddling machines, hay and corn sellers, Mining Boards, Wardens, Cobb's coaches, shanties, restaurants, newspaper agents, and other nuisances. The third was the era of quartz mining, wooden houses, mining speculators, town councillors, rail roads, Members of Parliament, Cabinet Ministers, auctioneers, Insolvent Courts, and other indications of an advancing civilisation.

A Digger's Wit, *Bendigo Independent*, 1875[1]

With his pick, shovel, washing pan and independent lifestyle, the free-spirited single male digger became and remains one of the great romantic touchstones of Victorian and Australian culture. So much so that, in World War I, the Australian infantrymen acquired the name of 'digger' as it was believed they were infused with the same qualities. Bate argues that this was because the years of the mining camps were 'a mass experience not rivalled until World War I'.[2] The contradiction between the independent, free-spirited gold-digger and a regimented Australian and New Zealand Army Corp (Anzac) infantryman is often lost in the romance of the telling. As always, the reality was far more complex. The mass experience of gold-digger life encompassed a shared pioneering experience that saw the chaos of the tented mining camps become the ordered urban environments of permanent homes and businesses, which women and children played a prominent role in creating.

The tongue-in-cheek piece in the *Bendigo Independent* located the mass experience in the first period of the gold rushes, yet this period was ephemeral and short-lived. By the time most of the migrant cohort had arrived on the goldfields, the independent digger working alone with tub and cradle was well and truly passing into romantic myth. The mass experience Bate speaks of is found in the necessity for cooperative labour, the sharing of resources, and the use of industrial skills to extract commercial quantities of gold. This necessity of working together resulted in the stubborn determination by most of the gold-diggers to take charge of their own communities, which resulted in 'a long struggle in Victoria between the digger migrants and their precursors'.[3] In the end, the digger communities had more in common with a disciplined Anzac brigade than the labels of 'independent' and 'free-spirited' suggest.

The enduring myth of the digger culture is focused almost exclusively on single young white males and ignores virtually everyone else. Wright challenges this notion and conclusively argues that we cannot ignore the contribution women and children made to digger culture.[4] The *Census of Victoria* taken in the years 1854, 1857, 1861 and 1871 supports her contention (see Figure 7.1). In 1854, women and children formed one-third (33%) of the goldfields population. By 1861, the number of women and children on the goldfields had increased to 46% of the total population. The 1871 Census Return shows women and children formed nearly two-thirds (62%) of the goldfields population.[5]

The bulk of the cohort's gold-diggers made their way to the goldfields either as part of families including children or were single young women. At least five of the adult women and one female child from the migrant cohort – Mary Ann Trickett and her mother, Mary; Charlotte Rigby; Mary Butler and her daughter, Ann Butler; and Jane Cornthwaite (née Wiseman) – worked for a time as diggers, either alone or alongside fathers, husbands or brothers.

Women from the cohort worked as shopkeepers, hoteliers, milliners and seamstresses, while the female children would later fill professional roles such as nursing and teaching. Almost all the male children, who migrated to the fields with their families, worked the diggings when still children, and then moved into farming or occupations similar to those in which their fathers had engaged prior to migrating. When discussing the 'mass experience' on the diggings, any discourse should include these women and children, their contributions to communal life, and how their experiences shaped the construction of the permanent communities that had emerged by the 1871 Census.

Figure 7.1. Population on goldfields by gender and age

Census year	Total goldfields population	Adult male no.	Adult female no.	Boy under 15 no.	Girl under 15 no.	Total children no.
1854	66,694	44,568	8168	7974	5984	13,598
1857	146,428	84,388	26,988	17,897	17,155	35,052
1861	222,181	122,175	41,454	32,517	32,035	64,552
1871	270,428	102,170	54,243	53,099	56,916	110,015

Census year	Total goldfields population	Adult male %	Adult female %	Boy under 15 %	Girl under 15 %	Total children %
1854	66,694	67%	12%	12%	9%	21%
1857	146,428	58%	18%	12%	12%	24%
1861	222,181	54%	18%	15%	14%	29%
1871	270,428	38%	21%	20%	21%	41%

Source: Census of Victoria 1854, 1857, 1861 *and* 1871.

Tracing an exact timeline for those of the cohort who migrated to the goldfields was often difficult. In some cases, such as that of John Francis and the Doody and Trickett families, moving to the goldfields likely occurred within a year of their disembarkation. Many others, including the Woods family mentioned in the previous chapter, and the Guy family, were much slower in taking that journey. Two of the single young adult males, Thomas Dickinson and his mate from Broughton, William Atkinson, demonstrated that not all single young men were intent on rushing to the goldfields. Initially Dickinson and Atkinson established a carpentry shop in Geelong. It would take over four years for them to finally make it to the goldfields in Creswick, where they settled permanently. One single young woman, Hannah Ashcroft, and possibly two others, Ann Foy and Charlotte Rigby, went to the goldfields unaccompanied shortly after disembarkation. The other single young females who settled on the goldfields did so only after meeting and partnering with men in Geelong and Melbourne.

Those from the migrant cohort were settling the goldfields and mining camps during the time of transition to the 'second epoch' or the 'organised prosaic industrial stage'. This stage involved greater injections of capital, industrial skillsets and the use of machinery to extract gold; the support of the growing agricultural, commercial and industrial sectors; and the expanding use of wage labour to mine.[6] It is a mistake, however, to view the shallow alluvial goldfields as exhausted by the mid-1850s, as this assumes that the independent digger had slunk off, their tail between their legs, as the diggings became more complex and mechanised, leaving large-scale capital to exploit deep lead and quartz. This was not the case.

Serle argues that the latter half of the 1850s and early 1860s were marked by a prolonged struggle as those who may be described as the 'independent diggers' fought to deny large-scale industrial 'absentee' capitalism a place on the goldfields. The success of the large-scale mining ventures and investment of Joseph Doody, the Tricketts and Mary Ann's husband Edward Morey, the Seddons, and several others from the migrant cohort demonstrates that there was plenty of room for the early diggers to prosper as the industrial stage of goldmining developed. In fact, it was more often the local diggers and investors rather than the absent capital who prospered.[7]

Gold: Timeline and Terms

The evolution of goldmining in Victoria involved a number of stages, the understanding of which is vital to appreciating the stories of the migrant cohort members who went to the goldfields. For instance, what did alluvial mining mean and what is the difference between shallow and deep-lead alluvial mining? Why are these processes different from quartz mining and processing? How did the increasingly capital- and machinery-intensive extraction of gold impact on those of the migrant cohort settling the mining camps that were rapidly becoming permanent townships and, in some cases, such as Ballarat and Bendigo, major industrial centres?

Mining Districts

The goldfields were clustered across much of central, northern and eastern Victoria. With the 1855 mining reforms, the areas containing the fields were divided into six mining districts: Ararat, Ballarat, Beechworth, Castlemaine, Maryborough and Sandhurst (Bendigo). A seventh, Gippsland, was added after the 1861 Census. These mining districts remained the essential administrative units for the goldfields throughout the second half of the 19th century. Each district was under the charge of a Warden who oversaw the government's administrative and enforcement units within a district. However, unlike the arbitrary and almost absolute authority of the Goldfields Commissioners whom they replaced, the Wardens were constrained in their authority by a remarkable experiment in democracy: the establishment of a Local (or Mining) Court in each district consisting of 12 miners nominated and elected by their fellow miners to oversee the mining district's operations (see below for further discussion).

New Chum Line of Reef, Bendigo.
Samuel Calvert, Illustrated Australian News, *26 May, 1888.*
State Library of Victoria, a/n: IAN25/05/88/109a.

Shallow Alluvial Mining

The initial rich gold finds were on shallow alluvial fields along or near surface waterways. Popular imagination paints a romantic image of the independent male digger sifting a creek bed with a pan and pick and washing out gold dust or nuggets. If such a person ever existed, he was quickly displaced by the reality that the most successful diggers were those who combined in cooperative teams of four to eight or more to exploit a range of mining licences across the alluvial fields. This cooperative digging rapidly evolved into mining on an industrial scale.

Puddling, which became the most effective way to separate gold from mud and stone, involved a capital expenditure of £200 or more, substantial efforts of labour, the movement of large quantities of alluvial soil and water to the puddling operation, and the dispersal of the waste afterwards. This is why the early gold rushes were such ephemeral affairs. Few had the inclination, skills, expertise or capital to exploit the shallow alluvial fields successfully. Gold yields were therefore to reach their peak well after the first short-lived epoch concluded (see Figure 7.2 below).

It is also a common misconception that the shallow alluvial fields were exhausted by 1854–1855. Serle notes that later alluvial rushes to fields in Victoria's west have never received their due.[8] The richest of these new fields were Fiery Creek (Beaufort) in 1855, Dunolly and Ararat in 1856, Pleasant Creek (Stawell) in 1857, and Back Creek (Talbot) and Steiglitz in 1859–1860.

Families from the cohort can be found joining all these rushes, whether from old diggings or from among those who had previously been reluctant to leave Melbourne or Geelong. James Guy, who established a brickworks in Geelong after disembarkation, abandoned the enterprise some three and four years later and, with his family, rushed to Ararat where he and his wife spent the rest of their lives.[9] The Woods family, who had also remained in Geelong upon disembarkation (according to the birth records of two children born there between 1853 and 1858), seemed settled on their own freehold market gardens.[10] Yet they suddenly sold up and joined one of the last great alluvial gold rushes sometime between 1859 and 1860. Their fourth Australian-born child, John, and all their subsequent children were born in and around Steiglitz between 1860 and 1871.[11]

Older alluvial goldfields in Castlemaine and Bendigo were also given new and profitable lives through increasingly sophisticated puddling operations. Large-scale puddler operations, such as the one the Seddon families ran in Castlemaine, were still operating profitably in the mid-1860s when Richard Seddon first made his way to the goldfields. A *Mining Surveyor Report* from

January 1863 states: 'In alluvial mining no new ground has been opened, but some good finds have occurred on the old workings.'[12]

A subsequent report six months later notes that there had been a substantial increase economic yields returned by puddling operations.[13] Large cooperatives of puddlers in the Castlemaine Mining District extracted more gold in the late 1850s to the mid-1860s from worked-over claims than was originally extracted from those claims during the three years 1852–1854, which were considered the heyday of the Mount Alexander rushes.[14] Such was the scale of the Seddons' operations, either as family enterprises or in association with other puddling companies, that a whole district on the outskirts of Castlemaine was named Seddon in the latter half of the 19th century.

Deep Lead Mining

James Esmond, whose discovery of gold at Clunes in July 1851 triggered the Victorian gold rushes, pioneered deep lead mining at Ballarat a couple of years later. Esmond had gone to the Californian goldfields in 1849 but was unsuccessful there as most of the gold-bearing lands had by then been staked out. However, he was a good observer, and with the Cavanagh brothers, who also had Californian experience, began sinking a shaft on a ridge above where the other diggers had staked out all the claims on the shallow fields. The other diggers thought they were mad, but by sinking a shaft approximately 65 feet deep that bottomed out on a layer of thin blue clay, Esmond and the Cavanaghs extracted 960 ounces of gold in two days. Bate ironically remarks that it was this discovery that truly 'brought madness in its train'.[15]

Deep lead gold had been washed down from quartz seams along ancient river systems that had then been buried as a result of later geographic activity, often volcanic. The fields around the Ballarat region became the most important deep lead mining area, yielding far more gold than did the shallow alluvial gold-digging. Extraction involved plunging shafts deep into the earth, and then pushing perpendicular tunnels out along what the diggers hoped were gutters of gold. Both the shafts and the tunnels could take months of digging, with no guarantee of a reward at the end. These mines also needed substantial quantities of timber to prop up the shafts and tunnels; sophisticated pumping equipment to drain the water leaching into the mines from the surrounding topography; draining of extant underground river systems; and, increasingly, the use of wage-earning miners.

Like quartz mining, the raising of capital and the engagement of wage labour would become essential to the process. The original cooperatives of diggers grew into business entities of up to 100 or more individuals as capital investment was sought either from local or, increasingly, from outside parties. The Tricketts and Moreys were among those families that became prominent miners and investors in deep lead operations. Others from the cohort, such as William Lancaster and William Mercer and their teenage sons, respectively Joseph and Smith, as well as the two orphaned teenagers, Thomas and John Proctor (originally known as Butler), would carve themselves a comfortable living as carters, loggers and splitters servicing the mines.

Quartz Mining

Gold originates as a geological product of quartz rock crystal formation. Alluvial gold, whether shallow or deep lead, is gold from eroded quartz rock reefs. In many of the goldmining areas, such as those in the Bendigo Mining District, the wealthiest seams of gold remained locked in quartz reefs. Initially, in areas such as White Hills, the reefs were exposed to the surface or close to the surface. Mining them still took substantial and often risky effort, with injury through the collapse of pits and shallow shafts being common. Even prior to the development of deep-shaft quartz mining, extracting the gold from quartz crystal rocks posed a substantial engineering and chemical challenge. The quartz needed to be crushed into a fine dust by mechanical stamping machines, usually steam-driven. The quartz dust was then reticulated and retorted using large quantities of mercury to separate the gold and turn it into gold amalgam.

In the early years of the Australian gold rushes, the mechanical processes used for quartz crushing and amalgamation were primitive or imported and expensive. Joseph Doody was one of those who locally developed and built efficient and sturdy quartz stampers, and used his experience in the dyeing factories of Lancashire to perfect amalgam technology. These local initiatives substantially reduced the cost of extracting gold from quartz. As with deep lead mining, as the years passed shafts had to be sunk deeper into the ground, sometimes up to 1000 metres below the surface, with tunnels radiating out to reach and raise the quartz. Such endeavours required ever-increasing amounts of capital and access to a waged workforce with previous underground mining experience, such as Cornish miners.

Great perseverance by the mining companies and patience on the part of their investors were also required. It was not unusual for a valuable quartz mining operation to take at least three to five years before any dividend could be paid. The experiences of Joseph Doody and his partners provide prime examples of the dizzying heights, stunning falls and sober recoveries that accompanied quartz mining ventures (see Chapter 8). In the final analysis, however, quartz mining proved to be the most profitable and productive of the three types of goldmining. Quartz mining continued profitably in the Central Victorian mining districts, yielding an average of 800,000 ounces per annum well into the first decade of the 20th century.[16]

Statistics from the Diggings

Gold production reached its peak in 1856, when 3,053,744 ounces were extracted from the Victorian goldfields. Annual yields would steadily decline thereafter until the early 1880s, when yields stabilised as the quartz mining industry became increasingly productive. However, the decline in production from 1861 to 1871 was not as rapid or dramatic as some, including Serle, have suggested.[17] Although the annual gold yield in 1871 was down by one-third on that of 1861, the year-on-year decline averaged 3.3% per annum.

In comparison was the dramatic transformation of the goldfields into well-established urban and agricultural communities. The 1871 Victorian Census marks the completion of this transformation of the mining areas from transitory mining camps into permanently settled urban and agricultural communities (see Figures 7.3 and 7.4). The transition to industrial goldmining may not have fully concluded by 1871, but in every other respect, especially the establishment of permanent urban communities, it was complete. Although down from an 1861 peak of approximately 80,000 diggers or miners (a decrease of nearly 40% by 1871), goldmining remained the predominant occupation in the mining districts. By 1871, digging or mining had been transformed into skilled industrial occupations – like other major occupations that are hallmarks of a developed economy.

Unless they were owner-operators, most miners worked for wages and lived in permanent homes in urban communities alongside people with other occupations. By 1871, the number of independent diggers, whether working alone or cooperatively, was down by more than 50% from the 1857–1858 peak. Many of those 14,000 recorded as 'Miners, Diggers' in the 1871 Victorian Census would have been working for wages in deep lead or quartz mines. Despite the growing importance of quartz mining, the numbers engaged in quartz raising, crushing and amalgamation remained relatively small. Improving industrial technology and the employment of experienced underground miners had made extracting gold from quartz reefs and its amalgamation considerably more efficient and cost-effective. However, as previously illustrated, both types of mining gave rise to work opportunities in ancillary occupations.

Figure 7.2. Gold yield per annum 1851–1871

Year	Yield (oz.)	Value (£) at 80/- per oz.*
1851	212,899	851,596
1852	2,286,535	9,146,140
1853	2,744,098	10,976,392
1854	2,218,483	8,873,932
1855	2,819,288	11,277,152
1856	3,053,744	12,214,976
1857	2,830,213	11,320,852
1858	2,596,231	10,384,924
1859	2,348,703	9,394,812
1860	2,224,069	8,896,276
1861	2,035,173	8,140,692
1862	1,730,201	6,920,804
1863	1,694,819	6,779,276
1864	1,622,447	6,489,788
1865	1,611,554	6,446,216
1866	1,546,498	6,186,992
1867	1,501,446	6,005,784
1868	1,684,918	6,739,672
1869	1,544,756	6,179,024
1870	1,304,304	5,217,216
1871	1,368,942	5,475,768

*Gold prices varied but this was the average export value over the period.
Source: Critchley Parker, Victoria and Its Mining Resources, 11–12.

Figure 7.3. Major occupations in mining districts
from the 1854, 1857, 1861 and 1871 censuses

Occupations	1854		1857		1861		1871	
	M	F	M	F	M	F	M	F
Goldmining	33,571	-	56,888	201	78,748	136	48,383	15
Merchants, Commerce & Trade	3742	-	9485	2200	13,056	1538	18,591	4592
Manufacturing	2538	-	5842	33	10,645	47	5737	71
Agriculture	729	-	2876	334	7648	935	12,348	608
Government inc. Military	1227	-	910	4	945	5	766	13
Professional	396	-	1097	291	1624	617	2035	1252
Domestic Service	411	-	1262	2647	1471	4605	1167	6994

Source: Registrar General /HCCDA/pages/VIC-1854-census-05_7, /HCCDA/pages/VIC-1857-census-02_46, /HCCDA/pages/VIC-1861-census_01-05_76, /HCCDA/pages/VIC-1871-census-18_40.

Figure 7.4. Goldmining occupations as returned
in the 1854, 1857, 1861 and 1871 censuses

Occupations	1854		1857		1861		1871	
	M	F	M	F	M	F	M	F
Puddling	-	-	3419	19	5755	9	1321	3
Sluicing	-	-	2160	7	4370	1	3836	2
Alluvial sinking	-	-	20,959	55	40,942	67	20,567	3
Quartz-raising	-	-	-	-	7336	10	8477	-
Quartz-crushing & amalgamating etc.	-	-	-	-	1038	5	579	2
Miners, Diggers (undefined)	-	-	30,141	120	18,366	42	14,284	4
Engineers, Engine-drivers, Carters & Slabbers etc.	-	-	209	-	941	1	639	1
TOTAL	33,571		56,888	201	78,748	135	49,703	15

Source: Registrar General /HCCDA/pages/VIC-1857-census-02_48, /HCCDA/pages/VIC-1861-census_01-05_78, /HCCDA/pages/VIC-1871-census-18_58.

Digger Democracy

Following the Goldfields' Commission of Enquiry, the colonial Victorian Government instituted one of the most remarkable and earliest experiments in democratic participation in a British colony. In 1855 the government established a Local Court (sometimes referred to as the Mining Courts) in each mining district to replace the Commissioners as the principal administrative and judicial authority. What was extraordinary was that these new courts were entirely elective bodies, with the members of the court nominated and elected by the miners in each of the districts at an open general meeting called and supervised by the District Warden.

The courts combined administrative, policy (or planning) and civil judicial functions in the single elected board. In today's terms, they could be seen as an amalgam of a local council and a magistrates' court. The diggers responded enthusiastically to this opportunity to participate in the future direction of the goldfields and of their personal lives. Henry Brown, who was an eyewitness to the first election of the Sandhurst Local Court in 1855, vividly captures the eagerness to participate in this rude democracy:

> Amongst those who were simply seeking their own importance in the excitement of the times, were one or two who really had the general interest of the people at heart. The most distinguished of these was one possessed of the idea that the earth was given to all men alike, and thought on the gold fields that all men should be equal; possessed of a considerable amount of eloquence, he constantly harangued the miners to choose only such men as would sweep away all distinctions … The next name was that of a man who had lately been a shoemaker, he was so over come with modesty when called upon to address the meeting, that his friends had to push him on.[18]

These elections to the Local Courts were to set the standard for Victorian democracy and thrust the independent diggers into the frontline of Victorian political culture.[19]

With the mining licence fee no longer an issue, debate turned to the role of capital in the development of the goldfields and the related question of the size and extent of mining leases. The growing need for capital and industrial machinery to exploit deep lead deposits and quartz reefs triggered calls to allow major outside capital investment in the fields. All parties to the debate agreed that 'capital would hold aloof' unless substantial leases across gold-bearing lands could be secured.[20] The greater majority of diggers, however, questioned the very need for the involvement of large-scale capital investment by men 'living without labouring, and living upon the sweat of other men's brows'.[21] The anger expressed by these diggers not only echoed British Chartist anger from the 1820s to 1840s, but was also firmly based on the idea of themselves as people who would not easily give up their 'freedom and independence in the gold fields of Australia' for the 'old European system of master and servant'.[22] The use of 'servitude' and 'slave' as descriptors for wage labour on the goldfields became common.[23]

Despite the rage and alarm often expressed, the independent diggers were not anti-capital or anti-machinery. They believed that they possessed the will and commanded the resources needed to continue to extract gold profitably by working together in increasingly larger cooperatives and small shareholding companies, to develop and construct the necessary machinery and technology, and to engage in small- to medium-scale capital-raising. Their fears were that government, banks and absentee capitalists were conspiring to dispossess them of the fields they were profitably working, and that outside capital would lock up the land just as squatters had captured much of the arable land in Victoria.

The Local Courts, or, as they later became known, the Mining Boards, were consumed by debate over the permitted sizes for mining leases. There were also many arguments among the diggers themselves as to what constituted a fair lease. Some wanted to maintain the original 12 square feet per claim per individual; others wanted leases based on frontage rather than block claims, or leases that covered substantial amounts of abandoned ground. The common elements agreed on by almost all diggers were that leases should only be available to diggers and miners who lived on the fields and actively worked the lease concerned, and should provide for a leasehold area no greater than what an individual or group of individuals could reasonably work.

Serle describes how the courts 'quickly reacted to the predominant needs of their district', resulting in 'a bewildering variety of regulations [being] developed'.[24] It is arguable that in each mining district those 'predominant needs' were established by the party who won control of a particular court. In Ballarat, for instance, control was won by representatives of the bigger deep lead mining interests, among whom Edward Morey, his wife Mary Ann, and her father, Alexander Trickett, were prominent. The court immediately began expanding the size of claims according to the number of men involved in a cooperative or company and the difficulties involved in working the claims. This particular court tried to eliminate 'shepherding', which involved the wasteful practice of sinking large numbers of shafts on independent claims to reach, or stop others reaching, the gutters of the deep lead deposits.

A remarkable experiment in democracy – a Mining Board election.
Samuel Calvert, Illustrated Australian News, *16 April 1857.*
State Library of Victoria a/n: IAN16/04/57/52.

This encouraged further amalgamation of cooperatives and companies, which often reached 100 or more working partners. Some of Ballarat's most famous companies emerged during this period, including Kohinoor, Band of Hope, Great Western and Great Eastern. Edward, Mary Ann and Alexander became significant partners in these companies.[25]

In Bendigo, the puddlers and the 'small men' won control of the court in 1855. These interests maintained control of the Sandhurst (Bendigo) Local Court through various iterations and reforms of the Mining Court system and effectively limited any great extension to the size of mining leases. The *Bendigo Advertiser* campaigned vigorously for a better balance, arguing that 'the members ... must have the firmness to discountenance anything like monopoly ... and the wisdom to offer legitimate inducement to capitalists to develop the resources of the district'.[26] Only one pro-capital quartz miner was elected to the first Sandhurst Local Court and that was Henry Brown's brother, William Brown. His attitudes and views were described by another member of the court as 'fanfaronade'.[27]

The Local Court in Bendigo, however, was far from effective in preventing the development of quartz mining. Joseph Doody was a major pioneer and investor in quartz mining and the necessary industrial machinery to make quartz mining feasible and profitable. The Brown brothers' big venture into large-scale quartz mining depended much on Doody's industrial skills and expertise. The Browns had imported a fancy stamping mill at great expense from Britain. It broke down on its first use, and it was Doody who came to the rescue with one of his locally built steam-driven stamping machines.[28]

The situation in Bendigo demonstrated the difficulties of combining regulatory and judicial functions in one small body of elected but voluntary members. In its first two years of operation the Sandhurst Local Court adjudicated some 1600 cases.[29] After 1857, the first elected government reformed the system and split the Local Court into two separate bodies. Regulatory authority remained with the still-elected Mining Boards, with members now being paid £50 per annum. A Court of Mines with an appointed professional judiciary was established to handle all civil judicial matters in the various mining districts. In response to a growing demand for outside investment by working miners, further legislative reform of mining leases in late 1858 and early 1859 saw even the Bendigo Mining Board capitulate and begin granting large leaseholds on quartz reefs. Joseph Doody and partners immediately took up substantial leases and floated several companies, including the Wellington Company, which began sinking a deep shaft in Long Gully.[30]

Legislation, together with the acceptance of expanded lease sizes and holdings by the Mining Boards, had the effect desired by the government of attracting substantial capital investment into mining. Unfortunately, it was entirely the wrong type of investment and triggered a catastrophic mining bubble. Serle states that over 100 public companies were formed in 1859, followed by another 100 in 1860, seeing 'well over £1 million … invested in about eighteen months by tens of thousands of the public'. By January 1861, this capital was 'almost annihilated', with only 14 of the surviving companies paying dividends, and of the 850 leases issued, only 270 actually being worked.[31] The people who fared best among these shipwreck companies were locally based miners and mining investors, particularly in Ballarat. When quartz mining started to produce substantial profits in Bendigo, it was the mines run by local men that generated such profits.

Nor did the independent diggers' feared loss of independence come to pass with the introduction of large-scale capital investment, advanced machinery and wage labour. They were not dispossessed and dispersed from the goldfields. The dogged fight these diggers had put up served them well in the next stages of the development of rural and regional Victoria, and few lower house politicians were prepared to ignore them. The large-scale capital-intensive deep lead and quartz mining operations also needed service towns and cities to support them and a rural agricultural industry to feed them. The members of the migrant cohort who remained on the goldfields proved adept at making the transition to the new urban and agricultural economies that emerged across the goldfields through the 1860s.

The Women on the Diggings

In *The Forgotten Rebels of Eureka*, Clare Wright tells the story of Martha Clendinning and her sister, Sarah Lloyd, who were determined to accompany their husbands to the diggings despite the husbands' vehement opposition. Wright describes Martha as a woman 'who knew her own noodle', and from Martha's own reminiscences we receive a picture of a shrewd and pragmatic woman who had a better understanding of the difficulties of the life of a digger than her husband, George, and brother-in-law, Tom Lloyd. George Clendinning was a doctor, but he went to Ballarat to dig, not to practise medicine. Despite having no experience beyond home duties, Martha wrote:

> Besides finding something to occupy our time, we felt we should much like some way of making a little money to help our husbands in their hard work. Teaching and needle work were out of the question ... At last the happy thought struck us. We should keep a store! A nice, tidy, little store!

The proposal was met 'with peals of laughter' from the husbands, but the two women stuck to their plans and the men became financially dependent on the women during the sometimes long months between gold payoffs.[32]

Wright continues, 'George did not realise that moonlighting to support their husbands was commonplace among Ballarat wives'.[33] Considering the Lancastrian origins of the migrant cohort, these men and women would not have found anything unusual in both the wives and female children obtaining additional money from moonlighting, but it is debatable whether they would have used a term like 'moonlighting'. And, as Chapter 4 demonstrated, the wife and older children undertaking paid work was a common occurrence in a working-class household. Yet there are no remaining reminiscences, diaries or letters from among the migrant cohort, so it is speculative as to how common the working woman would have been among the migrant cohort on the goldfields.

Bate says that on the goldfields 'a few women performed tasks unusual for their sex', pointing to a small number of women who in the censuses between 1854 and 1871 declared that they were diggers or worked in manufacturing (see Figures 7.3 and 7.4).³⁴ Bate did not elaborate on why he felt that this was unusual; perhaps he was expressing the common beliefs that digging involved physical labour beyond the strength of women and that manufacturing involved mechanical skills that only men were assumed to have acquired. The members of the migrant cohort would certainly not have found women undertaking physical labour or applying mechanical skills unusual. Many of the Lancashire women, whether married or single, were employed in manufacturing and other occupations that involved skills and, at times, brawn back in Lancashire.³⁵ For instance, later in the 19th century, power-loom weaving would come to be viewed as an occupation beyond the physical strength and skills of women. But in the first half of the century, it was an occupation dominated by women, and several women from the migrant cohort were employed as power-loom weavers or in other heavy and skilled manufacturing jobs in textile factories.

What is unique about the position of women is something that, among all the goldfields histories, only Wright discusses in any detail. Other historians, if they mention it at all, quickly brush over this feature of the diggings. Women were able – indeed, were required – to take out a licence if they worked in any capacity in the goldfield districts that involved maintaining a premises, whether alongside husbands digging, in trades or as professionals. A storekeeper such as Hannah Ashcroft (see Chapter 8) was required to pay a three-monthly licence fee of £15 in advance, regardless of the size of her business. It was a case of the 'hard-nosed' British bureaucracy accepting the pragmatic reality that women were integral to the goldfields and could be tapped as a source of revenue. The effect, Wright argues, was to give women 'the unalienable right of the property owner in a capitalist regime'. This effectively defined these women as 'small business people' alongside men, and thus was integrally entwined in the culture and politics of the goldfields.³⁶

The Goldfields Commissioners' licensing registers were destroyed some years after the end of the licensing system, so we do not know how many women were issued licences to mine or trade or how many of the women from the migrant cohort were issued mining licences to work alongside men as diggers. With the proclamation of the *Land Act 1869*, single women aged over 18 years were permitted to select, and many a father or brother had their unmarried adult daughters or siblings select adjacent blocks as a way of enlarging their farms beyond the maximum 320 acres per selector allowed under the legislation. It is probable that many male diggers, including some of the migrant cohort, had wives and daughters take out mining licences as a way of enlarging their claim beyond the 12 square feet allowed per individual. It is also probable that many of the women of the cohort worked actively alongside male family members on the diggings.

Mary Ann Trickett (see 'Mayoress of Ballarat' in Chapter 8) almost certainly had mining licences of her own in the early years, as she had in later years; and both she and her mother were known to have dug alongside her father, Alexander, and her husband, Edward. Mary Butler was working the diggings from almost the moment the family arrived on them, and, as her husband James was increasingly absent, she took over the claims and worked them with her young children (see 'Children of the Midden Heaps' in Chapter 8). No records exist to that indicate with certainty how many of the other married women may have joined their husbands in mining the diggings, although, considering their histories prior to migrating, probably a good deal of them did.

Participating in actual digging was not the only way female labour became an essential component of the digging life, especially for the women from the migrant cohort who had worked in domestic service in Liverpool and Manchester. As more and more women flocked to the goldfields, Wright says 'a curious thing happened'. Instead of domestic jobs being devalued, as usually occurred, the goldfields working woman became highly prized. 'I have become a sort of necessity', remarked one woman. Wives of men in cooperatives in which most of the other men were single were being paid in gold nuggets to provide domestic services to the whole team. Others established themselves as laundresses, seamstresses, menders of garments and cooks, and in other domestic services. Wright argues that this independence was a revelation to working-class women on the diggings: no masters, no contract, no terms of service and a lucrative living generated by the provision of freelance domestic services.[37]

Laundresses with prior experience, such as Elizabeth Woods, acquired a privileged and lucrative status, while garment-makers and seamstresses found themselves equally in high demand. Lucy Doody, who had been a skilled milliner in Manchester, is a prime example of the opportunities available to women on the goldfields, which are also demonstrated in this advertisement in the *Bendigo Advertiser*:

> **THE MISSES WISE,**
> **Milliners and Dressmakers,**
> In returning their sincere thanks to their numerous
> friends, beg to inform them, and the public generally,
> that they have removed their business to G. F.

Campion's Melbourne Home, Pall Mall, where they trust, as hitherto, to receive a continuance of their patronage.[38]

The 'Misses Wise' was a cooperative operation involving a number of Lancashire milliners and dressmakers. It was only one venture among many, whether solo or cooperative, run exclusively by women.[39]

Urbanisation of the Diggings

By 1871 only two couples among the cohort's gold-diggers were still actively engaged in mining, albeit as investors, company directors and mine owners: Mary Ann (née Trickett) and her husband, Edward Morey; and Jane (née Wiseman) and her husband, John Cornthwaites. On the other hand, just two couples and their children, and the dissolute wastrel, James Butler, had permanently left the mining districts. Jane Murray met a seaman, Fredrick Christian Dahl, on the voyage to Victoria and they spent 10 years on the diggings shopkeeping before moving to the Otago goldfields in New Zealand.[40] Charlotte Rigby, who most likely travelled to the goldfields unaccompanied, met but never married John Anderson Tait, a miner, at the Break O Day field and conceived two daughters with him.[41] At some point, Charlotte and John moved to Brisbane, where they lived in happily unmarried suburban bliss until the late 1880s.[42]

Males, including those classed as children at disembarkation, who had worked the diggings often took up occupations, such as mechanic or artisan, in which their fathers had been engaged prior to leaving Lancashire. The fathers, including Joseph Doody, James Guy, William Lancaster and Thomas Reynolds, provided informal apprenticeships and training for their sons as blacksmiths, brickmakers, builders and carpenters. This transition from digger to mechanic or artisan was probably not a sudden break, but a gradual shift in focus as the face of mining changed and communities within the mining areas developed. Such experiences were reflected across the mining districts as a whole.

Agricultural activities and opportunities also expanded, with the Doody boys and the Proctor brothers taking up farming after a profitable early career servicing quartz mines. Several other of the children in their adulthood moved into professions such as nursing, pharmacy and teaching, including William Mercer Jnr and two of the Lancaster daughters. Bate states 'that goldfields communities had easily the highest level of homeownership in the world'.[43] Figure 7.5 demonstrates eloquently the changing face of those goldfields communities and their modes of accommodation.

Figure 7.5. Population of mining districts by dwelling type in the 1857, 1861 and 1871 censuses

Census year	Tents and dwellings having canvas roofs	Stone, wood or iron houses	Slab, bark and mud huts	Houses of unstated materials
1857	124,241	42,309		
1861	82,208	98,308	19,352	3358
1871	2578	228,472	20,593	2067

Source: Registrar General /HCCDA/pages/VIC-1857-census-01_30, /HCCDA/pages/VIC-1861-census_01-02_27, /HCCDA/pages/VIC-1871-census-03_32.

Democratic participation in the development of the Victorian goldfields was achieved through the elections for the membership of the local mining courts and boards and through substantial engagement with the new Legislative Assembly as both electors and elected members. The diggers ensured that democratic participation in Victoria quickly became widespread and remained so through those early developmental years. They are the shining example of what Pickering refers to when he states that Australian democrats 'helped to make Chartism one of Britain's most successful, if unheralded exports'.[44] The enthusiastic participation in local mining court and board elections was not by the elites who earlier dominated colonial Victorian society, but by common people. Those who voted and were elected to the bodies were all diggers who had earned their medals doing hard labour on the fields, including those who were described as the 'large party miners' like the Doodys, Moreys and Tricketts. By exercising their right to vote in the first election of 1857 and subsequent elections, the diggers ensured that the Legislative Assembly was dominated by men like themselves. While women would not gain the vote in Victoria until 1908 (though they could vote in federal elections from 1902), they too had won themselves important and influential voices on the goldfields and within the communities taking shape in the 1860s and 1870s.

Both the men and women of the digging communities shaped the future development of the later gold-rich cities, such as Ballarat, Bendigo and Castlemaine, as well as many other regional towns and cities that transformed Victoria from a pastoral economy into a prosperous agricultural and industrial one. Digging communities finally embraced a future of goldmining as a large-scale industrial capitalist enterprise employing skilled and experienced wage-earning deep-shaft miners from places like Cornwall. But, overall, no matter how imperfectly or incompletely, the diggers managed to stay in control of the process, benefit from it and use the voice that they had gained to participate in the next stages of Victoria's development. For the migrant cohort, the skills and experience gained in industrial Lancashire, and the arduous work they performed as diggers, shopkeepers, artisans and mechanics, paid off as they stayed on in the mining areas to become deeply involved in the type of family and community formation described in *Gold Tailings*.[45]

Chapter 8

LIVES FROM THE DIGGINGS

The Great Western Company's quartz crushing and amalgamating mill.
Fredrick Grosse, Newsletter of Australasia, *1857.*
State Library of Victoria, a/n:NLA00/05/57/00.

There are some things wonderfully grand about the life of a gold miner. He will work from day to day with anticipation, and some years pass on. He is so happy while employed, and as I said gold, like love, does not grow on trees. But the gold miner has the same devotion while so employed. You can work for very little, and all at once you drop across a fortune. That is why it is so enchanting. You live in expectation, while being content for a living.

Mary Ann Tyler, *The Adventurous Memoirs of a Gold Diggeress*[1]

This chapter relates in greater detail some of the stories of families, single young women and men, and children from the migrant cohort who migrated to the goldfields after landing in Victoria. Historian Chris McConville coined the phrase 'the Existential Now' to describe the 'primal force of gold mining's attraction'.[2] A digger reminiscing about that compulsion described the following: 'not knowing what it would be like when we saw it, but fully expecting it every moment'.[3] Some have tried to compare this compulsion to that of the poker machine addict; however, there was something far more elemental about gold's attraction for those who lived the goldfields experience. And, as will be seen, the people in these stories do not seem to be goldfield addicts who wagered and lost everything, or hung on too long hoping finally to 'drop across a fortune'. In the main, the cohort's gold seekers seemed to have made a successful transition to other economic opportunities when the time was ripe.

The Master of Amalgam

To see the vagaries of goldfields fortunes and to understand the importance of industrial skills coupled with the necessary expertise to exploit them, we need look no further than the story of Joseph Doody, who landed in Melbourne in March 1853. Joseph, his wife Lucy and their two-year-old daughter, also named Lucy, were recorded as going off on their 'own account'.[4] Within days of disembarkation young Lucy died from a fever contracted during the voyage.[5]

An experienced plumber, Joseph would have had little difficulty in finding work as Melbourne was in the midst of a building boom. However, they did not stay long in Melbourne, possibly only long enough for Joseph to raise additional capital and equip himself for the goldfields.[6] Another daughter, Elizabeth, was born early in 1854 in Melbourne, but died a few months later in Bendigo.[7] On 7 May 1855, their first son, William, was born in Bendigo.[8] Joseph and Lucy seem to have been unlucky with daughters, but William and three other sons lived to ripe old ages.

It is remarkable how rapidly Joseph established himself as a leading player on the goldfields. In 1856, the *Bendigo Advertiser* reported on 'the improvement in the way of working both our quartz reefs and our alluvial workings' with reference to Joseph Doody: 'Mr. Doody's mill on the principle of dry stamping and crushing, with rollers, near Long Gully, deserves mention for the excellence of their final crushing and amalgamation.'[9] A year later the *Bendigo Advertiser* reported:

> The largest and finest lump of amalgamated gold which has ever been produced in this, or, probably, any other country in the world, was purchased yesterday ... The quartz was crushed by the Great Western Quartz Crushing Company, Long Gully, under the superintendence of Mr. Doody, who manipulated and retorted the amalgam. The careful and skilful manner in which the gold has been cleaned and retorted is most creditable to Mr. Doody, and we wish him all the success in his future efforts.[10]

Quartz milling was a major industrial operation. Joseph Doody and three partners had become leaders in the field in less than two years.

How Joseph Doody acquired this skill in manipulating and retorting amalgam – a highly skilled and prized art on the quartz goldfields – is doubtless related to his first job as recorded in the 1841 English Census: a young worker in a print factory and dye works. Manchester had established itself as the innovative leader in the chemical industry as it pursued better and more effective ways to bleach, dye or print textiles. Joseph would have been exposed to this innovation during his time at the print factory and dye works. Vast amounts of water were pumped in and out of these factories to be reticulated and retorted throughout the various bleaching, dyeing and printing processes. Joseph brought the industrial skills he had learned as a child and teenage worker in Manchester to the Victorian goldfields.

He also demonstrated an understanding of law and his legal rights, and a determination to work within a legal framework in upholding his rights. For example, as this court report states:

> When Justice Mollison was called to decide a case at Specimen Hill on Thursday last, between Charles Horst and Joseph Doody in a dispute over a claim that had been jumped, Doody proved to be 'an articulate and persuasive witness'.[11]

Within a short time, Joseph had become a leading player on the goldfields of Central Victoria and a torrent of information is recorded about him in newspapers and government records. In studying his ups and downs on the goldfields, much can be learned about goldfields life and practices. Between September 1857, when he won his claim jumping hearing, and January 1863, Joseph appears to have thrived.

In October 1857, his company opened a new quartz reef mine on a claim near Long Gully that for its first few years produced rich yields. He diversified into importing, assembling and operating water pumping equipment that was essential to successful quartz mining operations.[12] He even donated one pump to a local fire brigade.[13] By December 1862, he was in Inglewood working on a new claim at Maxwell Reef, which was reported as producing 'a rich yield'.[14] In January 1863, a hospital committee was formed to build a hospital in Inglewood, with Doody being one of its more substantial subscribers.[15]

This seems to be a high point of Joseph Doody's goldfields career. The *Bendigo Advertiser* captures his sunny optimism about the future:

> Mr. Doody leaves for New Zealand tomorrow, but retains all his interests in the various claims with which he is connected. Mr. Doody informs me his visit to the El Dorado is solely to have a look at the place, for which purpose his wife and family will be left behind until such time as he returns to Victoria. Mr. Doody has earned himself a respected name on these diggings … and I trust his trip to New Zealand may result as prosperously as he would himself wish.[16]

Shipping records tell us that he sailed for Otago, New Zealand, on the *Red Jacket* in January 1863.[17]

What the records do not tell is when he returned, but return he did. The big question is whether it was before or after a great tragedy struck. On 5 May 1863, Lucy Doody died. Her death certificate noted that it was the result of 'softening of the brain', and in brackets appears the notation '3 weeks'.[18] This suggests that the cause of death was a brain haemorrhage probably as a result of viral infection such as meningitis, which was rife in the mining camps at the time because of a lack of clean, fresh water. Lucy left four young sons, the oldest of whom, William, was just seven years old.

Life for a widower with four children would have been extremely difficult. Joseph Doody remarried within a year of Lucy's death.[19] His bride, Fanny Jameson, was also an assisted migrant from Lancashire. She was 22 years old when she left Bolton, arriving in Victoria in March 1857 with an occupation recorded as 'general servant'.[20] In the 1851 English Census we find her occupation noted as 'finisher' – another textile factory worker.[21]

Fanny had established herself as a successful and independent businesswoman in Bendigo by the time she married Joseph:

> **NOTICE**
> For Sale, a dwelling house and Refreshment
> Rooms situated near the Wellington Company works,
> consisting of two bedrooms, one sitting-room,
> refreshment rooms and Cellar, at present

doing a good business. The above will be sold cheap, as the present proprietor is leaving the district. For particulars apply to Mrs Doody.[22]

The cellar and its location, right at the heart of several quartz mining ventures including the Wellington Company owned and established by Joseph Doody and partners, suggests that it probably sold alcohol but was unlicensed. Fanny did not sell the business to become a stay-at-home housewife. She later became the active manager of the hotel and general store the Doodys established at Bears Lagoon.

The Wellington Company was a registered deep quartz mining operation with a nominal capital of £12,000, of which £9000 was paid up.[23] This company, and others with which Doody was associated, demonstrate the fine line between insolvency and riches that deep quartz miners straddled throughout the 1860s and 1870s. Joseph, like many others, was bankrupted as a result of his investment in and active role as manager of the Great Extended Eagle Company. Within a year of this bankruptcy the company struck very payable ground, and Joseph Doody and the company's other investors were discharged from bankruptcy.[24] This dramatic change in fortune underlines the haphazard, and very expensive, processes of making a living from the goldmines.

Eldorado Gold Mine, a Wellington Company's quartz mine.
Photographer: Algernon Hall.
State Library of Victoria, a/n: H1815.

Although he remained an owner of shares in mining companies that were producing and paying modest dividends, Joseph's discharge from bankruptcy is the last time his name is mentioned in surviving records in connection with mining pursuits until his death.[25] From 1868 onwards, Joseph turned his mind to more stable means of making a living, in particular, the establishment of the Bears Lagoon Hotel and General Store and selection of farmland near the lagoon (see Chapter 9). His pursuit of a fortune from gold, however, left him with Mad Hatter's syndrome. His last few years were a sad and tragic decline into dementia caused by his exposure to mercury during his mastery of the amalgam process. Joseph died in 1882 aged 52 years.[26]

Four Families

The stories of the four family (among others) presented in this section provide further illustration of Bate's argument that it was the urbanised, industrialised experience of the people who went to the Victorian goldfields that was essential to the rapid development of these fields from mining camp to established townships and cities which, unlike those of the Californian goldfields, survived beyond the gold rush days.[27] Each of these four families reappear in the following two chapters to illustrate the transition, or transformation, of the diggings into thriving permanently settled urban and agricultural communities.

Thomas Reynolds was recorded as a blacksmith in both the *Register* and the 1851 English Census; however, he was not a rural artisan. Prior to migration, he and his family were living in the heart of Oldham's industrial district on Soho Forge Square.[28] He would have worked for one of the engineering firms or foundries that dominated this particular area in Oldham, thus giving rise to the name of the square. Thomas, his wife Alice and their two sons, John (aged five years) and Thomas (aged three years), disembarked in Geelong on 3 September 1852.[29]

They travelled to the goldfields at Ballarat very soon after disembarkation; sometime in 1853 or 1854 Alice gave birth to a daughter named Diana in Ballarat.[30] Between 1857 and 1863, they had three more children, Nancy, James and William, all born in Ballarat.[31] The youngest English-born son, Thomas Jnr, was killed in a mining accident in 1868, aged 19 years.[32] Thomas Snr was working at one of the foundries that had sprung up in Ballarat during the 1860s, as well as continuing to mine with his two oldest sons. The death of the teenager probably stimulated the move away from digging. By the early 1870s, Thomas Snr had his own foundry on a small farm on the outskirts of Ballarat and was training his remaining sons to follow in his footsteps.

William Lancaster was probably one of the few Lancashire migrants whose occupation may be said to have matched rural artisan. In the 1851 English Census, his occupation was given as 'waller', that is a dry-stone wall builder, but he was also probably bricklaying. He was born in Broughton and was living there in 1851 with his wife Mary and five children, Mary Ann (aged 13 years), Joseph (aged 10 years), Jane (aged 7 years), Susannah (aged 4 years) and Thomas (aged 1 year).[33] William fitted the profile described by Winstanley of artisan/labourer transitioning from rural to industrial activities, along with Broughton itself.[34] At 40 years of age, William was one of the older of the assisted migrant, but as a large young family that included three girls the Lancasters were desirable migration material.

The family disembarked in Geelong on 20 November 1852, immediately going off on their 'own account'.[35] Early in 1853 Mary gave birth to a daughter in Geelong, Martha.[36] Sometime after that they travelled to the goldfields around Mount Alexander. In 1855, the oldest daughter Mary Ann, then aged 17 years, married a young 22-year-old miner, Henry Martin, who was also working the goldfields in the vicinity.[37] Henry was also an assisted migrant, having arrived on the *Derry Castle* in May 1853.[38] In 1856, both William Lancaster and Henry Martin can be found on the electoral roll exercising their new rights as miners. At this time, William and his family were residing in Fryerstown,[39] while Henry and Mary Ann had moved to Moliagul.[40]

By 1859, William and his family were living in Ballarat, where his wife gave birth to a daughter, Elizabeth, in the same year.[41] When his oldest son, Joseph, married in 1862, William and Joseph were working as woodcutters and splitters in Ballarat, probably supplying the deep lead miners with timber for their mining operations.[42] Daughter Mary Ann and Henry led the classic digger itinerant life, moving around various goldfields to the north and east of Ballarat. Their travels can be traced through the births of nine children between 1858 and 1876.[43] After the birth of their last child, Mary Ann and Henry settled down and purchased a lucrative hotel licence in Dean, a small gold township neighbouring Creswick, where they remained until their respective deaths in 1887 and 1893.[44]

William Mercer, his wife Maria and their three children, Smith (aged 15 years), Parysatis (aged 14 years) and William (aged 11 years), disembarked at Portland in Victoria on 4 December 1852. William Snr was employed by an Owen Reilly of Cashmere on a 12-month contract at £65, but there is no record as to what type of work William was employed to perform.[45]

By 1856, the family were on the goldfields at Amherst near the Adelaide Lead, where William, exercising his rights as a miner, was entered on the electoral roll.[46]

There is a significant gap in the records on the life of the Mercers on the goldfields, with several tantalising hints of a lucrative time on the fields and the forging of relationships that would benefit their children. James Henry Wheeler, a prominent Daylesford landowner who was a member of the Legislative Assembly (1864–67 and 1889–1900) and Minister of Railways in the Munro government (1890–92)[47], was one of the sureties in William Mercer Snr's probate documents.[48] James Wheeler made his fortune logging in the same region in which the Mercer family went to dig, and William, with his older son, Smith, may have been involved in that logging business. The youngest son, William Jnr, married one of Wheeler's daughters and lived next door to Wheeler on Raglan Street in Daylesford. William Jnr also became one of the first registered and licensed pharmacists in Victoria.[49]

James Woods was one of those who was slow to move to and settle on the goldfields. He, his wife Elizabeth and their two-year-old son, William, disembarked in Geelong on 22 December 1852 and left on their 'own account'.[50] They initially settled in the Geelong area, with James acquiring a small market garden farm. Three children were subsequently born in Geelong: Elizabeth in 1853, shortly after they arrived, Anne in 1856 and Mary in 1858.[51] For the *1856 Victorian Electoral Roll*, James qualified as a freeholder, representing yet another example of a migrant cohort member moving quickly into property ownership.[52]

James and Elizabeth give every impression of having established a comfortable and moderately prosperous life, yet, in 1859 or 1860, they abandoned that life to join one of Victoria's last major alluvial gold rushes. Their fourth child, John, and all their subsequent children were born in or near Steiglitz between 1860 and 1871.[53] What enticed James and Elizabeth to try their luck at this late stage is unknowable, but it is possible to speculate. James may well have had considerable contact with miners and shopkeepers on the goldfields by trading his produce with them. Cooperatives working the diggings, especially new fields like Steiglitz, were growing in numbers and sophistication of operation and machinery. The capital required to join a cooperative was upwards of £100. Many a trader, shopkeeper or merchant with goldfields relationships or networks was drawn into the new capital-intensive mining ventures on old and new diggings.[54]

Two Young Friends

Other than John Francis, whose short time on the goldfields was discussed in Chapter 6, there were just two single young men, William Atkinson, an agricultural labourer (aged 21 years), and Thomas Dickinson, a carpenter (also aged 21 years), who can be traced as migrating to the diggings.[55] They were childhood friends from Broughton on the outskirts of Preston, then a mixed area of growing industrial and remnant agricultural activities – classic Winstanley country.[56]

William Atkinson was living on his father's tenant farm at the time of the 1851 English Census. He and his siblings were all engaged in off-farm labour of various kinds, as would be expected in a district with a mix of rural and developing industrial enterprises.[57] Thomas Dickinson's father was a master carpenter in Broughton with his own shop, and Thomas was his apprentice. Thomas's mother and both his adult sisters, aged 19 and 16 years, were dressmakers.[58] Shortly after his arrival in Geelong Thomas married Jane Brewster, a 22 year old from Fife, Scotland, who was also an assisted migrant on board the *Borneuf*.[59] William never married, but was Thomas's faithful business partner until William's death from pulmonary disease in Creswick at the age of 52 years in 1883.[60]

William and Thomas were slow in leaving Geelong for the goldfields. Entries in the *1856 Victorian Electoral Roll* reveal both men living and running a carpentry business in Geelong.[61] William and Thomas's journey across the goldfields from 1856 until finally settling permanently in Creswick by 1862 can be traced through the births of Thomas's children.[62] We do not know if they participated in mining activities. However, Thomas died in 1886, aged 55 years, from the same pulmonary disease that carried off his mate, William, after what was described as a long and painful illness, 'the last nine weeks of which he was confined to his bed'.[63]

Pulmonary diseases caused by breathing dust and fine particles were common among quartz miners, suggesting that William and Thomas may have worked mines for a period. However, Broughton had a very large quarry, and the two men, as a result of living there, may have been more susceptible to the disease, or may already have acquired lung damage from living in the vicinity of that quarry before migrating. Well prior to their deaths, the good mates had established a successful and prosperous carpentry business in Creswick (see Chapter 9).

The Single Young Women

Surprisingly, the careers and occupations of those women who arrived in Victoria as single adult females and subsequently went to the goldfields are much easier to trace. Three young women from the cohort were to play significant roles in the growth of the mining camps into established urban communities, even if, as in the case of Hannah Ashcroft, it was as a pioneer shopkeeper in Ballarat. Two others left the Victorian goldfields, after many years of digging, having acquired partners and children, both demonstrating that they had not left behind with migration the working-class Lancastrian mores regarding marriage.[64] In this regard, they were far from alone among the single women in the migrant cohort, as will be seen in Chapter 10.

Hannah Ashcroft was the only single woman from the cohort who can be convincingly traced as travelling to the goldfields unaccompanied by family, husband or male partner. Hannah arrived at Geelong on the *Confiance* in April 1853. She was 25 years old, listed as a domestic servant, and went to work for a Mrs Wilson on a three-month contract at £30.[65] By early 1854, Hannah was trading goods, possibly including alcohol, out of a tent in Ballarat, and later that year she married Henry Munday, a miner in Ballarat. Unusually for a woman, her occupation was recorded in the marriage certificate as 'store keeper'.[66] As a shopkeeper on the goldfields, Hannah would have been required to have a licence costing the hefty sum of £15 per quarter. Hannah and Henry had four children between 1855 and 1863, two girls and two boys.

On the birth certificate of the last child, Henry's occupation was no longer recorded as 'miner' but as 'shopkeeper'. He was one of many diggers making the transition from active mining to a commercial occupation in an increasingly urbanised Ballarat, by joining his wife in her business.[67] However, in the first extant *Ballarat Rate Valuation Book* from 1865, it was Hannah who appears as owner of a shop and dwelling on Bridge Street, which was at the time developing as one of Ballarat's most significant small-trades and commercial-retail streets. Every other of the 100-odd premises on Bridge Street was a shop, shop and dwelling, or hotel. By the 1890s, when Hannah died, there were over 300 commercial premises along Bridge Street.[68] Hannah was clearly a doyen of the street and not someone who was going to lose her independence just because she married.

Ann Foy was another single woman from the cohort who may have gone to the goldfields unaccompanied. There is considerable confusion surrounding Ann's circumstances after she arrived in Victoria, for she was four months pregnant on disembarkation. She was discharged into the employ of Mr C. Thorne of Geelong, with a wage of 24 shillings for a three-month contract.[69] It is highly unlikely that she would have kept the employment once her pregnancy became noticeable. She gave birth to the child in May 1853, with the birthplace recorded as Geelong.[70] But, intriguingly, Ann married a young Irishman named John Mayne a few days after the birth of the child. On the wedding certificate John was described as a miner and the location of the marriage was recorded as Ballarat.[71]

Did Ann travel to Ballarat to escape the scandal, or did she meet John Mayne when he was visiting Geelong on some digger spree and he then 'rescue' her? John was an assisted migrant who arrived aboard the *Royal George* in November 1848 with his older brother, Thomas. He was then 19 years old and his trade was recorded as 'baker' in the *Register*.[72] The marriage seems to have been a successful one and Ann spent the rest of her life in Ballarat, with the couple having three children, all boys, who survived infancy.[73] John Mayne and his brother Thomas pursued their original baking trade alongside digging. This was not unusual, and it was probable that Ann worked alongside them baking.

John was still mining in 1868 when he was killed in a mining accident. Confusingly, his occupation was recorded as baker even though the cause of death was the mining accident.[74] John's death left Ann with three young boys, the oldest of whom was 13 years of age. Thomas probably took them in, with Ann continuing to work alongside him as a baker and the boys learning that trade. When two of her sons, John and Francis (Frank), died in Ballarat in 1926 and 1930 their occupations were recorded as bakers.[75] This is a clear example of a pattern on the goldfields whereby fathers, or in this case a father's brother, imparted to their children the skills acquired in their homeland. These skills would give them the means to participate in the development of commercial infrastructures in growing urban communities such as Ballarat. Ann also clearly possessed a resilience of spirit that allowed her to become part of the new developing community on the goldfields, having survived early misfortunes that could have condemned her to penury.

Jane Wiseman arrived in Victoria on the *Garland* in July 1852, disembarking in Melbourne. She was 23 years of age. Unusually for a single woman, nothing was recorded about where she went on disembarkation, probably because she was met by a young man awaiting her arrival.[76] On 25 April 1853, she married John Cornthwaite in Melbourne. Neither of their occupations is listed on the marriage certificate.[77] Jane knew John prior to migrating. He was also an assisted migrant from Liverpool, arriving in Melbourne three months prior to Jane.

John and Jane were on the goldfields at Alma by 1856 when the first of six children, William, was born.[78] A second son, Isaac, was also born in Alma in 1858.[79] Although the other four children are registered as being born in Maryborough, the Alma goldfield was on the edge of that regional town. Jane and John spent the rest of their lives in the Alma area. John died at the relatively young age of 45 years in 1877 and was active as a miner and mining investor until his death.[80] Jane lived to a ripe old age on the farm that their gold-digging and investing efforts had bought for them and their sons.[81]

The two other young women traced to the goldfields provide examples of families moving on after a period of prospecting – one family to new goldfields in New Zealand and the other to a suburban life in Brisbane, Queensland.

Jane Murray was on the same ship as Ann Foy. She was recorded as a 'domestic servant' in the *Register*. According to descendants on *Ancestry.com*, at some point after her arrival she married Fredrick Christian Dahl, a Danish crewman aboard the *Ann Thompson*, which carried Jane and her fellow passengers to Victoria. However, there is no marriage certificate.[82] Jane and Fredrick moved to Magpie Creek, on the outskirts of Ballarat close to Frenchmen's Lead, where they opened a grocery store.[83] While there, they had three children all bearing the anglicised family name of Dale.[84]

In 1862, they migrated to Otago in New Zealand on the *Blue Jacket*.[85] Jane died 18 months after their arrival in New Zealand. Fredrick opened a store on the West Coast goldfields and became a commercial and political rival of Richard Seddon, even though they shared a common political ideology inside the colonial liberal tent. Frederick's rise from common crewman to political leadership demonstrates the way earlier-arriving Australasian elites were being displaced by migrants to the various goldfields across the region.

Charlotte Rigby arrived in Melbourne in February 1852 and was taken into the employ of a Mr Petty, of Great Napier Street, as a domestic servant on a six-month contract at £26. When next sighted she was on the goldfields at Break O Day, where she gave birth to two daughters, Charlotte Christina in 1860 and Anna Gertrude in 1862. The father was named on the birth certificates as John Anderson Tait and his occupation given as miner.[86] There is no record of a marriage between Charlotte and John. In fact, the children bore the mother's family name all their lives. Descendants believe that Charlotte met John on the goldfields while mining on her own. At some point the family moved to Brisbane in Queensland where Charlotte died in 1887. She was still cohabiting with John. There is very little in the records to tell us how successful they were on the goldfields or generally in life, but Charlotte and John seem to have happily settled into suburban life in Brisbane without feeling the compunction to marry.[87]

The Mayoress of Ballarat

The Trickett family became involved in one of Victoria's great gold rush success stories, with the marriage of daughter Mary Ann to Edward Morey, described by Austin McCallum in the ADB as Ballarat's 'most spectacular investor and landowner'.[88] Mary Ann was considered to have had a lucky marriage and, so to speak, struck the deep lead. What no one has recorded is the extraordinary partnership that developed between Mary Ann and Edward, and how much of an equal partner she was in their success. Edward Morey could not read or write, but she could. Mary Ann worked the cradles in the early years, and went on with her father and husband to successfully exploit the deep lead, and later to build her own business empire in Ballarat. For a 17-year-old factory hand who had worked in a woollen mill alongside her father and mother in Bradford, it was a remarkable journey.[89]

On disembarkation in Melbourne, her father, Alexander Trickett, was employed by Joseph Beckett of Indentured Head.[90] Beckett's identity and trade is unknown, but at that time Indentured Head was a shipyard for small boats and punts operating in Port Phillip and on the Yarra River. Edward Morey was employed on these river boats after jumping ship in 1853 at about the same time that Trickett was employed by Beckett.[91] The Trickett and Morey relationship may have pre-dated their arrivals on the goldfields; they could have met on the river boats. The Trickett family were on the diggings around the Ballarat goldfields sometime prior to April 1855, for in that month Mary Ann married Edward Morey, who was by then mining at Specimen Hill.[92] Alexander Trickett, however, was one of the very few adult males from the cohort who does not appear on the *1856 Victorian Electoral Roll*.

Morey claimed to have been on the diggings and witnessed the Eureka Stockade Massacre in December 1854, and to being one of the first to tend the wounded diggers. Considering the likelihood that the Tricketts were also on the goldfields by this point, the family probably made the trek from Melbourne some time in late 1853 or early 1854. Alexander's wife Mary died on the diggings at Happy Valley, aged 53 years in 1864.[93] There is evidence that Alexander was involved in the cooperatives and companies being established by miners in the Ballarat region to pursue deep lead mining ventures. He was an initial shareholder in at least two companies that survived the bubble and went on to become profitable: the Prince Albert Mining Company and the Magpie and Frenchman's Mining Company.[94] On his death, Alexander was residing at Linton Park, a 2000-plus-acre estate outside the township of Linton, which was a rich mining area about 30 kilometres west of Ballarat. The estate was formally owned by Edward Morey. But there is some suggestion that it was acquired in association with Alexander and his daughter Mary Ann.

Morey did not hold on to Linton Park for very long after Alexander's death, which indicates that it was considered Alexander's property. Today the estate is riddled with the remnants of mining operations and was probably acquired to be mined. Alexander's occupation on his death certificate was noted as 'gentleman'.[95] This argues that he had done well enough to be considered of independent means, with his money probably accumulated from mining. There was no probate or will for Alexander. However, prior to his death, Alexander had ensured that all his property was already in the control of his daughter and her husband.

On her death in 1898, Mary Ann left a substantial estate in her own right.[96] The inventory in her probate documents values her real estate at £3192 and her personal property at £982. Included in the personal property are two parcels of shares for the Chalk Junction Gold Mining Company and the Ballarat Woollen and Worsted Mill. She was owner of a property with a 14-room house in Lyons Street, Ballarat; a 320-acre farm; and several parcels of land with cottages in Ballarat rented to tenants. She also had a 50% share in 400 acres on the Berry Lead, which in the 1880s was one of the richest deep lead mining districts.[97] At the time of Mary Ann's death, the Chalk Junction Gold Mining Company was still carrying on mining operations at Carisbrook.[98] This operation and the Berry Lead landholding mark Mary Ann as one of Ballarat's most significant and longstanding miners.

She was also a founding shareholder in the most successful of the Berry Lead mining companies, the Madame Berry, which extracted 387,313 ounces over its productive life, paying its shareholders a total dividend sum of £855,450 on a paid-up capital of £15,975 – a return of 5355%.[99] There also must have been something delicious for the 'factory girl', Mary Ann, becoming a founding shareholder in a woollen mill on the other side of the world.

Edward Morey's career was spectacular, and he was, along with two of his colleagues, Martin Loughlin and William Bailey, one of the more successful gold-diggers and miners in the Ballarat region. Morey, like Joseph Doody, was one of the few people closely associated with the migrant cohort families who struck wealth early in the alluvial gold period. He was apprenticed as a seaman at 13 years of age, and in 1853 jumped ship in Victoria. Sometime between 1853 and 1854, Morey travelled to the goldfields in the company of a group of boatmen he had been working with on the Yarra River.

He and his partners provide an excellent example of the importance of cooperative labour and industrial skills on the goldfields. Working as a cooperative of a dozen or more, they extracted gold in substantial quantities while some neighbours less than 20 metres away found nothing. According to McCallum, the partners' last known alluvial claim in the Jewellers' Shop yielded one ton of gold. Morey went on to become a successful deep lead miner and investor in large-scale mining ventures.

Morey was an investor and director of the New Australian Mining Co.; Last Chance Co.; Queen's Jubilee Co.; New Koh-i-Noor Co.; Northern Start Co.; the Prince of Wales, Bonshaw Co.; and the Madame Berry, mentioned above. He was also a founding director of the Phoenix Foundry and the Ballarat Woollen and Worsted Mill. He was a member of the Victorian Legislative Council from 1897 to 1901 and Ballarat's mayor in 1894.

Morey understood early the links between successfully exploiting deep lead mining, industrial-scale machinery and mechanisation, and capital. His energy ensured that all three were available on the Victorian goldfields.[100] On his death he left an estate valued at £62,950.[101] Mary Ann Morey's role in his ventures should never be overlooked. Edward was illiterate and it was Mary Ann who provided the literacy skills within their partnership. She also positioned herself as a prominent patroness and supporter of numerous foundations and community building projects, including hospitals, schools and benevolent organisations. Mary Ann's story is further explored in Chapter 10.

Children of the Midden Heaps

Stories abound of children abandoned or orphaned on the goldfields who yet managed to survive by scrapping through the midden heaps for missed gold dust.[102] Often told by missionaries and priests waxing lyrical in righteous indignation against the Devil's baneful presence on the goldfields, it is hard to ascertain the truth behind these tales.[103] The three Butler children (who renamed themselves Proctor) provide a real-life story, and it is a fascinating one. Their mother, Mary, died on the goldfields when they were young and their father, James, abandoned them soon after; yet they not only survived but thrived.

The three children, Thomas (aged eight years), Anne (aged four years) and John (aged two years), sailed from Liverpool with their parents on 10 July

1852 aboard the *Wanata*, disembarking in Melbourne on 4 October 1852. The *Wanata* was one of the three ships that had an exceptionally high death rate, with 15% of the children who boarded the ship dying from 'scarlatina' or measles on the voyage. The experience, according to Thomas's children and grandchildren, had a deep and lasting traumatic effect on him.[104] Thomas was the only migrant from among the cohort for whom there is evidence of sustained Christian belief.

The children all travelled under the name of Butler, but James and Mary were not married until 1850, and it is one of the reasons why the children later reverted to using their mother's maiden name. In the 1851 English Census, Thomas, then aged seven years, was recorded as living with his grandmother, Mary Proctor, a widow, with his family name recorded as Proctor.[105]

By 1853, James and his family had gone to the goldfields. Theirs was a nomadic life that can be traced through the birth of five more children: Mary in Ballarat (1853), James in Ballarat (1855), William in Pleasant Creek (1857), Margaret at Ararat (1859) and Robert at Red Bank in Dunolly (1861). On all the children's birth certificates James's occupation was noted as either miner or digger, though he was often absent for months on end, and it was Mary and her older children who worked the claims.[106]

Descendants of the Proctors believe this portrays Mary Butler and three of her children.
S. T. Gil for Macartney & Galbraith, lithographer.
State Library of Victoria, a/n: H17089.

The family was still on the goldfields in 1867 when Mary, their mother, died, aged 44 years, at Peter's Diggings. She left eight children, the oldest of whom, Thomas, was 17 years old and the youngest of whom, Robert, was five.[107] Soon after Mary's death James deserted the goldfields and his family for good. He had been coming and going for several years while working as an itinerant agricultural labourer and drover. When James died in Geelong from liver failure aged 64 years in 1888, he was described in his death certificate as single with no known relatives.[108]

The personal reminiscences of this story are derived from *Destiny of Gold* by Shirley Ward, a descendant and local historian. Ward's outline of assisted migration and goldfields history is not reliable, and she assigns events and acts to James and Mary Butler that did not occur. However, the oral reminiscences by the children and grandchildren of the Proctor siblings, which can be confirmed in part by primary documents, ring with an element of truth.

Among these is one story in which Thomas, at the age of 12 years, after a savage beating by his father, leaves the family tent to live with a puddler named 'Captain' Baker. Baker later discovered a rich Bealiba Reef known as the Queen's Birthday Reef, which established both Baker's and Thomas's fortunes. Thomas also re-adopted the maternal family name of Proctor. From about the age of 16 Thomas had his own mining licences on the St Arnaud quartz gold reefs. He also worked for other bigger quartz mining companies, establishing a carting business carrying quartz rock to the stamping mills.[109]

When his younger brother John was old enough and big enough, he joined Thomas as a carter and logger. John went with logging parties to the Murray and carted back timber for the voracious appetites of the quartz mines and stamping mills. Ann found work as a barmaid at the age of 14 and rose to become the manager and then owner of the hotel in St Arnaud, and raised the younger Australian-born Butler/Proctor children. The children all irrevocably broke with their father, with the English-born siblings re-adopting the Proctor family name. On reaching adulthood the Australian-born children drifted away to goldfields in Western Australia and even South Africa, according to Ward. The English-born children, however, remained close and established prosperous lives for themselves after the Victorian gold rushes in and around St Arnaud. Their story is taken up again in the following two chapters. All three can be numbered among the assisted migrant success stories, and they do not seem to have been handicapped by the uncertain status of their births, or the very difficult and tragic experiences they endured as children on the goldfields.[110]

The stories of individuals that feature in this chapter all do so because there is evidence of these migrants succeeding, or at least making a go of it, on the goldfields. Most were also successful in transitioning their lives and occupations when moving on from gold-digging. Only one of these migrants can be said to have failed in making a go of it on the diggings and that is the wastrel James Butler. He does stand as a reminder of how not to make a go of it on the diggings, an example his children did not emulate. Doggedness and determination were important qualities for miners who made lives for themselves and their families on the diggings and in the communities that arose out of the goldfields. All the migrant cohort who went to the goldfields, whether to dig, operate stores or ply trades servicing the diggings, went there with industrial and commercial skills acquired in Lancashire, or were children of parents who possessed such skillsets. The only exception were perhaps the Proctor children, but they demonstrated the ability to attach themselves to those who had such skills and were willing to pass them on.

Successful mining or digging, and the building of the townships and communities to support the diggers, was a shared cooperative experience. When Bate argues that the goldfields experience was 'a mass experience not rivalled until World War I', he fails to acknowledge that women and children played prominent roles in the shared pioneering experience that saw the chaos of the tented mining camps become the ordered urban environments of permanent homes and businesses.[111]

The 'mass experience' shared on the goldfields developed out of the shared values the migrants brought with them from southern Lancashire: mutuality, kinship and family obligations, and cooperativism. These values were central in the drive to establish permanent and stable communities for the goldfields generation's betterment. Most of the cohort featured above reappear in the following two chapters, because they were part of the family and community building that came to dominate life, culture and society on the goldfields and, indeed, across the rest of regional Victoria. They were part of what David Syme described as a generation who, in 'advancing civilization', created a 'transformation more marvelous … than the changes which have taken place in Europe', a transformation that made unrecognisable the pastoral society that they had descended upon.[112]

Chapter 9

FREE SELECTION AND FREE GRASS

The ideal of the yeoman farmer.
This engraving romanticises the selector as the sturdy yeoman farmer.
Alfred May & Alfred Martin Ebsworth, Australasian Sketcher.
State Library of Victoria, a/n: A/S25/09/80/244.

> *These three principles – free selection, the abolition of auction, and open pasturage over the unalienated lands of the Crown – were all they insisted on. They are the principles laid down by Gibbon Wakefield, and they would carry them out, for the benefit of the free citizens of this country.*
>
> From the opening address to the Victorian Land Convention, 15 July 1857[1]

It is by exploring the land issue that we may understand how a key aspiration of Lancastrian Chartism played out in Victoria during and after the gold rush years. And the biggest question here is: what exactly were people aspiring to? British Chartism looked back to an older pre-industrial concept, which may never have existed, whereby every man should have three to four acres on which he and his family could subsist, tiding them over during economic downturns. Wakefield created a program for the settlement of temperate anglophone colonies around the ideology of the yeoman farmer. It was to become, and perhaps remains today, the most significant political, social and cultural force in the development of Victoria and Australia. The problem with the ideal of the yeoman farmer is that no one could ever agree on what it meant, but it stirred the imaginations of migrants as much as did gold.

It is therefore not surprising to find that about 50% of the migrant cohort's diggers settled on rural properties after digging on the goldfields, despite having little or no experience in farming. This could be taken to suggest a closer connection to rural Lancaster than the existing English data suggests. However, few of these ex-gold-digger landholders seem to have invested their future livelihood solely in the business of farming. Farming was often ancillary to other commercial activities, with the small blocks of land purchased, frequently on the outskirts of the goldfields towns and cities, housing artisanal industries such as blacksmithing, wheelwrighting, brickmaking and carpentry, and often subsidised by earnings from the diggings.

It is only after the passage of the *Land Act 1869* that a small handful of families from the cohort's diggers undertook farming with serious intent on increasingly bigger properties. The *Land Act 1869* was the most successful of the various 'selection acts' intended to bring the concept of the sturdy yeoman farmer to fruition in Victoria.[2] But the reality was that farming, like digging, needed to be treated as a commercial business operation involving many of the same values shared and applied on the goldfields – mutuality, kinship and family obligations, and cooperativism.

There were only four families from the cohort who successfully selected, but the selection files of each provide a vivid picture of how selection worked. They also reveal aspects of the selectors' personal lives because these four families frequently needed to engage in extensive correspondence to secure their selections. In this correspondence they often opened their heart in direct and intimate ways. These selectors learned to take the business of farming seriously, but the attachment to the land they displayed was profound. This explains why the concept of the yeoman farmer remains so deeply rooted in the Australian psyche.

Joseph Powell, in discussing the connection between Chartism and the land reform movements of the 1850s through to the 1880s in Victoria, wrote:

> Previous attitudes towards land disposal, especially those concerning geographical concentration and the hallowed connection of land sales

and an immigration fund, were rendered anachronistic during the gold rushes. Busy towns replaced the miners' tents on the diggings, and Victoria harvested her richest crop of political exiles. Chartists and other reformers in Britain were at the time demanding 'land for the people', and some of this fervour was carried to Australia by those who came in search of gold.[3]

Powell goes on to argue that much of the tension that developed in the Victorian political system – between the Legislative Assembly and the Legislative Council, and between pastoralists and small farmers – was the result of multiple conflicting visions of the 'agrarian myth' in Victoria. He points to Hofstadter's assertion that an agricultural society developed in the US that was career-directed, not tradition-oriented, based on a farm management philosophy characterised by a 'business-like' attitude, rather than a 'craftsmen's' approach and an emotional attachment. Powell holds this is an appealing argument that contains many lessons for the student of Victorian developments.[4]

Fahey is more specific about the rational trajectory the development of Victorian farming took in the wake of the gold rushes:

> The yeoman idea had been enshrined as an Australian ideal in the 1850s when settlers, who had recently achieved manhood suffrage, were able to challenge the monopoly on land held by the first pastoral settlers or squatters. By the end of the nineteenth century, the term had narrowed in meaning and it had come to exclusively denote small freeholders. By this stage, the yeoman was an anachronism, and the Australian farmer was becoming capital intensive and market orientated.[5]

'Capital intensive' enterprise and challenging the 'monopoly' of the squatters, whether over land or political power, were activities that the gold-diggers had become highly experienced in pursuing.

Those of the cohort, be they adults or their children, who took up rural land, whether by selection or outright purchase with earnings from the diggings, were remarkably effective in maintaining and expanding their property holdings despite, on the whole, possessing no agricultural experience. The available evidence suggests that their success was the result of them entering into land ownership already in possession of, or quickly acquiring, the 'business-like attitude' described by Powell and Fahey. As Fahey notes, prior to 1870 and the widespread opening of new lands, 'the small farm section was strongest in the goldfields counties' and on farms purchased by successful diggers.[6] An idealised memory of a rural England had little place in the world of the hard-nosed Lancashire gold-digger.

Before Selection

Small farmers initially established themselves in close proximity to Melbourne and Geelong, providing them with ready access to farmers' markets in these cities. As the goldfields townships grew, so too did small farming around those expanding markets. These early farmers were perhaps as close to the yeoman farmer as Victorian farming would ever get. The holdings were small, on average 40–60 acres, and usually acquired from the Crown via an auction process that made the land relatively expensive. To rise above a subsistence level of farming, small farmers relied on intensive cropping, raising chickens, keeping a few pigs and a couple of dairy cows, and needed to be located in close proximity to markets to sell a small surplus.

The migrant cohort showed little interest in this type of farming prior to the 1860s. They were, after all, urban dwellers, not farmers. Those who did not migrate to the goldfields settled in the coastal cities and townships, where they engaged in industrial and commercial trades similar to those they had pursued in southern Lancashire. The only exceptions were two families who took up farming almost immediately after their arrival in Geelong. One was the Woods family, with James selling up his market gardens and taking his family to join one of the last gold rushes (refer Chapter 7). The other was the Rainford family, who settled down in what was a classic example of the small yeoman farming communities that developed around Melbourne and Geelong.

Like so many others from the greater Liverpool area, Joseph Rainford was described as an agricultural labourer in the *Register*.[7] The 1851 English Census shows he was born in Liverpool City and was simply described as a labourer. He lived in one of the newer dockside developments and all his neighbours were labourers, carters or artisans, such as masons, bricklayers or joiners. His subsequent career does seem surprising, but perhaps he was not as far removed from rural experience in Lancashire as the records suggest. He may well have performed seasonal work on nearby agricultural estates. His wife, Elizabeth, and her sister who lived with them were dressmakers. Joseph's younger brother, James, who at the age of 20 years migrated with Joseph and Elizabeth, also laboured on the Liverpool docks.[8] Joseph, Elizabeth and their children, together with James, disembarked in Geelong in October 1852. During the voyage a child named Thomas was born.

The family left the Migrant Depot on their 'own account', although James went to work for a Mr John Moore at Moorabool on a three-month contract worth £60 plus rations.[9] Joseph was enrolled as an elector on the *1856 Victorian*

Electoral Roll, as leaseholder of a dwelling house in Riddle's Paddock, Geelong, with his occupation recorded as gardener.[10] In August 1857, Joseph and James jointly acquired by auction an allotment of 42 acres in the Duneed Parish on the outskirts of Geelong.[11]

Marked out on the parish map are a handful of large allotments of land at the northern end, but most allotments are 100 acres or less, with 40–50 acres being the average size. Their proximity to Geelong may have allowed these small farms to rise above bare subsistence on the back of crops and dairy products, but the experience of Joseph and James suggests that they both undertook off-farm work. Joseph had acquired an adjoining allotment of another 40 acres by the time he died in 1893, aged 67 years, and James can later be found living in Geelong and working as a labourer and carter, perhaps for the farming community where the Rainfords had established themselves.[12]

There is evidence that, at the time of Joseph's death, he and James were operating a carting business from the farm. Joseph died intestate and his widow was granted probate for the estate.[13] The probate provides a good snapshot of his farm and the living derived from it. Joseph had expanded the farm's landholding to 84 acres and built on it a four-roomed house of stone and wood with a total probate value of £520. He had 4 horses, a cart, 3 cows, 3 heifers, 2 pigs, 25 fowl and 30 tons of hay. The horses and cart are evidence of off-farm work as a carter, while the large tonnage of hay suggests that this may have been another source of income for Joseph. He also had £210 in savings, indicating that the family was making more than a subsistence living from the farm.[14]

Did Elizabeth Rainford take up her old occupation as a dressmaker to supplement the family income? There is no evidence of this. She died 13 years after Joseph in 1904, aged 80 years.[15] She made a will leaving the bulk of her estate to her two Australian-born sons: James, who was still farming the property; and John, who was farming a nearby property. The residual went to her surviving Australian-born daughter, Alice, who had married another neighbouring farmer.[16] The original farm had been expanded to over 100 acres under James's care. John and other neighbouring farmers had also consolidated their blocks to 100 or more acres, as others found the small blocks too difficult to work profitably, or moved onto the new lands opened up for selection after 1869. Thomas, the ship-born son, was not mentioned in Elizabeth's will, but farming was obviously not for him as he had left home aged 17 years to become a teacher (see Chapter 10).

Land Reform and the Land Acts 1860–1869

Powell argues that a social, political and economic revolution was an inevitable consequence of the Victorian gold rushes because:

> Land issues were not divorced from the broader reforms demanded by radicals of all kinds, but there is no doubt that land reform was seen as the catalyst of wide change. The opening of the lands was the prerequisite for a program of encouraging settlement and immigration, especially with the decline of mining. More simply, some held that the establishment of a 'yeomanry' on the public domain was the highest of ideals of a growing nation.[17]

Popular demand for land, particularly among the early diggers, who from 1854 onwards found that the alluvial fields were not bringing the riches they had longed for, found a voice in the Victorian Land League, formed in December 1856.

The reality – a selector's new home.
Photographer: C.H. Kerry.
State Library of Victoria, a/n: H21486.

A series of fiery meetings held in the Eastern Markets in Melbourne opposite the new Parliament House crystallised around key Chartist platforms including universal male suffrage, free land and free commonage on the squatters' pastoral runs. In June 1857, the Secretary of the Victorian Land League invited a Congressional Assembly of Delegates (known as the Victorian Land Convention) to formulate a program for constitutional and land reform. On 15 July of that year, 89 elected delegates representing mainly communities from the goldfields met for the first time, again opposite the young Victorian parliament. This convention claimed to be more representative of the people than was the parliament, which still had not yet granted universal male suffrage.

It was around land reform, however, that the most controversy would be generated, leading to a riot when Parliament was invaded on 18 August 1860.[18] The Victorian Land Convention proposed three major resolutions that would remain the centrepiece of all legislative attempts at land reform until the early 1880s. They were:

1. That all exclusive occupation of unalienated Crown lands for pastoral purposes should cease, and such lands be open as free pasturage for the public;
2. That every adult person should have a right to select a claim of land not exceeding (number of acres to be determined) acres at a uniform price without auction;
3. That the right of free selection to be exercised by the actual cultivator should not be confined within the surveys, but should extend over all unalienated lands, surveyed or unsurveyed.[19]

The Victorian Land Convention ran out of steam after the granting of universal male suffrage. But many of the Convention and Victorian Land League's leaders became leading players in later Legislative Assemblies and various government cabinets, playing essential roles in subsequent attempts at land reform in the colony.[20]

The first major Selection Act was passed in September 1860 by the Nicholson government. This was a seriously flawed Act that created two classes of land: 'special', which could be acquired via auction by existing landholders; and 'country', which provided for unoccupied land to be surveyed and then up to 640 acres acquired by selection at a fixed price. An estimated 60,000 acres was taken up by genuine selectors under this Act, mainly around goldfields towns. Most of the goldfields allotments were 40–50 acres or less, often occupied by miners and tradesmen who combined income from other occupations with that of their small farm.[21] The take-up of these allotments could be viewed as aligning with the yeoman or Chartist ideal. At least three, or possibly four, of the migrant cohort were among those who selected under the *Land Act 1860* and the slightly amended 1862 version.

Two of these individuals were William Atkinson and Thomas Dickinson (refer Chapter 8). In 1862, they jointly acquired four allotments of land comprising 12 acres on the edge of Creswick. They established a successful business as wheelwrights and carpenters on the property. William died without wife or children and left no will or probate, but, considering the lifelong attachment between the two men, it would appear that William did not feel the need to make a will. However, Thomas did leave a will on his death. Thomas's will and probate demonstrate the range of commercial activities carried out on the property. There was a six-room cottage, the workshops, a stable, a piggery and over 100 chickens.[22] These documents provide clear evidence of a property being used to combine trades with limited farming to create a reasonable income. When Thomas died in 1886, three years after William, the *Creswick and Clunes Advertiser* remembered him fondly as an 'old and well respected resident'.[23]

In 1861, James Woods, who settled in Stieglitz with his family, acquired a 20-acre allotment on the outskirts of the township under the mining title provisions of the *Land Act 1860*. According to his youngest son Peter, who inherited the property, James 'farmed it after giving up mining'. The probate documents for James's estate do not record what type of farming James undertook on the property, as Peter did not get around to applying for probate until 1942 – some 26 years after his father's death.[24] Peter and his two older surviving brothers, William and John, appear to have had little interest in the property, leaving it abandoned for all those years, as they all had acquired their own substantial rural properties. We can only speculate on the role played by the gold dug up by James and his sons in the acquisition of their properties, but gold-digging success often resulted in the acquisition of substantial properties.

The fourth individual is William Mercer. William died in 1877, aged 58 years, from 'fatty degeneration of the heart'. His occupation was described as farmer.[25] He left, by the cohort's standard, a complicated will. But among his estate was a property: Allotment 12, Section 11 in the Wombat Parish, County of Talbot. This was a tiny block, maybe 10–12 acres at most, yet it was valued at £1000 in his probate. This is probably because of its location right on Wombat Creek at the very southern boundary of what became the Mineral Springs and Ornamental Parklands, which in the latter half of the 19th century was a major tourist resort and remains so to this day. The parish plan is unusually blank as to the ownership of all Section 11 allotments.

Their position beside the creek suggests that they are mining claims that were converted to freehold, probably under the 1860 or 1862 Land Act.

The probate documents are quiet on what activities Mercer undertook on his farm; however, it is likely to have been market gardening supplying the nearby township.[26] What is important is that William's children and grandchildren, propelled by the start he gave them, made the transition from the goldfields to urban professionals and shopkeepers. Progressively, his descendants acquired property in Daylesford and later Melbourne, including homes, rental properties and shops.

It was the squatters who most benefited from the *Land Act 1860*. An estimated five-sixths of the land opened up for selection had been acquired by squatters within a year of the Act's proclamation. Using techniques such as 'pea-cocking', where a squatter selected a prime section of property that denied others access to water or roadways and the like, and 'dummying', where agents would select the land, the squatters consolidated control of their existing pastoral runs and added to what they already possessed.[27]

One of the migrant cohort, James Butler, by family legend is said to have found that dummying resulted in easier money than the demanding work of digging. According to Ward, James was 'a waster and a heavy drinker', and it was through dummying that James found his true calling. When son John came to select after earning a good living hauling timber to the quartz mines, he found that he had already selected in the early 1860s when still a child. On further investigation, John discovered of his father that 'he had used all the family names to collect dummy selection fees' and the family suspected that many more identities had also been used.[28] This story and circumstantial evidence in the case against the squatter John Ettershank (see discussion under 'The Battle for Bears Lagoon' below) suggest that squatters were not the only ones to benefit from dummying.

The *Land Act 1869*

The bulk of the migrant cohort who acquired rural properties did so in the 1870s after the passage of the *Land Act 1869*, which finally resolved the land question in favour of the selector. The Act was pushed through the Victorian Parliament by a Scotsman, James McPherson Grant. Grant had fought as a volunteer in the 1844 war with the Ngapuhi in New Zealand, trained as a lawyer in Sydney, and successfully defended the Eureka Stockade rebels in court. He was a belligerent opponent of wealth and privilege, and wily in pursuing his objectives. This combination of traits bought him success where others had failed in confronting the opposition of the squatters and merchant elites.[29]

His solution was to make bona fide settlement of the selection precede its alienation. There was an initial licence period of three years in which a number of measures had to be taken to prove that the selector was actively living and working on the property. The measures included the construction of a permanent residence, fencing of the perimeter of the selection, cropping of at least one-third of the property and other improvements to the selection. After the expiry of three years, if the residential and improvement requirements were met, the land could be converted to freehold by paying the balance of 14 shillings per acre, or converted into a lease for seven years.

The 1869 Act allowed for selection prior to survey but limited the size of any one selection to a maximum of 320 acres. The legislation also provided the Minister of Lands and the District Lands Offices with retrospective discretion to disallow selections granted under the previous Land Acts. The result was that nearly 15 million acres were released to the small farmer and cultivator in the 1870s.[30] While the size of selections and the inexperience of many selectors would give rise to other problems, the *Land Act 1869* did transform farming in Victoria.

Not all the cohort moved onto rural properties via selection. One consequence of the 1869 Act was that a lot of land, particularly in older settled districts, came onto the market and was snapped up by those who were prospering from goldmining. Those from the migrant cohort who purchased or selected freehold farms were in the main successful in the management of their properties, despite most of them having no previous agricultural experience. This is exceptional as the failure rate for inexperienced farmers, especially on selections, has been put at up to 50–60%.[31] The small handful from the migrant cohort who took up farming seriously were among some of the most avid experimenters in the adaptation of a sustainable system of European agriculture to the Victorian environmental conditions and to the running of farms as businesses in a market economy. The most plausible explanation is that years of hard work on the goldfields, coupled with the entrepreneurial skills the migrants either brought with them from England or acquired as diggers, allowed them to approach farming with the same mindset they applied in profiting from the goldfields.

Thomas and John Proctor

At first blush, the Proctor boys, Thomas and John, appeared among the least likely to survive the goldfields (refer Chapter 8), let alone go on to be among the cohort's most successful and prosperous farmers. Through hard work,

Thomas and John prospered sufficiently on the goldfields to secure good farmland, which by their deaths they had enlarged into substantial farm holdings engaged in the most progressive and scientific agriculture.[32]

Thomas commenced his farming career in 1871 with his marriage to Mary Jemima Cross, which resulted in her father leasing him 296 acres at Kooreh.[33] By Thomas's death in 1926, the original lease had been transformed into a substantial freehold farming and grazing property of 2725 acres, which he named Ulverstone.[34] At probate, he also had substantial shareholdings in three farmers cooperatives, one dairy factory and a meat works. In Thomas's name were £1500 in interest-bearing fixed deposits and about £1200 in various other savings accounts. The 1926 wool clip sold for £1776. The farm's livestock and unsold crops were not valued in monetary terms but were catalogued by number; nevertheless, all were substantial, including more than 2500 merino sheep.[35]

Thomas's assets were divided between his widow and children. Under the will's terms, his wife was to receive approximately 40% of Ulverstone, with its stock, crops, farm machinery and other implements to be held in trust for her benefit during her lifetime and upon her death to be reverted to a tenancy-in-common in equal shares in favour of their four youngest children. The remainder of Ulverstone and its assets were to be divided equally between Thomas's three older sons. However, the eldest son had already been established by his father on a neighbouring farm of nearly 1000 acres; so in exchange for a waiver of all debt owed to his father's estate, this son relinquished any claim on the estate, apart from a personal bequest of £1000.[36]

Thomas made his name as a 'progressive landholder and farmer', and by the time of his death was, according to the *Age,* known as 'the grand old man' of St Arnaud. He was active in the St Arnaud Manchester Unity Lodge; the local Anglican parish; the St Arnaud Hospital, of which he was vice-president and a life governor; and the regional agricultural society, where he was an enthusiastic promoter of experimental and new methods of farming.[37]

Thomas is one of the few from the cohort for whom there is direct evidence of an actively demonstrated strong religious belief. Thomas's religiosity may have been influenced by his traumatic migratory journey on the *Wanata,* with its unacceptably high mortality rate among the children on board. He built his local parish church using rock discarded from local quartz mines and was remembered by his children and grandchildren as particularly devout – although they seem to have adopted the mindset that developed in rural Victoria that saw Sunday church activities as a social occasion that provides a welcome respite from the drudgery of farm work. Thomas's family was a very large one and he doted on all of them.[38] To die widely respected as the grand old man of St Arnaud was a rise in status for an illegitimate boy of uncertain parentage conceived in a boarding house in a railway town in Lancashire.

While Thomas was not a selector, his younger brother John was. John's selection story, as does that of his wife Jane, exemplifies some of the fascinating personal accounts that can be found in the selection files. As related earlier, John's name had been used by his father as a dummy for a squatter. Some 15 years later John had to persuade the St Arnaud Lands Office that he could not have possibly selected in 1860–61 as he was only 10 to 12 years of age. The production of his original birth certificate from the UK finally convinced the Lands Office. In 1878, John was allowed to select 320 acres in Bealiba in the land district of St Arnaud.[39] He selected next door to a woman who was to become his wife, Jane Marchant, who was aged 18 years when she selected in 1875.[40]

Unmarried women aged 18 years or over were permitted to select, and men often used their adult female children to accumulate additional farmland beyond the maximum 320 acres they were allowed.[41] From the correspondence in her selection file, it is quite clear that this was the case for Jane Marchant's selection. But Jane was a daughter who refused to accept that her father should control the land. In 1878, when Jane applied for the licence to be confirmed, her father mounted a sustained campaign to prevent her receiving confirmation because of her marriage to John Proctor. She wrote to the Lands Board in response, stating that 'she had married against her father's wishes' but as a result 'she had escaped his domineering control'.

The notes scribbled on this letter by the officers of the St Arnaud Lands Office demonstrate a remarkable sympathy for her position. Her father's application was rejected. It is also clear from the correspondence in both John's and Jane's selection files that John's migrant childhood, his orphan years on the goldfields and his status as a survivor who had succeeded meant something to the men in the St Arnaud Lands Office.

The pair faced one more hurdle before securing their two selections, and that was the requirement of a permanent residence on both properties. Jane and John chose to meet this requirement by building a sprawling home that straddled the boundary of both selections.

The 640 acres they acquired through these selections was only the start of their acquisitions. By the time of John's death in 1918, the couple owned a total of 2076 acres of land.[42] In his will John left 640 acres to his oldest son, Henry, and 617 acres to his other son, Francis. The balance, including the original selections, was placed into trust for Jane, to be divided between their three daughters after her death. In bank deposits, shares and life insurance policies John had built a portfolio valued at £3500 to be held in trust by Jane and divided equally among their children upon her death.[43]

Like his older brother, Thomas, he was an enthusiastic modern agriculturalist. Despite receiving no education himself and being unable to read or write, John ensured that each of his children received a good education. In one letter regarding his selection, John argued that a permanent residence on the selection was not possible if he wanted to provide his children with that good education: 'my reason for shifting the family off the farm is I have a young family and no school within six miles of my land'.[44] On completion of his sons' formal schooling, John sent them to Rich Avon, a large pastoral estate with an excellent reputation for training young men in all aspects of modern farm management and techniques.[45]

The Proctor boys were huge successes, but the stories of the three families below were more typical of those who became farming families following time spent on the goldfields.

Thomas Reynolds and Family

Thomas Reynolds fits the classic portrait of a gold-digger turning to small farming on the outskirts of a major goldmining town. By the time of his death in 1894, Thomas owned four blocks of land. Two were urban allotments in West Ballarat, and the other two were contiguous blocks of farmland of 57 acres and 38 acres on the outskirts of the Ballarat township, with a total value of £1047. The second block and one of the township properties were leased out at the time of his death. Each of the four blocks had a solid stone and brick cottage. He had little else in personal assets, so it is probable that all his gold earnings and later income had been ploughed into the properties by way of investment.[46]

Although his death certificate recorded his occupation as 'farmer', Thomas had returned to his old Lancashire occupation of blacksmith, which would have considerably supplemented the income from his farming activities. Thomas trained his sons to follow in the trade, as both Australian-born sons were later employed as smiths. He left the larger of the farms to his oldest surviving English-born son, John. The other properties were to be sold and the proceeds divided equally between the remaining children.[47]

John's migration story ends tragically. Between 1903 and 1909, he left or lost the farm and ended up working as a labourer in Ballarat.[48] Then in 1912, John was killed in an accident while riding his bicycle home, possibly from work but more likely from the pub. He was knocked unconscious, fell into a large puddle of water and drowned.[49] As there are no probate documents in existence for John, it is likely that he died penniless.

His Australian-born siblings Diana, Nancy and James were to do much better than John. Diana married a Ballarat fruiterer, Henry Slater, who was originally an assisted migrant, and they moved to Geelong where they set up shop and continued to prosper.[50] Nancy married a farmer and grazier, Samuel Shillington from Wendouree, also an assisted migrant, who had accumulated over 500 acres by the time he died. The Shillington landholdings may well have included the block that Thomas and then John farmed.[51] James became a boilermaker at the Williamstown Railway workshops.

William Lancaster and Family

At some point in the late 1860s, William Lancaster, his wife Mary, their youngest son Thomas and their two Australian-born daughters Martha and Elizabeth left Ballarat and moved east to the County of Anglesey. William may have moved to follow new mining opportunities, but in 1872 he selected 300 acres in the Parish of Molesworth near the township of Yarck. William did not immediately live on his selection; instead, he resided in Yarck, taking up his old career as a drywaller and bricklayer. This was to cause him considerable difficulties in securing the tenure of his selection. But William employed men to make the improvements required to secure the selection.

One of the men who built the home on the property lived in it during the three-year licence period. This was a not uncommon practice, particularly among ex-gold-diggers who had the money to pay others to work for them, which the local Lands Office helpfully notes in Lancaster's selection file.[52] However, the practice did leave those so doing open to extortion or, if such an arrangement was discovered by the authorities, to having their licence annulled because, as the selector, they had not fulfilled the residency qualification.

This is what happened to Lancaster when a James Bright wrote to the Lands Office in June 1874 claiming that all the improvements to Lancaster's selection had been done by himself and that he had not been fully paid for them, and further that Lancaster had not lived on the property during the previous three years. Bright also took Lancaster to court. Lancaster settled with Bright; however, there is no record of how much Lancaster paid. In October 1874, Bright withdrew his objections to Lancaster being granted the licence for the selection. But the Lands Office was not so easily satisfied. There was another six months of correspondence before the Lands Office accepted evidence that Lancaster's son Thomas, as his father's proxy, had been the primary occupant and improver of the selection.

William completed purchase of the freehold in December 1880, albeit not without some struggle. 'Failure of crops', 'drought' and an 'inability to sell cattle' all caused periodic cashflow crises, necessitating William seeking approval for mortgages during the period of the leasehold.[53] Perhaps it was more struggle than it was worth, for at some point between the acquisition of the freehold on the selection and his death in 1896, William sold the farm to a neighbouring selector, Peter Dunn. As part of the sale, Dunn owed William £1000, which was secured against the property by way of mortgage in favour of William. At his death, this was William's only asset.[54] With no children by then to provide for, the interest on this mortgage would have provided a modest retirement income for him and his wife.[55]

In his will, William bequeathed the exact amount of £1000 – with his youngest son Thomas receiving £300; his oldest son Joseph receiving £200; and his oldest surviving English-born daughter Jane Barry also receiving £200. The two Australian-born daughters did not fare as well. Elizabeth Halliday, the youngest daughter, received £100, but Martha, the first Australian-born daughter, received only £10. The remaining sum of £190 was left in trust for her son, William's grandson Gordon William Lancaster, to receive on reaching the age of 21 years.[56]

It would seem that Gordon was the product of an illicit relationship as his 1893 birth certificate recorded his mother's full name but noted the father as just 'Lancaster', in other words no father.[57] Martha had married a farmer in Yarck, Thomas Aldous, in 1873.[58] She is found on various electoral rolls still residing with him in the early 20th century,[59] and her death certificate lists Thomas Aldous as her husband.[60] Yet clearly Aldous was not Gordon's father, and William chose to express his displeasure with Martha while ensuring that his grandson would be provided for.

Thomas, the youngest of the four English-born Lancaster children, who was just three years old when the family migrated, provides another example of a migrant child striking out on his own as a farmer. Thomas Lancaster was part of the movement away from Melbourne, Geelong and the goldfields townships as the *Land Act 1869* helped open up new lands for settlement. This movement occurred 'in two major directions: north across the dividing range onto the Wimmera and Northern Plains, and south to the coastal and hilly forests of the Gippsland'.[61] In Thomas's case, he moved to Gippsland and acquired farmland in Moondarra, a once heavily forested valley that, when cleared and grassed, became a rich dairy district.

Rate records and land title records do not seem to exist for this district, but birth records for Thomas's children suggest that he did not move there until the early 1890s, around the time his father died. There is also something slightly odd about the move. His wife seems to have died or vanished in mysterious circumstances. He never remarried and neither did his older son marry; and the two lived out their lives as single men on the farm Thomas purchased in Moondarra. The property would have been purchased from a selector or group of selectors who had already undertaken much of the hard work in clearing the land and seeding it with grass, indicating that Thomas had a decent amount of capital when he made this move.

Both Thomas and his son, Edward, were entered on the *1903 Australian Electoral Roll* at the same address, with Thomas recorded as a farmer and Edward as a labourer.[62] By 1917, Edward had taken over the farm and Thomas had retired to the nearby township of Warragul.[63] Thomas had two other sons who took up farming on their own properties in the Gippsland region. Thomas died in 1934 in Warragul but there is no will or probate; he had probably already handed over the property to Edward before retiring to Warragul. Edward died in 1971, aged 90 years and unmarried. He also left no will and there are no probate documents, even though Edward's occupation on his death certificate was recorded as farmer and his address given as Moondarra.[64]

Jane Wiseman

Jane Wiseman was the only single young woman who could be traced through marriage to the goldfields and then to a rural property. As discussed in the previous chapter, Jane married John Cornthwaite soon after landing in Victoria and moved with him to Alma, a goldfields region, where they had six children. At some point, Jane, John and second son Isaac jointly acquired a 1100-acre property in the Alma region, where both John and Jane lived out their lives. John died at the relatively young age of 45 years in 1877, but appears to have been active as a miner and mining investor until his death.[65] As there is no probate for him and he did not leave a will, it is difficult to assess John's success. Jane died 23 years later in 1900, still living on the property.[66]

Jane Cornthwaite also did not make a will and there is no probate. However, as was the case for the other migrants who died with no will or probate, this did not mean that Jane and John had not achieved success in their ventures in Victoria. When Isaac died in 1925, the farm property was valued at nearly £4000 and among his assets were a substantial number of goldmining shares recorded as first being purchased by John.[67] Jane and John's eldest son, William, and his youngest brothers, George and John Jnr, moved to Thorpdale in the Gippsland region, noted for its rich farmland, where they selected contiguous blocks of land. Noteworthy is the rapidity with which they met the requirements for development of their selections in securing freehold on their properties, suggesting a significant level of capital resources acquired on the goldfields from mining.[68] Both William and George were successful farmers and left their children prosperous small farms.[69] John Jnr, however, vanished, perhaps moving interstate or overseas.

The Battle for Bears Lagoon

Joseph Doody first selected land in the area of Bears Lagoon under the *Land Act 1865*. This Act was the first attempt by the then Minister of Lands, James Macpherson Grant, to fix seriously flawed earlier Land Acts and to open up Victoria's rural hinterlands to the small farmer. Doody was granted a lease over 71 acres on Allotment 158B, Parish of Janiember, in the county of Bendigo on 17 December 1869. On 20 February 1873, he was granted freehold title for the land under Section 33 of Grant's second and more effective land reform legislation, the *Land Act 1869*, after it was certified that Doody had 'made substantial and permanent improvements to the value of One Pound for every acre' on the allotment.[70] On this land Joseph Doody and his wife Fanny built the first Bears Lagoon Hotel and General Store, as well as meeting the cultivation requirements for freehold title.

After a successful career as a miner and investor, Doody had been declared bankrupt in April 1868 when he and fellow investors had overreached themselves on quartz mining ventures at Inglewood.[71] That he could select the land so soon after his bankruptcy is evidence of the vagaries of fortune experienced by the gold-diggers. Joseph would have had to have been discharged from bankruptcy to be able to select (refer Chapter 8).

In 1872, Joseph and his 18-year-old son William selected a further 560 acres in four allotments to the south of Doody's original selection. This land had originally been selected, under one of the earlier land acts, by Henry Henrickson. In 1870, Henrickson travelled to New Zealand to join his brother. He forfeited his selection but requested that the four allotments be transferred to the Doodys in return for them compensating him for the improvements he had made and the rents he had paid. The Lands Office gazetted the forfeiture and then allowed the Doodys to re-select the blocks under Sections 19 and 20 of the *Land Act 1869*.[72] However, it is highly probable, although there is no direct evidence of such, that Henrickson selected the blocks as a dummy for John Ettershank. Certainly Ettershank considered the land to be rightfully his, as demonstrated by correspondence in the Doodys' selection files and another file titled 'Correspondence Regarding Selections of Mr John Ettershank – Sandhurst

Land District'.⁷³ His fight to reclaim that land and many other adjoining allotments in the Serpentine Creek/Bears Lagoon area, and the Doodys' and other selectors' fight to retain their title to the land they believed they had validly selected, resulted in what I call here the 'Battle for Bears Lagoon'.

Builders of a new nation.
Bears Lagoon women dressed in all their finery to celebrate the birth of a new nation.
Courtesy of the East Loddon Historical Society.

Although a relative latecomer to the ranks of the pastoralists, John Ettershank came to represent, in the public mind and in the view of the colonial liberal governments, all that was bad about squatters. The *Age* described Ettershank and his brother as 'land-grasping gentry' who resorted to 'dubious means' to satisfy their 'appetites'.⁷⁴ His name also crops up in parliamentary records in connection with alleged bribery and improper appointments.⁷⁵ Ettershank's migratory trajectory ironically crosses with Joseph Doody's at several points before they both finally arrived at Bears Lagoon and came into conflict.

John Ettershank was of middle-class Scottish origins and a qualified civil engineer. He moved to Manchester soon after gaining that qualification, where he was involved in the construction of new engineering works and warehouses – on some of which Joseph may have worked as a plumber and glazier. Ettershank did not stay in Manchester for very long. He migrated to Victoria with his new wife Christina, older brother Edward, and Christina's brother, William Eaglestone, as unassisted migrants. They arrived in Melbourne in December 1852.[76] Ian Itter claims, and various obituaries attest to this, that they came out to work on the construction of the Alfred Graving Dock at Williamstown.[77] Construction of the dock, however, did not start until 1864, and it was then that a branch of the engineering firm established by the Ettershank brothers was awarded one of several contracts put out to tender[78]

It is probable that the whole family group migrated to participate in the gold rush and travelled to Ballarat soon after arriving in Victoria. Whether they actually dug or mined on these fields is impossible to ascertain. But the Ettershank brothers and Eaglestone saw the opportunity to put their engineering skills to work – importing parts and assembling or constructing engines, pumps, boilers and other engineering machinery increasingly required to extract gold. Joseph Doody was engaged in similar enterprises in Bendigo, and their paths may well have crossed when the Ettershanks opened a branch of their engineering works in Bendigo towards the end of the 1850s.

John Ettershank quickly realised that he could make greater profits as a stock agent delivering sheep and cattle to the hungry miners. Although he did not pioneer the stock routes, which saw sheep and cattle driven from NSW and southern Queensland down the inland corridor, he turned this work into a very lucrative business that broke the monopoly Sydney stock agents had previously held over the stock trade. It was this business that first brought Ettershank to Bears Lagoon.[79]

Bears Lagoon is a narrow gash in the alluvial flood plains located about 55 kms northwest of Bendigo, formed by a fracture along a fault line in the underlying rock. It is now silted up as a result of an irrigation channel running through it and is wadeable, but was once very deep, supporting abundant game and fish. It may have been fed by an artesian water supply as well as the network of creeks that drain into the Serpentine Creek and then the Loddon River. The area around it is flat and was covered in native grasslands. Conveniently located midway between the Murray River crossings and Bendigo and Ballarat, it was an ideal location to rest and fatten cattle and sheep before driving them south down the Serpentine Creek and then on to Ballarat or Bendigo.

The first Europeans to settle around the lagoon were the managers and shepherds of some of Victoria's biggest squatters, including John Bear, after whom the lagoon was named. From 1862, attempts were made to break up the pastoral estates and open up the land in the Sandhurst district for selection. John Ettershank used the flaws in the early Land Acts to place a number of employees on blocks throughout the East Janiember Parish, which is centred on Bears Lagoon. He would then assist these dummies with finance for improvements and lease payments. The improvements were often minimal and the blocks were used exclusively for pasturing sheep and cattle.

After the *Land Act 1869* was passed, a substantial number of these early selections came under investigation from the Lands Department, and much of the early material in the correspondence regarding the selections of John Ettershank consists of affidavits, letters and statements in relation to these investigations. It may have been the Doodys who stirred the Lands Department to look at those selections. At least one affidavit was obtained by Joseph Doody from a shepherd who used to work for Ettershank. Between 1872 and 1874, several of the pre-1869 selections were forfeited for non-payment of rent, non-compliance with the provisions of the Land Acts, and non-performance of covenants in the respective leases. In at least one case, a widow, Margaret Horan, was permitted to re-select the allotment under Sections 19 and 20 of the 1869 Act. On other allotments new selectors quickly took up the forfeited selections.

Ettershank came out fighting, claiming that on all the selections concerned he had right to title, as all the original selectors had assigned title to him in return for being advanced sums of money.[80] This was the beginning of a long legal struggle that went all the way to the Privy Council in the UK, where Ettershank won one case on appeal and lost another.[81] Protracted negotiations between the Lands Department and Ettershank and his lawyers continued until 1886, when they finally agreed on a settlement. In return for paying rental arrears and penalties of £1172.10, Ettershank was granted Certificate of Title on 1212 acres selected in 1865. Among the people displaced was Margaret Horan, who received £300 in compensation from the Lands Board. Ettershank did surrender his claim to several other titles for which selectors had ownership and grant of title already confirmed.[82] This included the Doodys' selections.

Whether people like Margaret Horan eventually lost their selections to Ettershank, while others like the Doodys would successfully fight off Ettershank, came down to the relative influence the various parties could wield. It could not have been an easy fight for Doodys. At the very beginning of William Doody's selection file is a letter from Ettershank addressed to the Assistant Commissioner of Land. It reads:

> Sir, I have the honour to send you on the leaf the different allotments of land which the President agreed he would not present to be selected pending the adjudication and settlement of my claim to them.

A pencilled note on the letter says, 'not to be selected pending settlement of Mr Ettershank's claim'. This indicates that Ettershank could wield influence at the highest levels of the public service. Yet, subsequent to that note, the Sandhurst Lands Office did proceed with the applications for selection by Joseph and William, suggesting that there was considerable division within the Lands Department.[83]

Joseph and William were prolific and literate correspondents, who demonstrated a considerable understanding of their entitlements and rights. Despite starting work sometime around the age of 9 or 10, in a dyeing works in Manchester, Joseph seems to have acquired a good elementary education and absorbed much of the radical political and Chartist thought prevalent during his childhood and teenage years.[84] His son William was born and grew up on the goldfields. William's letters are well-written in a neat and legible handwriting, suggesting that the educational opportunities on the goldfields were far from inadequate, as so often portrayed by contemporary writers and later historians.[85]

The Doodys' struggle for their selections coincides with a time of considerable political upheaval in Victoria as the liberal groupings of the lower house battled to assert their dominance over the upper house and implement their reform programs, particularly around land and electoral reform. Joseph seemed to have ready access to James Grant (previously Minister of Lands, and then Minister of Justice in the Berry government) and Francis Longmore (Minister of Lands at the time and, like Berry and Grant, committed to breaking up the great pastoral estates through a punitive land tax). There were also letters in their selection files from various members of the Legislative Assembly querying the Lands Department as to why the Doodys were having such difficulty in gaining final freehold title to their selection, when they had made their improvements and paid the money due on their leases.

In the latter half of 1876, the Minister of Lands directed that title be granted expeditiously to both the Doodys. Although the grants of title to Joseph and William were dated, respectively, 22 July 1876 and 10 February 1877, they did not receive the certificates of title for another two years. The Sandhurst office, so supportive in the early years, seems to have fallen under the influence of Ettershank and found one excuse after another to not issue the certificates. The last excuse was based on the receipt of an anonymous letter reporting that Joseph Doody was running businesses on his selection: the Bears Lagoon Hotel, general store and Post Office and a blacksmith shop. Although the letter of the law said that this could be cause for forfeiture of a selection, the Lands Department on the whole tended to ignore the establishment of such businesses as they were vital to the development of viable rural communities. An exasperated and terse order from the Commissioner finally resulted in the issuing of the certificates. The Doodys were then officially able to join their fellow selectors in developing what was initially a thriving community similar to many springing up across Victoria at the time.[86]

Joseph Doody died in 1882.[87] He was 54 years old. He spent time in the Kew Asylum before returning to Manchester to seek a cure for the Matter Hatter's syndrome (mercury poisoning) acquired during his days as a gold miner. In Manchester he was told that nothing could be done. He made a will and returned to Victoria, and lived out his life between Bears Lagoon and Inglewood, where he owned a home and still had mining interests.[88] Joseph's sons and grandchildren would go on to play influential roles in the community at Bears Lagoon, establishing a school, a mechanics institute, an agricultural cooperative and other institutions. We can follow their involvement in the building of a viable township and community in the pages of the *Bendigo Advertiser*.[89]

Strikingly, John Ettershank also became involved in supporting this growing community. He contributed substantial sums annually to the local school and was a founding contributor to the Mechanics Institute. More importantly, he became a powerful and wily defender of local small farmer interests, demonstrating that we should not unthinkingly demonise the squatters. Ettershank's defence of local farming interests when the bureaucracy attempted to construct an irrigation channel cutting across and dividing many of the local farmers' blocks of land, including William Doody's, was determined and successful. He also built a massive red-brick woolshed, one of the first mechanised shearing sheds in Australia. It was viewed as another example of his empire building; yet Ettershank encouraged other farmers to use it.

Although selectors had to make the effort to crop their land to secure their selection, this region was sheep country. With the support of Ettershank and his red-brick woolshed – to which the small farmer could take his herd for a day's shearing, sorting, grading and transport to the markets – sheep became an increasingly important part of the farming system in the region. Finally, in the 1890s, in what can only be seen as a last middle finger at the Lands Department, Ettershank began auctioning off his land to local farmers. He had been offered £5 an acre for much of his estate by the Lands Department so they could pursue new schemes for closer settlement in the area. He rejected this, instead selling the land for between £3 and £5 to experienced local farmers at an interest rate comparable to that offered by the Lands Department. William Doody was among those who purchased additional blocks of land.[90]

In coming to Australia Joseph Doody was seeking independence and a pathway to property ownership denied to him and his peers in Britain. The discovery of gold and the availability of land in Victoria presented the possibility of achieving that dream of independence and property ownership. The goldfields and the land became battlegrounds on which a new social democratic society took shape. The struggle to unlock the land, which the Doody family's personal struggles humanise, created a new and substantial small-property-owning business class that had a significant investment in the success of both this evolving new social democracy and of the country as a whole. In making his migratory journey to Bears Lagoon, Doody imbibed along the way new political and social cultures that provided him and his sons with agency in their struggles against an oligarchy determined to preserve its entrenched privilege.

The Doody family's experiences are far from unique in this migratory story. For all the migrant cohort followed in this collective biography there are similar migratory journeys. The result was an evolution into a small-business-owning and property-owning class enabled by the social democracy that they were overlaying onto the pastoral and mercantile oligarchic society that existed prior to their arrival. This transition was not unique to the goldfields or to the agricultural communities being created across regional Victoria; it was also changing the values in society generally and influencing the cultures of the townships and cities, including Melbourne. By the end of the 19th century, Victoria was predominantly an urban and suburban society, which Donald Horne described as 'the first suburban nation'.[91]

Chapter 10

AN ADVANCING CIVILISATION

Bridge Street, looking east from Sturt Street, Ballarat, c. 1886-1887.
Photographer: Fred Kruger.
National Gallery of Victoria, a/n: PH337-1979.

> *We have witnessed transformation more marvelous in one respect than the changes which have taken place in Europe. We have within a quarter of a century effected a social and industrial revolution which it has taken many centuries to achieve elsewhere.*
>
> David Syme, Publisher and Editor of the *Age*,
> on the 25th anniversary of its founding

Syme saw growth of the urban centres in regional Victoria as the end product of 'an advancing civilisation'. He waxed lyrical on how 'four great stages of human progress', from 'savage roaming the wilderness' to 'manufacturer following the agriculturist', were all 'brought under our eyes' and 'better still they have been bloodless progressions in a little more than a quarter of a century'.[1]

170

Victorian Aboriginal people will dispute the use of 'bloodless' to describe the processes Syme celebrates as for them it was far from bloodless. However, as Davison argues, the goldmining generation created and accelerated industrial and commercial growth, which, on the back of the expansion of the 'octopus' tentacles of the railways, 'stretched into every section of the colony'.[2]

What Syme celebrates, and Davison sketches, matches the descriptions by Darwin and Belich of the explosive expansion of settlement across the American frontier of 'the exploding Wests'.[3] Darwin described it thus:

> The remarkable feature of the American frontier was not so much the torrent of farmers who moved west, but how rapidly towns followed in their wake. Towns grew much more quickly in size than the population as a whole. Towns attracted artisans with industrial skills. It was the dynamic fusion of Old and New Europe that underlay its success. In Australia and New Zealand … the same stimulants can be seen at work.[4]

While Melbourne became the pre-eminent industrial and commercial urban centre of Victoria, the growth of other prominent industrial and commercial centres such as Ballarat, Bendigo and Castlemaine substantially contributed to the industrialisation of Victoria and the associated accelerated commercial growth.

Most of the cohort, whether they went to the goldfields or not, did not follow rural pursuits, but settled in and were involved in the creation of the urban industrial and commercial centres of Victoria. Some individuals who went to the goldfields stayed on in cities such as Ballarat, Bendigo, Castlemaine and Daylesford, and through the application of their expertise as skilled industrial workers provided a critical contribution to building urban and community infrastructure. Davison writes of how Victoria's industrial economy developed around 'import-substituting industries that generated a variety of subsidiary trades'.[5] He argues that this arose with the assistance of protectionism, which became an article of faith of various governments from the 1860s.

However, import-substituting industry and trades were a feature of the industrial and commercial development of the goldfield towns from at least the second stage of the gold rushes. Bate and Serle argue that the isolation of the major goldfield townships, the poor state of the roads (if the rutted tracks to the fields could be called roads), and the length of the journey necessitated these towns developing their own industrial and commercial capacities.

The abundance of artisans, mechanics and craftsmen working as diggers on the fields made this viable. Joseph Doody provides a prime example of this with his Bendigo-made stamping machines, steam engines and pumps. His great rival at Bears Lagoon, John Ettershank, also established engineering and foundry businesses in Ballarat and Bendigo. Not all of this industrial development was confined to small factories and artisan workshops. The Bendigo Iron Works; the Phoenix Foundry, Ballarat; and the Ballarat Worsted and Woollen Mill were examples of industrial development that rivalled anything Melbourne was then undertaking. Keech Castings (a direct descendant of the Bendigo Iron Works, and producer of steel products for the agricultural, defence, mining and railways industries) and the Ballarat mill complex now operated by Rivers are still important industrial works in Bendigo and Ballarat.

Arriving in Ballarat, Bendigo and Castlemaine in 1862, the railways played a critical role in regional economic development, enabling some towns, like Castlemaine, to thrive, while others, including Bears Lagoon, originally a central hub for the inland stock routes, lapsed into rural backwaters. The railways also became important pathways into skilled occupations. The stories of two children from the migrant cohort demonstrate how the railways provided them and their male children with a pathway into skilled and permanent employment, and offer a glimpse into the route back to the major cities that started as a trickle and ended as an avalanche. Both James Guy and James Reynolds turned their experience working alongside their artisan fathers into skilled jobs with the railways.

James Guy became an engine driver, first in Ballarat, before being based out of both Melbourne and Seymour, a critical railway junction. James Reynolds was trained by his father as a blacksmith. After marrying, James moved to Footscray and found employment in the railway workshops at Williamstown. It was at these workshops that the first militant union movement in Australia was founded, primarily by Lancashire migrants. By the time James retired, he was a boilermaker.[6] He also owned his own home at 71 Moore Street, Footscray.[7]

While all his sons followed him into the railway workshops, one of his daughters enrolled as an undergraduate at Melbourne University.[8] The experiences of Reynolds and his children demonstrate the how permanent railways jobs provided advancement in Victoria for those employed and their families. James Reynold's daughter is not the only example of an Australian-born female child of the cohort entering higher education. Yet it was exceptional to see a child of a boilermaker, let alone a female child, gain admission to a university in the early 20th century.

Railway Dreaming

On 15 October 1862, a train carrying the Governor, Sir Henry Barkly, and other distinguished guests pulled into Castlemaine at just before 1 pm to a tumultuous welcome from the townspeople. The *Mount Alexander Mail* declared, 'this momentous event was well and worthily celebrated. Never has the township been the scene of such excitement as was exhibited on this occasion'.[9] With this inaugural rail journey, what had previously been an arduous three- to five-day trek to the goldfields was reduced to four to five hours.

Castlemaine had every reason to celebrate. In *Lost Relations*, Davison observes that if the railway had bypassed Castlemaine 'the town was doomed'.[10] These celebrations marked the completion of the first stage of the Melbourne to Murray River Railway, with the line then terminating at Bendigo. At the time it was the most expensive public project ever undertaken in Australia. Originally, the intention was for the line to be financed by private enterprise; but after the failure of the private development company and long debate, the Victorian Government stepped in and established a precedent for financing public works out of the public purse.[11] The public financing of the Victorian rail network became the pragmatic reality of colonial development.

Castlemaine and its townsfolk had to fight very hard to have the railway diverted through the township. The town was not on the most logical or natural route to Bendigo, demanding a diversion that Serle described as a 'great extra expense'.[12] The diversion involved carving two tunnels, building three expensive bridges, embankment works and constructing a long causeway to bring the line into the centre of Castlemaine. Local community and political leaders, including John and Joseph Seddon, who were establishing themselves as important merchants and tradesmen in Castlemaine, fought long and hard to have the railway pass through Castlemaine. John Seddon was probably involved in the railroad construction works. A by-product of the alluvial diggings was washed clay. John and his sons established themselves as brick makers recycling this waste from the digging. The viaduct and the substantial Castlemaine Railway Station were built of brick from this waste, and still survive today.

The importance of this Castlemaine victory can be demonstrated today by looking at how once-thriving goldmining townships such as Harcourt, Maldon and Newstead languished, while Castlemaine remains an important regional centre. 'It is not unreasonable to conclude that a large proportion of … money will find its way into Castlemaine', the *Mount Alexander Mail* triumphantly observed.[13] Davison notes that:

overnight, the mining town got an industrial base … The new jobs called for more brain than brawn, more precision than force, more punctuality than perseverance, more prudence than risk, more literacy, numeracy and knowledge of the wider world.[14]

The railway initially brought the riches to Castlemaine over which the *Mount Alexander Mail* had exalted, but this prosperity was relatively short-lived.

By the early 1880s, the Castlemaine city fathers were begging the government to build a regional rail workshop in then-abandoned industrial works. The railways had opened up Victoria's interior to wheat cultivation, a revived wool trade and what would later become a thriving dairy industry. However, the short rail trip to Melbourne ensured that Castlemaine was increasingly bypassed for the larger processing centre and port. 'The townspeople of Castlemaine would not rest until railway workshops were established in the town,' Mayor J.A. James declared.[15] But this was a forlorn hope. The power Castlemaine once wielded with gold was long gone. The railways, like almost everything else, had become centralised in Melbourne. This affected not only the Seddons in Castlemaine but others like Ann Wheeler, who saw the family brewing business destroyed by cut-rate competition from Melbourne brewers.

The department store that the Seddon family first founded in the gold rushes staggered on until the 1930s, trying but never succeeding to emulate the Myers' success in transforming their Bendigo drapery into an Australia-wide department store chain. John's and Joseph's children had by then well and truly joined the flood of young people migrating to Melbourne in search of work and better prospects. They were lucky in that they had capital dug out of the ground by their fathers to take with them.

Ironically, the railway is now contributing to a revival of Castlemaine's fortunes. New improved track works and a regional rail link to Melbourne provide a service that takes about an hour to the central city. This is turning Castlemaine and surrounds into desirable commuter dormitory suburbs for Melbourne.

Dairymen

To fully appreciate the connection between the railways and the various regional centres that emerged to service agricultural industries, we only need look to the Bailey family and their relationship with the town of Terang. Thomas Bailey (aged 36 years), Elizabeth (aged 30 years) and their four children, Robert (aged 8 years), Margaret (aged 5 years), Martha (aged 2 years) and Mary (aged 1 year) sailed from Liverpool on 20 June 1852 aboard the *Araminta*. They landed at Geelong on 4 October 1852.[16] Prior to emigrating, the Baileys were living in Prescott, a township northeast of Liverpool, in 1851. Now firmly part of Liverpool's outer suburbs, it was then a market town with a thriving coalmining sector. Prescott was surrounded by rich, shallow seams of black coal and was an important supplier of the coal driving Lancashire's industrialisation.

In the *Register*, Thomas was recorded as being an agricultural labourer. However, in the 1851 English Census his occupation was listed as labourer and there is no mention of any agricultural workers, including tenant farmers, in the several pages either side of the page containing the Baileys' returns. The area where Thomas lived was a densely settled urban, working-class, residential area. Labourers predominate in these pages, but there was also a high proportion of skilled workers, artisans and tradesmen. It is also an area where over 50% of wives are noted as having occupations. Elizabeth Bailey was not one of these women, but this does not mean that she was not in employment.[17]

After disembarkation in Geelong, Thomas found employment while still at the depot with B. Downing of Elephant Bridge, now the township of Darlington in western Victoria.[18] The Elephant Bridge Hotel, a historic bluestone pub built in 1855, to this day maintains the name of the early township. The region was natural grasslands and squatters dominated with large sheep-grazing runs. There is no record of a B. Downing among existing records of squatters and their landholdings or in the Victorian *1856 Electoral Roll*. However, Thomas was recorded as a shepherd on 'Mr Cole's Station, Cloven Hill' on the birth certificates of his three children born between 1854 and 1861.[19] This makes Thomas a remarkable exception among the migrant cohort – he did what the colonial administration desired of fathers with large young families and undertook work on a pastoral estate. And this was not to be the only exceptional move by the Baileys. The Baileys are the only family from the cohort who neither migrated to the goldfields nor stayed on in the big cities of Melbourne or Geelong.

In 1863, shortly after the birth and infant death of the youngest son, the family moved to Terang, where they settled permanently.[20] Terang was a service township for the surrounding pastoral and agricultural districts. By the end of the 19th century it had become an important dairy town.[21] Significantly, when the township was surveyed and various allotments put to auction, Thomas Bailey acquired, between 1869 and 1870, two allotments adjacent to the railway line and station then marked out for Terang.[22]

This was an astute investment on his part and provided his family with a direct connection between the dairy factories and the railway. On his death in 1899, aged 83 years, Thomas's occupation was still recorded as labourer, but the allotments had a combined value of £210. A brick warehousing and cool store facility had been constructed on one of them. He also had shares and bank savings to the value of £220.[23] The industries in which Thomas laboured are unknown. He may have undertaken a number of jobs in which work became available. However, at some point his children tied themselves closely to Terang's developing dairy industry.

His Australian-born son, Frederick, worked all his life as a dairyman in one of the dairy factories established in Terang, and two of the English-born daughters married dairymen. Phoebe Bailey, the Australian-born daughter, married a dairy farmer. However, it is the oldest of the children, English-born Robert, who would most prosper, establishing a thriving teamster business that connected the dairy farms to the factories and then to the railway. The Bailey family prospered by becoming part of a developing industry early, recognising the importance of the railway to that industry's growth, and realising that potential through astute property purchases and business interests.

Cobrico Cheese Factory, Terang, c 1900.
This may have been one of Robert Bailey's teamsters.
Photographer: Ernest Bugg. State Library of Victoria, a/n: H83.47/39.

Success and Satisfaction

In migrating directly to an agricultural region and township, the Bailey family was unusual among the migrant cohort. However, the Baileys share many common experiences with those who stayed on either in the goldfields or in the cities and big townships. The similarity lay in the application of skillsets acquired in industrial and entrepreneurial southern Lancashire to achieve at least a modest prosperity in a post-gold rush era. Some, like the Guy family, would find pathways into skilled trades for their migrant and Australian-born children, putting these children and their descendants on an upwardly mobile trajectory.

As with the rest of the migrant cohort, the story the Guy family story raises questions about success and satisfaction in regard to the migratory journey they from Lancashire. Can any judgement on whether their migration brought them success be made? What criteria should we use to measure such success or failure? Surely we should not apply the common criteria used to measure success today. Did the migrant cohort believe they were better off through their decision to migrate? Were they satisfied, comfortable or even happy in their new life in Victoria? These questions are almost impossible to answer without access to letters or diaries that express the migrants' feelings on the matter. Even where letters or diaries do exist, the research that draws on these sources indicates that in this writing the migrants at times appear to be trying too hard to convince family in their homelands, or themselves, that migration to Australia was good for them.

At first glance, James Guy's story does not appear to be one of economic success on the goldfields. Yet his descendants celebrate his decision to migrate and demonstrate considerable pride in their own success stories as Australians. They believe that James and his family's decision to migrate to the new world brought opportunity and comfort that they would not have found in Lancashire. James (aged 35 years), wife Bridget (aged 27 years) and two sons, John (aged 3 years) and Henry (aged 1 year), sailed from Liverpool on the *Flora McDonald* on 21 April 1852. After a voyage of nearly four months, they arrived on 18 August 1852 in Portland, Victoria. After disembarkation, the family was recorded as leaving the migrant depot on their 'own account'.

In the *Register*, James Guy's occupation was recorded as agricultural. labourer.[24] In the 1851 English Census, the Guy family was recorded as residing in Crosshall Street, which is at the upper end of Liverpool, close to what has evolved into the city's civic and cultural centre. Although Crosshall Street was a working-class street, it was a cut above the tenements down the hill and towards the docklands. James was recorded in the 1851 census as a labourer working in the brickmaking industry. Two of his brothers were also employed as brickmakers. His neighbours were all tradesmen, mechanics or artisans engaged in the manufacture of goods of various types.[25]

James seems to have initially planned to build a brickmaking business in the Geelong area. 'James Guy, brickmaker', was entered on the *1856 Victorian Electoral Roll* for the Portland electoral district. He qualified as a voter through occupancy of a freehold premises.[26] After his death many years later, among his property assets were two small allotments in Portland Bay, which were probably the original freehold property.[27] The allure of gold, however, captured James and his family and they appear to have never returned to Geelong.

By April 1856, James and Bridget were at Mount Ararat. A daughter, Elizabeth, was born there in that month.[28] Between 1858 and 1866, James and Bridget had another six children, all born in Ararat or its neighbouring gold settlement, Cathcart.[29] Ararat and Cathcart remained prosperous gold-mining towns until the late 19th century. The records are unclear on whether James took out mining licences or prospected, but at his death he owned two properties near Commissioners Hill, suggesting that he had obtained mining leases in the area early on.

On his death in 1877, aged 62 years, James's occupation is recorded in both his death certificate and probate documents as labourer.[30] However, the valuation papers for his assets note that 'the deceased was a brickmaker' and a brick kiln is listed among the assets.[31] Like many other gold-diggers, James probably used skills acquired in Liverpool to obtain a secondary income. As Ararat evolved from mining camp into settled city, James Guy followed a pattern common among gold-diggers of turning to old occupations. A distinct local brick remains a feature of Ararat's architecture.

In his will, James made his wife executor and sole heir.[32] He left her four properties. Two of them were in Ararat near Commissioners Hill. The first was a two-acre block with a brick dwelling valued at £25. The second was a six-acre block described as having 'no building fence or other improvements on it', valued at £10. The final two properties were the previously mentioned allotments in Portland Bay, with an unimproved value of £5. There was no other property of any value. He had £5 in miscellaneous debts, giving his estate a total value of £35.[33] Although this could be regarded as close to failure as one could come, James would not have seen it as such. By his death, he had acquired land sufficient to provide security and capacity for subsistence living to tide his family over when there was insufficient income from the diggings, his trade or labouring work.

Bridget died in 1893 in Ararat, aged 69 years.[34] She left no will, but had two properties to the value £105, and £50 on deposit in a savings bank. The first property had a weatherboard house on it, so she was not living in the brick house James had built. As both blocks were small, it is likely that she sold the land James owned and lived on the interest on the capital thereof. Their oldest son, John, who came out from Liverpool as a three year old, died aged 26 years just before his father's death.[35] There was no will or probate for John Jnr. Bridget's estate was divided equally between Henry, her surviving English-born son, and the six surviving Australian-born children, three boys and three girls.[36] There was no probate for Henry or two of the Australian-born boys. They also appear to have been unmarried and labourers all their lives.

Only one, the youngest boy James Jnr, moved into a skilled occupation as an engine driver. He died at the age of 84 years in the suburbs of the railway town of Seymour, where he owned his own home.[37] Two of the girls married men who, like James Jnr, had skilled occupations. Both these families moved to Melbourne, where they and their descendants established themselves permanently. The third daughter, Mary, remained unmarried, and also moved to Melbourne, where she acquired a freehold home in Richmond. This raises the question of whether James Snr and Bridget had accumulated more assets and property than was shown in their wills and probate, enabling the daughter, Mary, to purchase the home. Did they succeed enough to allow each of their children to enter into property ownership prior to their death? It is among the descendants of James Jnr and of the two married daughters that we find the celebration of the Guy family's decision to migrate, and pride in how much the family had achieved in Victoria.[38]

Successful Independent Businesswomen

Two women established very successful careers independent of their husbands in post-gold rush cities and towns. One was classified as a single young adult woman upon arrival in Australia, even though she was travelling with her parents, as she was 17 years old. The other was a child of five years when she landed. Their successes are often overlooked because their husbands were also successful, one as a goldminer and investor, the other as a brewer. Yet the evidence is clear that these two women did not ride on the coattails of their husbands but built their own independent fortunes through astute investment and business decisions coupled with a lot of hard work.

Mary Ann Morey died on 24 July 1898 from a cold caught in Melbourne. She was 63 years of age.[39] Such was the length of her funeral procession in

Ballarat that 'special provision was made by Sergeant Biggs, of the City police, for the regulation of the traffic as the cortege passed along the streets'. Two bishops conducted both the funeral and burial services. It would be easy to dismiss this as a turnout to honour her husband Edward Morey because of his influential position as one of Ballarat's leading and most successful citizens. However, the *Ballarat Star* makes it clear that the turnout was a mark of respect for Mary Ann and an acknowledgement of the 'great esteem' Ballarat citizens held her in.[40]

Earlier chapters have discussed Mary Ann's influential role alongside her father and husband in goldmining and investment endeavours. In later years she was a partner with her husband in the construction of a substantial office building and row of shops on Lydiard Avenue and Chancery Lane in the centre of Ballarat. At her death, Mary Ann left a large estate in her own right (see Chapter 8). One of the more interesting share parcels she owned was for the Ballarat Woollen and Worsted Mill. She was an original investor in the mill along with her father and husband.[41] She also played an influential role in the transformation of Ballarat from frontier gold town into a settled urban centre with art galleries, schools, hospitals and benevolent institutions.

A charming titbit from the *Ballarat Star* celebrates what its citizens saw as a sophisticated urban society developing in Ballarat – over which the one-time Lancashire factory girl, now Lady Mayoress, presided:

> Mrs Morey, the esteemed wife of the Mayor of the City, Cr E. Morey, M.L.C., last night held a reception on an elaborate scale at the City Hall, which proved altogether inadequate to accommodate the large number of citizens who attended to pay their respects to the kindly hostess. Excellent arrangements had been made and the guests, who numbered considerably over five hundred, were most hospitably entertained. The mayoress, who was handsomely attired, and held in her hand an exquisite bouquet, received the visitors in the mayor's room.[42]

Mary Ann was a life member of the Old Colonists' Association and, against the norm for wives and women in this period, she held a seat on its main committee for many years, rather than being relegated to the ladies committee. Among other functions, the Old Colonists' Association played an important role as a benevolent institution supporting diggers, or more importantly the wives and children of diggers who had been left destitute by circumstances beyond their control. Among the many organisations and institutions to which she lent her support, Mary Ann was a patron and benefactor of the Ballarat hospital, art gallery and public library.[43]

Ann Proctor is the other of the two migrant girls who built themselves independent business careers in post-gold rush regional centres. She did so despite starting her life on the goldfields at the tender age of five years, being orphaned at age 14, illiterate and innumerate, and effectively becoming mother to her five Australian-born siblings. On her mother's death in 1867, Ann found work as a barmaid at the Victoria Hotel in St Arnaud, and quickly rose to become manager of the hotel. She taught herself to read, write and gain competency in arithmetic by sitting in on the school classes she forced her reluctant younger siblings to attend. By her mid-20s, she was able to purchase the hotel and used it as the foundation from which to launch a business career that saw her acquire a substantial real estate portfolio in the then thriving township of St Arnaud. She did this in her own right, despite marrying William Wheeler, a successful brewer and hotel owner, in 1869.[44]

When William Wheeler died in 1894, his estate was valued at £14,000, with £8900 in real estate and £5100 in personal property. The real estate included two hotels, a brewery, a large brick family home in St Arnaud and a substantial farm property outside the township.[45] He bequeathed the income from the estate to Ann during her lifetime, with the estate to be divided equally between their children on her death.[46] Ann seems to have been a shrewd investor and good saver. By the time of her death, she had accumulated her own real estate portfolio valued at £7920 and personal property worth £1448 separate from the trust established by her husband. Ann's personal property portfolio consisted of the original hotel purchase (the Victoria Hotel), eight tenanted properties and one general store on the main street.[47] She also substantially increased the value of the estate Wheeler had left in trust. However, the one thing she could not save, as hard as she tried, was the brewery business.

The loss of the brewery business stands as a prime example of the way economic patterns were shifting from the later 1870s onwards. If the railways had originally breathed new life into townships like Castlemaine and St Arnaud, over time they began to suck industry out of them and back into Melbourne.[48] Brewing exemplified the way economies of scale and the railways allowed Melbourne-based industries and manufacturers to deliver in quantity to regional cities and townships, undercutting the local competition. Sometime before Ann's death, the family surrendered in the face of increased competition and sold the brewery to a Melbourne competitor. They received a good price for the business and it appears they believed that the brewery was going to be maintained as a going concern. It was not. Within months of the sale the brewery was closed, and now all that remains is a pile of rubble and a brick chimney next to a stream. Melbourne had begun to assert its absolute predominance in the industrial and commercial evolution of Victoria.

Education and Health

Central School, Bendigo, or – as it became known – Camp Hill School, is an enduring and magnificent monument to the importance placed on education in the new colony by Victorian settlers, including the migrant cohort. The school sits on the heights above Bendigo's central business district and is a striking and imposing two-storey, red-brick gothic building. It was built in the mid-1870s and opened in 1878 with an initial enrolment of 1290 pupils. The school still dominates the Bendigo skyline and is a mark of the robustness of public secular education.

Central School (Camp Hill School), Bendigo opened in 1878 with 1290 pupils. It dominates the skyline of Bendigo, shouting the importance of education to colonists.
State Library of Victoria, a/n: H90.140/1400.

Father Backhaus, then in charge of the Catholic parish of Bendigo, opposed the construction outright because of the school's secular and public nature. A substantial number of protestant ministers, including James Bonwick, believed that children on the goldfields were uneducated, illiterate and godless.[49] Yet several of the children, such as the Doody boys, Ann Proctor, Thomas Rainford and William Mercer, had acquired considerable literacy and numeracy skills by adulthood. They also became highly articulate defenders of what they believed were justice and their natural rights because of the education they gained in these public schools. They felt much the same about health and saw it as the role of government to provide for the health of their children and their communities. Indeed, health and education were considered essential elements in the building of a 'better Britain'.

The commitment to establishing good educational and health systems in the townships in the latter half of the 19th century cannot be overestimated, particularly as they provided a pathway to advancement. There are four examples from the migrant cohort of children taking this pathway on disembarkation to become teaching or health professionals in regional Victoria. They did so during the period when Victorian governments implemented policies and legislation regulating the education and health industries, and institutionalising the training and professionalisation of teachers, nurses and pharmacists.

The Teacher

Thomas Rainford, who was born on the voyage to Victoria, did not join his father, uncle or younger siblings in the farming business. He became a teacher and then headmaster of various government schools in some of the townships that evolved from mining camps or agricultural settlements to become important regional hubs. Entries in the *Teachers Records Books* regarding Thomas provide a rare glimpse into the personality of a migrant cohort member.

The route to becoming a teacher in the schools of this period was through showing enough promise while attending school to be given a position as pupil teacher on graduation and then to be trained on the job. Did Thomas resist pressure from his father to leave school as soon as possible to join the rest of the family on the farm? Or was Thomas encouraged by his parents to pursue this career as a way of advancement? The records suggest that he had a stubborn and independent streak. On 17 January 1869, Thomas was entered on the *Teachers Register* as having the lowest classification of fourth class, at the age of 17 years. Within six years he passed the required examinations to be promoted to second-class status and was considered 'quite equal to the sole management of a school of this type … in every way deserving of promotion'.

Two years later, in 1877, Thomas was classified as a first-class teacher and was transferred to head a multi-teacher school at Echuca in 1878.[50] At this school he met Alice Mary Barker, whom he married in 1881.[51] She was a pupil teacher at the school and employed as an assistant teacher in January 1879.[52] He appears to have had a glowing career, and in 1891 received the ultimate accolade 'of the right stamp'.[53] Alice, on the other hand, according to reports in her record, was an indifferent and disinterested teacher. She resigned several times without proper notice, sometimes because of pregnancy. Alice would always return to her duties, until 1903, when she resigned for good.[54]

Following Alice's resignation there was a breakdown in the relationship between Thomas and the Victorian Department of Education. Did his wife's resignation have something to do with it, or was there a major change in the management of the department? Between 1 August 1903 and 3 October 1905, a series of reprimands were placed on Thomas's record for 'unorthodox teaching methods'; failure to maintain 'pupil discipline in approved manners', despite the department's admission that his pupils were 'well-behaved and attentive'; and neglect of his administrative duties. In a final warning, he was fined £3 and threatened with dismissal. Early in 1906, it was recorded in heavily underlined capitals that Thomas 'RETIRED' due to 'ILL HEALTH'. A final entry below these words, although mainly illegible, suggests that officials in the department engaged in some sort of debate about Thomas's retirement and came to an agreement that led to an honourable exit.

There is also a suggestion that Thomas threatened the department with legal action if his departure was not handled to his satisfaction. The dispute was resolved with the grant of a substantial annual indexed pension of £145 14s 2d (based on Thomas's annual salary for the previous three years of £242 17s per annum).[55] The detail of the records for both Thomas and his wife, Alice, which was replicated across the *Teachers Records Books* from the mid-1870s onwards, emphasise the diligence the Department of Education applied to the training, observation and inspection of teachers in its employ during the latter half of the 19th century in establishing a robust, secular and comprehensive public school sector across all of Victoria.

Thomas retired to Geelong, where he purchased a home. He is entered on the *1909 Australian Electoral Roll* as being of 'independent means', and his wife as occupied with 'home duties'.[56] His ill-health was clearly a convenient excuse for all concerned as Thomas lived to the ripe (and by all accounts, energetic) old age of 88 years, dying in 1940.[57] His death certificate, will and probate describe his occupation as 'gentleman'.

He owned two small properties in Geelong of little value. However, there was a substantial investment portfolio valued at £4949, of which £2715 was by way of mortgages over properties returning between 5.5% and 6.5% in interest per annum, and £2013 in savings accounts.[58] Alice had predeceased Thomas, but five of their children survived him. He bequeathed each child £500 and left the remainder of his estate to be shared equally between the Geelong and Western District Protestant Orphanage and the Geelong and

District Kitchener Memorial Hospital.[59] Throughout his long retirement, Thomas dedicated his energies to those institutions.[60]

The Nursing Sisters

Two English-born sisters, Jane and Susannah Lancaster, who arrived in Victoria as children, became nurses at the Ballarat Base Hospital, which had been established in 1855–1856 as a hospital for the deserving poor from among the digging community. Over the latter half of the 19th century, the status of nurses was elevated from something akin to a domestic servant to a commendable professional career that could be pursued by respectable young women.[61] As nurses 'fought to become approved trained professionals', the Lancaster sisters would have benefited from that elevation in status. However, as to their training, medical historian Trembath observes that during this period training and qualifications 'were diverse and varied to say the least'. He notes that Ballarat and Sandhurst (Bendigo) hospitals established some of the earliest and better regarded training programs for nurses.[62]

A considerable part of the problem lay within the hospital system itself. Unlike education, where the government established a state-run school system under the control of a central government bureaucracy, hospitals and the benevolent institutions supporting them operated as locally based charities providing for the care of the deserving poor who could not afford private medical treatment. In theory, the hospitals were financed through voluntary subscriptions. The reality was that three-quarters of the cost of hospital building and day-to-day operations were being borne by the Victorian Government. Despite three Royal Commissions recommending drastic changes to the 'voluntary system', the hospital committees vigorously resisted the idea of state interference on the grounds that greater government involvement would 'stop the flow of those streams of private benevolence which enrich the moral qualities of the giver'.[63]

Yet, as the 19th century drew to a conclusion and the bigger hospitals, including Ballarat and Sandhurst, were increasingly seen as providing superior medical services to that offered by private practitioners there was increasing demand for these hospitals to be opened up to fee-paying patients. Public versus private systems of health care would be fought over until well into the 20th century. Nonetheless, by 1904, with the establishment of the Victorian Trained Nurses Association, a uniformly trained and accredited nursing profession was firmly in place across all registered hospitals in Victoria.[64]

Jane and Susannah Lancaster were not the only children from the migrant cohort, or from its Australian-born children, to enter the nursing profession. Two Seddon daughters became trained and accredited nurses, and one of

Frances Harley's daughters became a registered nurse at the Royal Melbourne Hospital. What is vividly evident from the Lancaster sisters' experience is how the elevation in the status of nurses provided them with the financial capacity and community standing to strike paths independent of their parents and family. They also stand out because, as nursing gained respectability as a profession that reputable women or gentlewomen could undertake, there was a drive to limit the recruitment and training of nurses to 'young ladies whose social backgrounds were first rate'. Ballarat and Bendigo hospitals, reflecting their digger background, resisted this notion and argued that 'respect' was earned through 'superior training', and that 'there are people who are not rich in this world's goods, who are capable of nursing'.[65]

This certainly applied to Jane and Susannah, who were aged nine and seven years when they disembarked in Victoria with their parents. The *Register* also states that neither could read or write, although before becoming nurses they must have acquired both abilities. The Lancaster family was almost a perpetually itinerant goldmining family, but clearly at some point the two girls had enough, staying on and settling in Ballarat when their father uplifted the rest of the family to move to newer goldfields. There are no records of when the sisters became nurses and they may have entered the hospital's employ first as domestic servants. However, by the late 1870s, both are recorded as employed as nurses and remained in the nursing profession until Susannah's death in 1887 and Jane's death in 1925.[66]

It is striking, considering the increasing importance placed on the moral character and standing of nurses throughout the latter half of the 19th century and early 20th century, how little emphasis the female migrants put on gaining respectability through marriage, as exemplified by the Lancaster sisters.[67] Jane initially married a miner, Stephen Barry, in 1858, when she was just 15 years old.[68] There was one child born very shortly after the marriage, doubtless indicating the reason for the marriage.[69] Stephen did well as a miner, but Jane was not to benefit from it. By 1879, she was living with another man, William Oriel, but was not married to him. They had a son that year and on his birth certificate her name was recorded as Jane Barry.[70] Jane and William never married, but by 1903 she was using Oriel as her surname. He was labouring, and she was recorded as a nursing sister.[71] This meant that, while the two Lancaster sisters may have begun their nursing careers as domestic servants, by 1903, Jane, at least, had gained the required qualifications to be recognised as a nursing sister.

Susannah, the younger sister, died of cancer aged 40 years. She married Richard Williams just a few days before her death. There is next to no information discoverable through extant records about Richard beyond his occupation, which was noted on the marriage certificate as 'labourer'.[72] There were no clues as to the length of their cohabitation, but presumably they decided to stop living in sin and to marry when Susannah's death was imminent. There were no children from the relationship.

The Pharmacist

William Mercer is another example of a child from the migrant cohort growing up on the goldfields and establishing themselves in one of the newly developing professions. William arrived in Victoria aged 11 years. According to the *Register*, he could read but not write.[73] This was unusual for a child of this age growing up in southern Lancashire who was attending school, so may be another example of how misleading the *Register* could be at times. The 1851 English Census records that he was a 'scholar' and attending school. By the time William was 10 years old, his studies would have included basic writing and numeracy skills, which were becoming increasingly important in that industrial region.[74] We know nothing of what schooling he received on the goldfields, but it must have added considerably to the grounding he received in Lancashire. The relevance of this is that William became a registered pharmacist, owning and operating his own pharmacy in Daylesford.

According to Michelle Knehans, the pharmacy profession flourished in Victoria during of the gold rushes. The lure of the goldfields attracted many young chemists who had served their apprenticeships with licensed chemists in Britain. They found dispensing medicines on the goldfields to be far more rewarding than digging for gold. Both trained chemists and medical practitioners were soon demanding government regulation to protect and distinguish them from the many quacks touting homemade remedies on the goldfields. The *Medical Practitioners' Act 1862* was passed to distinguish the trained and educated from the fraudulent, creating a system of registration for medical titles and rights of practice. This included chemists as a separate profession from doctors. The training and education standards required for both professions were high.[75]

William would have had to serve a lengthy apprenticeship with an existing registered chemist in Daylesford, although there are no records as to such an apprenticeship. He would also probably have been expected to demonstrate advanced levels of literacy and numeracy skills, which argues that he, like other children from the migrant cohort and their Australian siblings, was not lacking in educational opportunities on the goldfields.

The *Pharmacy Act 1876* provided for the regulation of the pharmacy profession, including protection from fraudulent practitioners, and established a divide between pharmacy and medicine.[76] William became a registered pharmacist under this Act, with the right to call himself a chemist. He was recognised as a registered pharmacist in all official documents and on electoral rolls up until his death. By 1886, when his older brother Smith died, William owned and operated his own two-storey chemist shop on one of the Daylesford properties owned by the three siblings.[77]

In 1875, William married Ann Circassia Wheeler.[78] She was the daughter of James Henry Wheeler, a prominent Daylesford landowner, Member of the Legislative Assembly (1864–1867 and 1889–1900) and Minister of Railways in the Munro government from 1890 to 1892.[79] The Wheeler/Mercer family relationship was a longstanding one. Wheeler was one of the sureties in William Mercer Snr's probate documents.[80] James Wheeler made his fortune logging in the same area that the Mercer family first went to dig, and William Mercer Snr and William Jnr's older brother may well have been involved in Wheeler's logging business. William Jnr and James Wheeler were next-door neighbours on Raglan Street, a prominent residential street in Daylesford. William Jnr and Ann had four daughters and one son who survived into adulthood.[81]

This son, the third William Mercer, followed his father into the pharmacy business and served for years as his pharmacist assistant until he too qualified as a registered chemist. The daughters, however, all pursued higher education opportunities in Melbourne and established careers in music and the arts – a fairly unusual occurrence for regional-born women of the period.[82]

In 1904, William, his wife and his son followed the daughters to Melbourne, where he and his son opened a new pharmacy on Chapel Street, South Yarra.[83] He was living in East Malvern when he died in 1919, aged 83 years.[84] There is no will or probate documents for William Jnr, as by the time of his death the pharmacy business was in his son's name, the substantial Melbourne residence was in his wife's name, and the balance of his personal property had been transferred to his wife and daughters. When Ann Circassia died in 1936, she had only that rather substantial home worth £1000 to leave to her two unmarried daughters.[85]

William Mercer and his family are the final examples from the migrant cohort goldfield subset of migrants who carved themselves a place in the new agricultural, commercial and industrial sectors that emerged in regional Victoria following the gold rushes. Unlike the Californian mining camps and townships, which mainly vanished when the gold had been exhausted, the goldfield migrants of Victoria built economically viable and sustainable communities, townships and cities across rural and regional Victoria, particularly so on the goldfields. In cities like Ballarat and Bendigo they established substantial industrial works that in some cases are still central to these cities' economies today. They also created opportunities for their children and grandchildren in not just the trades, industry and agriculture, but also in emerging professions like teaching and health. They repeatedly elected to parliament men who had been diggers or the sons of diggers like themselves, several of whom were prominent in the various ministries of governments during the late 19th century, ensuring that their voice remained a powerful one in government.

The migrant cohort ran the gamut from very prosperous to humbly competent. Nevertheless, they all shared commonly held aspirations that they strove to achieve in building lives for themselves and their children in the communities they helped to build. However, despite their best efforts, the tide that swept hundreds of thousands of migrants onto the goldfields would steadily recede from the mid-1880s on. With the completion of the so-called Octopus railway network, Melbourne's industry and commerce stretched into every section of the colony, and, via the city's trading seaport, throughout the Pacific. Melbourne established such an economic hegemony over the rest of the colony that, when it caught financial pneumonia, as it did in the early 1890s, it severely affected the rest of Victoria. It is to 'Marvellous' Melbourne that this story turns to complete the collective biography of the migrant cohort from Lancashire.

Chapter 11

MARVELLOUS MELBOURNE

Marvellous Melbourne.
One of the great suburban land auctions of the 1880s.
S.C. Morrison, Illustrated London News, *19 January 1889*.
State Library of Victoria, a/n: H98.143.

I found Melbourne a really astonishing city with broad streets full of handsome shops and crowded with bustling well-dressed people. The whole city, in short, teems with wealth, even as it does with humanity. Well, you may say, what is there wonderful in all this? Melbourne is the prosperous capital of a prosperous British colony. What is there to marvel at in its possession of all or nearly all the features of the most advanced civilisation? But there is much that is marvellous in Melbourne. The city is not 50 years old.

George Augustus Sala in 'Land of the Golden Fleece', a series of articles first published in the *London Daily Telegraph* in 1885[1]

George Augustus Sala, a prominent figure in the London circle of journalists known as the 'young lions', undertook a lecture tour throughout the eastern colonies of Australia in the mid-1880s. The by-then-elderly lion's lectures were not well attended, and he was mainly ignored by Australian society. But, in August 1885, the *Argus* syndicated a series of articles Sala wrote for London's *Daily Telegraph*, including one titled 'Marvellous Melbourne'. The Melbourne populace was enraptured by his vivid prose describing Melbourne's astonishing growth over 50 short years into what had come to be seen by some as the 'first city' among the British colonies. The article was received enthusiastically by Melburnians as an absolute endorsement of their city and colony, and its bold title 'Marvellous Melbourne' became the city's enduring epithet.[2]

In the article's opening paragraph Sala provides the warning that 'astonishment does not imply unqualified admiration', but many of the good citizens of Melbourne either missed or chose to ignore the ironic intent of the title and, indeed, the overall ironic tone of the article.[3] Although not all! Those Melburnians less than impressed with various aspects of the city's progress and ethos would with classic larrikin humour coin their own versions of the title: 'Marvellous Smellbourne', 'Murderous Melbourne', 'Barbarous Melbourne' and, after the great financial crash of the early 1890s, 'Marvellous Smellboom'.[4] Historians such as Asa Briggs, Michael Cannon, Jill Roe, Graeme Davison and Geoffrey Serle were also alive to the ironic connotations of Sala's title. However, much like the way the ironic intent of Donald Horne's *The Lucky Country* is now lost in the public's imaginative mythologising of Australia, so too has the sting been lost from 'Marvellous Melbourne'.

Sala concluded his article with the observation that, after the gold rushes had run their course, 'there was left a residuum of "real live men", as the Americans say, and those live men and their sons have made Melbourne what she is'.[5] Davison confirms Sala's view of the spectacular growth of Melbourne's commerce, industry and trades. He argues that Melbourne's prodigious development was to a great extent a product of diggers and their children making their way there after doing time on the diggings, and establishing themselves in new commercial and industrial trades.[6]

However, as observed in previous chapters, other than exceptions such as William Mercer, the migrant cohort members who went to the goldfields tended to remain in the townships and farmlands that developed in those districts. It would be the native-born children and grandchildren who joined the flood to Melbourne in the last decades of the 19th century and into the 20th century. Those from the migrant cohort who permanently settled in

Melbourne did so soon after disembarkation; they never went to the goldfields, and lived and died in Melbourne.

Those who settled in Melbourne became shopkeepers, trades men and women and industrial artisans. They participated in the breakdown of classic British hierarchal trade structures; developed some of the small factories that formed the backbone of Melbourne's import-substituting industries; disrupted the commercial order previously dominated by the old, large mercantile houses; and, through their determination to own their own homes, were the engine that drove Melbourne's suburban growth.

Donald Horne claimed for Australia the title of 'the first suburban nation'.[7] It was a title that would be disputed by Kenneth Jackson in *Crabgrass Frontier: The Suburbanization of the United States*. However, Jackson did concede that Australia, Canada and New Zealand, 'all countries with strong frontier traditions, small populations and a British-induced dislike of cities', had in many ways equalled the US in the development of home-owning suburban societies.[8] Davison suggests that the 'claim to be the "first suburban nation" is a variant of American (or Australian) exceptionalism'. However, he then acknowledges that the 'claims … [when] examined in a more rigorous way … are capable of illuminating what is distinctive and more general in our national urban histories'.[9]

Davison argues that what distinguished Australian suburbs from their British and North American counterparts was the swiftness with which the barriers to entry for the working classes came down in Sydney and Melbourne, particularly after the gold rushes of the 1850s. He claims that 'high among the goals of the self-improving workingman was a home of his own' and that it was nowhere more obvious than in Melbourne.

> The free, skilled immigrants of the 1850s, often imbued by Chartist ideals of small proprietorship and respectability, and lured by the prospect of rapid social mobility, had given the once-aristocratic suburban idea a radical democratic twist.[10]

The impact of the newly emergent lower-, middle- and upper-working classes on Melbourne, with their aspirations and ideas, was as dramatic as that of the gold-diggers, even though their contribution to the development of the city are often overlooked in comparison to that of the diggers. Among these Melburnians, who became part of the backbone of a 'do-it-yourself, property-owning democracy', were members of the migrant cohort, and their stories illuminate Victoria's contributions to Australia's national urban and suburban heritage.[11]

Labourers, Tradesmen and Artisans

The Holt family illustrates in so many ways the socioeconomic trends occurring in Melbourne during the latter half of the 19th century. Their one point of departure is that the family was not of the gold-digging generation, those whom Davison argues were the main engine of Melbourne's industrial, economic and suburban growth from the late 1850s onwards. As far as can be ascertained, the Holt family never went to the diggings. Their whole lives were defined by the borders of the old Melbourne city and the newer suburbs of Collingwood and Fitzroy where they lived, worked, married and died.

Edward (aged 40 years), wife Harriet (aged 37 years) and five boys, John (aged 15 years), Edward (aged 11 years), Richard (aged 8 years), David (aged 6 years) and Samuel (aged 2 years), disembarked in Melbourne on 8 December 1852. Samuel died within a few days of arrival from a fever contracted aboard the ship.[12] The *Register* recorded Edward's occupation as agricultural labourer and his son John, who as a 15 year old was classified as a single adult male, as a groom. Edward was employed by Hugh Guthrie of Melbourne on a six-month contract at £70 with rations.[13] Guthrie appeared regularly in the *Register* as an employer and was entered on the *1856 Victorian Electoral Roll* as a customs agent.[14] Considering Edward's actual occupation in Liverpool, Guthrie probably employed Edward in some capacity as a waterfront worker.

Like most of the other males among the cohort, Edward Holt had little connection with agriculture. In 1851, Edward and his family were living in Bootle on Mersey Street, now called Regent Street, which spans the length of the docklands from Liverpool through Kirkdale and Bootle to Seaforth. The side of the street opposite the docks was lined with terraces housing the better skilled waterside workers (refer Chapter 4) and Edward was recorded as being such a labourer. John was listed as a scholar.[15] John's subsequent early career in Melbourne suggests that he may have been employed in a part-time capacity looking after horses for one of the carters servicing the Liverpool docks.

Both Edward and John were entered on the *1856 Victorian Electoral Roll*. Edward, occupation labourer, qualified as a freeholder with a home in Cecil Street, Collingwood.[16] John is a surprising addition to the roll as he was not anywhere near the qualifying age of 21 years at the time. He is, however, listed as a carter receiving an annual salary of £100 from 'Rishton' in 'Smith Street'.[17] Charles Rishton was entered on the *1856 Victorian Electoral Roll* as a grocer owning two properties at 127 and 129 Smith Street.[18]

Rishton was born in Lancashire and migrated to Victoria as an unassisted migrant sometime in 1850–51. He quickly established a substantial grocery business and several of his employees were on the *1856 Victorian Electoral Roll* with the exact same £100 annual salary as John. £100 per annum was the minimum salary a man needed to earn to qualify for enrolment in 1856. From this we might surmise that Rishton intended to establish a political career or to be influential in politics and was ensuring that his employees could vote; or it could be a reflection of the importance Lancashire migrants placed on being able to vote. The entry of John Holt onto the *1856 Victoria Electoral Roll* raised some initial scepticism; however, other evidence, including a parish marriage record of his marriage, confirms that the John Holt on the electoral roll was the same young man.[19] He lied about his age to gain entry on the electoral roll in 1856, perhaps with the cooperation of Charles Rishton.

The father, Edward, and his wife, Harriet, disappear from the story after 1856 until their deaths: Harriet in 1877 and Edward in 1881. Edward's death certificate records his occupation as quarryman and he was still residing at Cecil Street.[20] Cecil Street is up in the northwest corner of Collingwood on the border of Carlton and Fitzroy, close to the bluestone quarry where he worked, which later became something of a family business. There is no will or probate for Edward. It is with his sons that the family's story becomes illustrative of the remarkable upheaval in the socioeconomic lives of the children, whether native-born or not, of the migrant cohort.

By 1865, Edward's four boys had achieved some prominence in their commercial and industrial occupations, and had acquired four adjoining properties on Hoddle Street, which was rapidly becoming one of the important centres of the 'small factory' industrial development described by Davison. John, the oldest, had taken over a grocery store and grain and feed business on the corner of Hoddle and Vere streets; while David, the youngest boy (then aged 18 years), had established a wheelwright business in the adjoining premises.[21] Edward Jnr, the second-oldest son, aged 24 years, was living in the same premises as David, but was a partner in Foulds & Holt, smiths and wheelwrights, located at 145 Little Lonsdale Street.[22] Richard, who was aged 21 years, was one of three listed partners in Briscoe & Co., iron and steel merchants, with business premises located at 245 Elizabeth Street and 11 Collins Street.[23]

What is telling in this account is the age of the three younger boys and the pinnacles of business ownership they had reached in skilled industrial trades. This would have been unthinkable in the England of their birth, where master craftsmen in artisanal trades fought relentlessly to maintain their position at the top of the hierarchy by adopting practices that made it very difficult to scale the ladder or to take ownership of a craft workshop of one's own.[24]

In Victoria and Melbourne, however, the youthful did not find their pathways blocked by hierarchal tradition. The Holt brothers' story and the development of Hoddle Street illustrates the breakdown of the classic British hierarchal trade structure that occurred in Victoria, and the predominance of the small manufacturing workshop in Melbourne's industries in these formative years.[25] When John and David first moved to Hoddle Street in 1863, it was lightly populated. The street's main businesses were feed and grain stores, together with a variety of firms catering to the horse, cart and carriage trades, including a wheelwright (Roberts and Fergusson) and two carriage makers. There was a smattering of butchers, grocers and greengrocers catering to local residents, and three hotels. At this time, Hoddle Street felt very much like it was at the edge of the city.[26]

Hoddle Street early 1860s.
State Library of Victoria, a/n: H25131.

Hoddle Street, 1886.
Photographer: H. Hume.
State Library of Victoria, a/n H2009.169/1.

Ten years later, Hoddle Street was a densely populated street of small businesses, commercial enterprises, industrial works and trade workshops. John had moved on and his corner store was now operated by William Taylor, grocer and wine and spirit merchant.[27] In the 1872 *Collingwood Rate Book*, John Holt is listed as the owner of the corner store building and three other premises, including the one from which David operated his business. There are 41 properties on that rate book page: a hotel, a butcher, a grocer and a greengrocer, and another 37 premises described as either 'shop and residence' or simply 'shop', of which 14 (37.84%) were owned by the occupant. The occupants were tradesmen or small business owners including a bookmaker, cabinetmaker, cab owner and builder, couch maker, draper, fettler, French polisher and printer.[28]

From 1870 onwards, both Edward Jnr and Richard were no longer listed in the *Melbourne Directory* as partners with either Foulds or Briscoe & Co. They had joined their brother John and father Edward at the Fitzroy Bluestone Quarry. John was working at the quarry from at least 1867.[29] His father and brothers, Edward Jnr and Richard, appear to have joined John at the quarry sometime between 1870 and 1871.[30] What caused the move to the quarries by Edward Jnr and Richard and whether it arose from a downturn in their lives is unknown.

Bluestone quarry where John Holt was to become foreman, c 1866.
State Library of Victoria, a/n: H635.

However, John prospered at the quarries and was the senior foreman by the 1890s, while Richard had purchased a substantial cottage in a new development in the north of Collingwood by the early 1880s for himself, his wife and their four children.[31] Edward Snr, John, Edward Jnr and Richard all worked at the quarries until their deaths. David continued the wheelwright business in Hoddle Street, with the other three properties rented out to other tradesmen. In the 1876 *Collingwood Rate Book*, David is listed as owner of the four properties.[32]

For all the extraordinary developments in Melbourne, there was much that was critically under-developed. Both 'Marvellous Smellbourne' and 'Murderous Melbourne' were coined in response to the stench of an unsewered Melbourne and the epidemics of typhoid that resulted from such poor sanitary conditions. David died suddenly at the age of 31 years in 1877 of typhus, a victim of the lack of progress in the delivery of clean water and removal of sewage.[33] He had married an Anna Maria Padley in 1868, but they had no children.[34]

The 1878 rate book still recorded David as the owner of the four properties on Hoddle Street.[35] After that, the properties are recorded as owned by others, at least two having been occupants of the properties prior to David's death. There was no will, and a thorough search has failed to locate probate documents for David. Probate would be expected even if he had died intestate and his widow or family wished to claim title on the properties to sell or otherwise dispose of them. This suggests that John Holt was still co-owner of the properties on Hoddle Street, even if not listed in the rate books as such. Shortly after David's death and the sale of the properties on Hoddle Street, John began to acquire properties for himself and his children in the new developments sprouting in North Fitzroy.

John had moved to North Fitzroy after his marriage. In the first *Fitzroy Rate Book* (1861–1864), John and Jane Holt were recorded as residing in a small cottage on Westgarth Street, which, like much of North Fitzroy, was then sparsely populated.[36] The cottage was owned by his father-in-law, Thomas Morell, who also owned a largish parcel of land in North Fitzroy close to the quarry in what is now known as Edinburgh Gardens. Thomas Morrell's occupation is noted as labourer on John and Jane's marriage certificate, but in the *1871 Fitzroy Rate Book*, the first rate book in which Morell's occupation is recorded, he is described as a 'pensioner'.[37] He was most likely a military pensioner. Life on a British pension was pretty miserable and he would have needed to labour to make ends meet. Morell had possibly come to Victoria as a serving soldier in one of the two British regiments sent out in the early gold rush period. British soldiers on discharge were encouraged to remain on in Victoria with the offer of blocks of land of between 10 and 50 acres, depending on length of service and rank.[38]

From about 1870, North Fitzroy experienced a boom in population. According to the *Collingwood Observer*, 'when young Collingwoodians get married they migrate to comfortable and respectable cottages erected by enterprising capitalists at North Fitzroy'.[39] Davison argues that a similar pattern could be found across the eastern suburbs, as many newly married couples from among 'the children of the gold rush' left the old inner suburbs for the next outer ring of new suburbs.[40] In the view of the *Argus*, those 'who on entering the married state … transformed from boarders to householders' were chiefly 'working men or artisans'.[41]

Morell may not have been one of the *Collingwood Observer*'s 'enterprising capitalists', but he benefited from the influx into North Fitzroy. He maintained ownership of two sections at 2 and 4 Watkins Street, and subdivided and sold off the balance of his property. John built a double-fronted, five-room weatherboard cottage at 4 Watkins Street, North Fitzroy, which on his death was valued at £400.[42] The *1878/79 Fitzroy Rate Book* notes Thomas Morell as the owner of both properties, but in the following year John was listed as owner/occupier of 4 Watkins Street and owner of No. 2.[43] Neither Thomas nor his wife, Mary, died in Victoria. It is possible that, with the money earned from the sale of his land to John and others, the couple returned to Ireland to live out their last years.

By 1889, the streets surrounding John and Jane's home had become a densely populated suburban estate of households headed by men mainly in the building trades: bricklayers, blacksmiths, carpenters, masons, plasterers, quarrymen and sawyers predominated, with a smattering of butchers, bakers, grocers and other shopkeepers to supply local residents. The cottages they occupied were big by the standards of the older inner-city suburbs they had vacated and were solid structures of brick, stone and weatherboard, every bit the 'comfortable and respectable' homes described by the *Collingwood Observer*.[44]

John's family's local property acquisitions did not end with the purchase of 2 and 4 Watkins Street. By 1900, all of his four sons were noted in the rate books as owners of properties in or near Watkins Street. Only his oldest son, George, who was married, occupied his home. The other houses were rented out and the sons resided with John and Jane.[45] The *1903 Electoral Roll* had six of John's adult children residing with him and Jane. All the adult children, including George and the Holts' three daughters, had occupations in the skilled trades. The three daughters, Alice, Bella and Nellie, were all dressmakers, although whether they operated their own business, worked in a factory or were outworkers is unknown. Two of the sons had followed their father into the quarry business, while the other two were a tinsmith and a bootmaker, respectively.[46]

Of the four Holt brothers who migrated with their parents Edward and Harriet, only one, the second son Edward Jr, despite his early promising years, seemed unable to finally settle down. He never married and died in North Melbourne hospital in 1890 of kidney failure. His death certificate records his parents and siblings as 'unknown'.[47] John was the only one of the family who made a will. He bequeathed all his real and personal estate to his wife Jane, which consisted of the freehold property at 4 Watkins Street valued at £400 and furniture valued at £10. He had already provided for his sons. There is no evidence that John similarly provided for his daughters, who had married and settled down with men in the trades in the same North Fitzroy suburb they grew up in.

The Reverend James Ballantyne, addressing working-class readers in England, asked rhetorically, 'What can I gain by going to Victoria?', and answered, 'He will be able to … secure a comfortable freehold for himself … what every Englishman glories in – a house which will be his castle'.[48] If Ballantyne had known the Holts and their neighbours, he would have pointed to them as prime examples of his promise. The Holts demonstrated that migrants did not need to go bush or gold-digging to chase their aspirations. They pursued their urban dreams quite successfully. The 'castle' metaphor became an apt one with the great bust of the early 1890s. The prudent early purchases by the Holts and their neighbouring working-class home owners in Fitzroy would place them among those Melbournians best situated to weather the decade-long deep economic depression that followed the bust.

The Mack family provides another example of those of the migrants who, as far as can be ascertained, never went to the goldfields. The Macks were also the only known example from the migrant cohort of a family who returned to England permanently, in their case seven years after they first arrived in Victoria. There is scant evidence as to what William and his wife did while in Melbourne. He is not recorded in any *Melbourne Directory* between 1857 and 1860. William was entered on the *1856 Victorian Electoral Roll* as a freeholder with a home and carpenter's workshop in Liverpool Street, Abbotsford.[49] The directories do not list a Liverpool Street in Abbotsford, but that is not unusual – Hoddle Street was not listed in the street directory until 1860. Liverpool Street probably ran alongside the Yarra River. Neighbours of the Mack family were boatbuilders, chandlers, river punt operators and the like. Considering his background on the docks of Liverpool, William was probably a carpenter involved in the Yarra River boat trade.

Between 1855 and 1859, the Macks had four children, all boys – William (1855), Thomas (1856), John (1858) and James (1859) – and all born in Collingwood.[50] Thomas died shortly after birth, but the other three sons returned with their parents to England. The family returned to Liverpool on the *Eagle*, departing Melbourne in April 1860. They could afford a second-class cabin for the return voyage so they must have done reasonably well during the seven years they were in Melbourne.[51] They settled down in one of the newer waterfront districts in Kirkdale. Their neighbours were all in the building trades or employed as carters and other types of waterfront workers at the top end of the skilled trades. William Mack also purchased the terrace house they lived in on the family's return to Liverpool.[52] The two youngest of the Australian-born sons, John and James, returned to Victoria in 1888; however, it cannot be ascertained whether they settled permanently in Australia or just visited.[53]

James Seddon, unlike his sibling John or cousins Joseph and Thomas, did not make a beeline for the goldfields at Mount Alexander on arrival in Victoria. Rather, he settled in Collingwood, where, by 1856, he owned a freehold property and was pursuing his trade as a carpenter.[54] While James and his family made Melbourne their permanent home, establishing businesses and homes on the corner of Hoddle and Gibbs streets, they took advantage of the construction of the railway between Melbourne and Castlemaine to establish familial and business contacts with their relatives working the goldfields around Mount Alexander.

In the 1860s, James was paying rates on a property in Castlemaine that was located close to where John and Joseph resided, and had invested in various goldmining companies alongside the two.[55] James's oldest son, William, had a printing business with branches in both Hoddle Street and Castlemaine, while a younger son, Robert, died aged 28 years in an industrial accident in Castlemaine in 1876.[56] This argues for a close connection between Melbourne and regional centres such as Castlemaine, Bendigo and Ballarat, especially after the railways arrived in the early 1860s.

With the Seddon families we see yet another example of so-called agricultural migrants who were in fact Davison's 'self-improving working men' from industrial England. These men were able to exploit openings within the industrial and commercial environment in Melbourne and beyond to establish themselves as small business and property owners – an opportunity not available to them in Britain.

James died in 1871 in Collingwood, aged 57 years.[57] He was another from the migrant cohort who either left no will or was considered to have died intestate. By the time of his death, his oldest son William was listed in the rate books as the owner of the Hoddle Street property, where he operated his printing business. When William died in 1917, he owned two properties, the original Hoddle Street property in Melbourne and one in Castlemaine. The properties were valued at £440 and £105, respectively.[58] James's widow Ruth and his second son, James Jnr, disappear from the records after his death.

Family lore has it that James Jnr and his family, accompanied by Ruth, migrated to the US where they settled among Lancashire kin in Pennsylvania. There was a substantial migration into New England and Pennsylvania by skilled and semi-skilled industrial workers from southern Lancashire in the 1850s through to the 1870s. Among them were several Seddon families. Tom Seddon, an American Seddon who moved to Australia, and was CEO of Bendigo Heritage Attractions for 15 years, believes that in the latter half of the 19th century, there was considerable Seddon family mobility between the northeast of the US, Australia and New Zealand, and that the Seddons maintained extensive contacts across the oceans.

There is important historical research to be undertaken regarding the interconnectedness of working-class families who migrated to seemingly distant areas of the anglophone worlds. James Jnr and Ruth's story, however, does confirm that the migrant cohort were not stuck in Victoria and that continued mobility and migratory movement were a significant part of the cohort's experience.

Single Young Women

Whereas only a few families stayed and settled in Melbourne immediately after migrating, the majority of single young women from the cohort chose to do so. Even those young women who disembarked at Geelong or Portland rapidly made their way to Melbourne. They also tended to get married or settled into de facto relationships quickly and a significant minority established themselves in trades. Three single young women who stayed on in Melbourne have stories that are of particular interest.

The first of these is Emma Louise Hugo. Emma's early family story illustrates how in a city like Liverpool unconventional family structures could thrive. She married a man in Victoria who was from the middle classes, in fact of the Imperial colonial class (his father being a colonel of a British West Indies regiment). Emma, whose occupation was recorded as dressmaker in the

Register, arrived on the *Hope* in November 1852, disembarking at Portland. In the *Register*, she was recorded as employed by a Mrs Harrison of 6 Stephen Street at £20 with rations for a term of at least one month.[59] As a dressmaker she would have stood out out among the single women as a person with a skilled trade, and one wonders how long she stayed with Mrs Harrison. The shortness of the tenure suggests that neither party expected Emma to stay longer than was necessary to enable her to find her feet.

Emma is recorded in the 1851 English Census with the occupation of dressmaker's apprentice. She lived with her mother, Emma Snr, and two younger sisters at 10 Fairview Place, Toxteth Park – an area of Liverpool containing high-end artisans, tradespeople, dockworkers, clerks and seamen. Emma's mother described herself as a widow and an annuitant – that is, in receipt of yearly payments, presumably from the father or fathers of her children.[60] When Emma married in Victoria, her father was named as John Hugo, gentleman.[61] However, this John Hugo remained something of a mystery, as did whether Emma Snr was ever married to him, or indeed to anyone else. The 1841 English Census finds Emma Snr residing in Saint Anne Street in the heart of Liverpool with three sons, the oldest of whom was aged 14 years, and two of the three daughters noted as residing with her in the 1851 Census, Emma and Lucy. There is no adult male recorded as residing with Emma Snr, husband or otherwise. Her occupation is recorded as 'teacher'.[62] Between 1841 and 1851, Emma Snr bore at least one more child, Fanny.[63] It has not been possible to identify a John Hugo in either Liverpool or Wales, where he was said to originate, who could remotely be a match for the father of her children.

On 3 February 1855, in Melbourne, Emma Jnr married William Henry Ferris, a produce merchant, who was born in Antigua in the West Indies. His father was a colonel. According to the parish marriage records, among the witnesses was a John Hugo. Initially I thought this could be Emma Jnr's father, but on further investigation I believe this John Hugo to be Emma's oldest brother.[64] What John was doing in Victoria, or when he arrived there, is not recorded. That he does not appear in the inwards shipping records is not unexpected. John also does not appear on the *1856 Victorian Electoral Roll*. However, a John Hugo of the right age to be Emma's brother departed from Melbourne for Liverpool on the *Morning Light* in November 1856, approximately 18 months after Emma's marriage.[65] If Emma was disappointed that the brother she had possibly followed to Australia returned to England, she nevertheless settled down in Richmond, Melbourne, with her husband.

William Ferris was entered on the *1856 Victorian Electoral Roll* twice. He was entered in the Melbourne electorate with a premise at 91 Flinders Street

West and described as a 'produce merchant'. He was also entered on the roll for the electorate of Richmond and described as a 'shopkeeper, 39 Cremorne Street'.[66] However, this address appears to have been their residence rather than a shop. The Melbourne trades directories confirm that Ferris had a warehouse and operated a business as a produce merchant in Flinders Street between 1857 and 1865.[67] Ferris was also listed in the *Melbourne Directory* between 1866 and 1880 at a series of residential addresses, but no occupation was provided.

However, by the end of the 1870s, William Ferris had established himself as one of a new and growing breed known as 'commercial agent'. The rise of the commercial agent mirrored a rapid growth in the independent commercial and financial services sector and the number of people engaged in providing those services, such as accountants, brokers, insurance agents, real estate agents and mortgage brokers. Davison argues that the increase in the number of these independent operators in the provision of financial and commercial services helped undermine the old commercial structures dominated by the big mercantile houses, and by the 1890s had made a permanent impression on Melbourne's financial and commerce worlds.[68]

The growth of independent agents and mid-level commercial and financial employees was never more evident than in a new subdivision in Caulfield Shire where William and Emma finally settled. In the 1870s, the couple acquired a large block, which they subdivided into three sections. They built a house at what became known as 48 Cubitt Street, Richmond, and sold two other sections in the early 1880s. This subdivision is strikingly different from that of the Holts. The Ferrises' neighbours were middle-class professionals employed in commerce, finance and insurance. They were not magnates, but managers, upper and middling clerks, or self-employed like William Ferris.[69]

William and Emma were still living at this residence when they died within three years of each other. William died first in 1895 and his death certificate notes his occupation as salesman.[70] But he described himself as a 'gentleman' in his will and is similarly described in his estate's probate and administration files. William left a small estate, with real estate valued at £310 and a personal estate of £93, to Emma as the sole beneficiary.[71] His estate was rather small considering his career, but it is also likely that he, like many others engaged at a mid-ranking level in the financial and commercial services sector, suffered disproportionately during the great depression of the early 1890s.

When Emma died in 1898 the value of the Cubitt Street property had declined to £226, which is consistent with the fall in real estate values throughout the 1890s caused by this lengthy and severe economic downturn.[72] William and Emma had three sons, all of whom were employed as middle-class professionals by the time of the couple's deaths. There is some suggestion that William assisted each son, once married, to become a home owner. There is also a very touching note in Emma's will. She divided her estate equally between her three sons, but states that two of her sons had been providing her with money 'from time to time to meet my daily necessities' and that the amount 'recorded in an account book by me' should be repaid prior to the division of her estate.[73]

The second of these young women, Elizabeth A. Smith, could be described as an archetypical female cotton mill worker of the first half of the 19th century. Elizabeth's father was a master craftsman, but she, her mother and her sisters were shut out of the artisan guild system even more effectively than were young males. According to Clark, in the cotton-weaving towns of South Lancashire, single young women became 'heroic' as they established a measure of financial independence as textile workers in the first half of the 19th century.[74] Elizabeth was just 18 years of age when she arrived in Victoria on the *Hope* in November 1852.[75] She was the daughter of James and Elizabeth Smith and at the time of the 1851 English Census resided with them in Clayton-le-Moors, a village on the outskirts of Blackburn and Accrington.

Clayton-le-Moors was a cotton mill township. There was a smattering of male coalminers in the neighbourhood but almost everyone else, including women and children aged over 12 years, were employed either in the mills or in associated work. James Smith's wife and two daughters, Mary and Elizabeth, were all employed as power-loom weavers in the cotton mills. James was a tailor.[76] That the family and their neighbours were longstanding cotton industry workers was confirmed in the 1841 English Census.[77] Elizabeth is another example of an individual whose occupation as recorded in the *Register*, that of domestic servant, is distinctly different from their real occupation in Lancashire. It is difficult to imagine that Elizabeth's referees and, for that matter, the CLEC were unaware that she did not meet the selection criteria.

Within five years of her arrival in Victoria, Elizabeth had become the tailor she could not be in England and established a millinery and drapery business at 74 Park Street on a site now occupied by the Royal Melbourne Hospital.[78] In 1854, Elizabeth conceived a child with a Thomas Burton, named Annie Elizabeth Burton in the birth records.[79] Between 1855 and 1874, Elizabeth had another nine children, with their birth certificates all naming Thomas Burton as the father.[80]

Remarkably, despite having those 10 children, Elizabeth continued to run her own business until well into the 1890s. Thomas was a bootmaker and was first listed in the *1859 Melbourne Directory* with a small workshop on Bridge Road, Richmond.[81] By 1865, he occupied three adjoining premises at 176, 178 and 182 Bridge Road, and was described as a boot and shoe dealer, as well as an importer of quality leather boots and shoes. Elizabeth, however, was still pursuing her own independent business, having moved to La Trobe Street in the city where she was still described as a tailoress.[82]

Elizabeth and Thomas continued to run their businesses in separate locations until 1880, when they purchased adjoining properties in Burwood Road just as it began developing into Hawthorn's main manufacturing and retail strip.[83] Thomas continued as a bootmaker, shoe dealer and importer of leather footwear. Elizabeth, however, now described herself as a 'fancy dealer'. The properties they occupied were palatial by 1880s standards, with each consisting of eight rooms combining both shop and residence. Yet the couple never stopped listing themselves as owner/occupiers of their separate residences and maintaining the illusion that they were independent householders.[84] Was this a case of Elizabeth the Lancashire power-loom weaver continuing to assert her hard-won independence?

The last of the three young women, Frances Davis, also established herself and her children successfully in the 'rag' trade. In the 1851 English Census, she was living in the house of Ann Catherine Williams and was described as a house servant. Williams had three male lodgers – a general clerk, a glass cutter and a hatter – indicating a fairly substantial boarding house premises.[85] After disembarkation in Geelong, Frances left the depot to work on a one-month contract for Mrs McCallum of Geelong.[86] By 1855, Frances had moved to Melbourne and married a John Harley in Carlton.[87] They had two children, a boy named John in 1856 and a girl named Frances in 1858.[88] But shortly after that John Harley vanished from the records.

Rate book records establish that Frances Harley owned and occupied a premises on O'Shanassy Street in North Melbourne from at least 1858, but there is no indication of her type of work. However, much later records, from the first decade of the 20th century, confirm that Frances and her children operated a tailoring and garment-making business out of the premises.[89] Frances was another tradesperson who colonised the new suburbs of Melbourne. In 1891, she purchased a substantial block of land in Northcote and quickly began subdividing it. By 1896, she had four properties with tenants and another two occupied by herself and her family.[90]

Frances's financial circumstances at her death are unknown as there was no will or probate.[91] However, she and her children had clearly prospered. In the first *Australian Electoral Roll*, following Federation in 1903, there were families of mainly female Harleys living and working as neighbours where O'Shanassy and Courtney streets in North Melbourne intersect.[92] These include the address originally occupied by Frances and her business. Davison notes that this area of North Melbourne was a centre of the garment and bootmaking trades.[93] The two cottages occupied by the Harleys have survived being engulfed by the Royal Melbourne Hospital precinct, but only tenuously so. When Frances died, she was residing with Millicent Francis and Ellen Marion Harley at 52 Martin Street, Northcote, who were respectively described as 'costumiere' and 'milliner' in the *Australian Electoral Roll*. The Martin Street premises was one of the houses that Frances originally owned, but was by then in the names of Millicent and Ellen.[94]

In *Marvellous Melbourne*, Davison tends to circle two census years, 1881 and 1891, as marking apexes in Melbourne's economic, political and social development during the latter half of the 19th century. The first of these years could be viewed as the high point of the gold-digger generation's disruption of the old political and economic frameworks and orders within Melbourne. Earlier chapters have examined how the planting and propagation of new ideas by urbanised industrial and commercially oriented working and lower-middle classes radically transformed socioeconomic conditions on the goldfields and agricultural lands, and in regional urban townships and cities.

The stories above illustrate how similar significant developments in Melbourne broke the dominance of the old mercantile and commercial classes, creating a pathway for a home-owning, business-running artisanal culture to flourish in the city. The 'free-wheeling independence of the goldfields', which became part of the cultural inheritance of the child migrants and the native-born children, contributed to a breakdown of the old hierarchal structure of the classic British trades, allowing for a diversified and accelerated growth in import-substituting industries and a wide variety of subsidiary trades.[95] Thus, we see young women become the tailoresses they never could have been in the home country, and young men barely out of their teens establish themselves in small factories and craft workshops as owners and partners.

The radical liberalism of an earlier generation had become accepted received wisdom among liberals and moderate conservatives, often working in coalition, embracing protectionism and the benefits of government financing of essential public works. In Melbourne, this resulted in the establishment of a comprehensive railway and tram system spread out across a rapidly growing suburbia, sewerage and water works, and world-class public hospital and education systems.

The other significant trend that occurred in Melbourne could be seen as a product of all of the above. There was a massive building boom and explosive growth in new suburban developments in both the older and newer suburbs. The migrants whose stories are told above all participated in this boom, buying property and building new houses for themselves and often for their children too. The Holts in northern Collingwood and Fitzroy, the Harleys in Northcote, the Burton-Smiths in Hawthorn, and, exemplary of the emerging commercial middle classes, the Ferris parents and sons being among the first residents in these new suburban developments.

The 1880s were a time of exuberant confidence – a confidence shared by the middle classes, tradespeople, artisans, and a substantial proportion of the working classes. It was the decade when the belief that home ownership should be a right and within the reach of all became firmly fixed in the Australian psyche.

The year 1891 marked the point when the smiling facade began to crack and the blind faith in a marvellous future proved to be a mirage. Blainey sums it up well:

> In Melbourne in 1891 new skyscrapers began to advertise for tenants. New cottages and villas standing in paddocks in the suburbs called out for buyers. It seemed, to those who had read the signposts, that half the city was 'To Let' ... The common belief was that Tomorrow would pay the debts, but suddenly Tomorrow became Today.[96]

The striking thing about the economic crash of the early 1890s is just how much what occurred in Melbourne has parallels with the Global Financial Crisis of 2007–2008 in the US.

Unsustainable lending, dodgy financial practices and outright corruption led to a banking disaster in 1893 when, in the space of six weeks, 13 Australian banks closed their doors and two-thirds of all deposits in trading banks were unable to be withdrawn.[97] The stench of financial and political corruption surrounding this great disaster resulted in Melbourne acquiring the epithet 'Marvellous Smellboom'.

The resulting economic depression of the 1890s disproportionately affected the working classes, independent trades and crafts, and small factory enterprises. Businesses and factories consolidated into increasingly large conglomerates, with owners no longer working alongside their employees. At one point it was estimated that one in five breadwinners were out of work, and over 60,000 people left Melbourne to look for employment elsewhere.[98] In the decade that followed, various liberal governments sought solutions to the crisis through retrenchment and budget cutbacks – all of which only deepened the depression. As a result, the working classes, and many in the trades, guilds and unions, abandoned their long-time support for the colonial liberals for an emerging and invigorated Labor Party.

Perhaps surprisingly, those from the migrant cohort whose stories feature above seem to have survived the crisis relatively intact. John Holt and his sons still owned their respective properties in 1900, and those whose names were recorded in the rate book pages surrounding the Holts in 1890 appeared on the whole to still be in possession of their homes in 1900.[99] The Holts' neighbourhood was still one where men working in the building trades predominated. The Harleys still owned the business premises and homes established by Frances in North Melbourne and Northcote in the early 20th century. Some of the children of Elizabeth Smith and Thomas Burton maintained thriving retail businesses in the adjoining premises on Burwood Road in Hawthorn well into the 20th century. William Seddon, on his death in 1917, left his wife and children a substantial printing business and residence in the building on Hoddle Street that his father had first purchased in the 1850s.

Did they feel the drastic slump in property prices, or were they, in effect, immunised from it? They do not seem to have borrowed heavily to enter the property market, and, because they entered it with a lifetime in mind, may not have been much affected by the slump in property values. They were secure in the knowledge that their homes were their safety net – as in the old Chartist dream.

Chapter 12

WE DID NOT COME ALL THIS WAY TO TUG FORELOCKS

A Conclusion

Berry's hard working sons of toil.
Eight hour demonstration in Melbourne's Zoological Gardens in 1864.
Samuel Calvert, Illustrated Melbourne Post, *18 May, 1864.*
State Library of Victoria, a/n: !MP18/05/64/1.

Then away with the useless discussion of an abstract principle, and let us, as reasonable men discuss what fiscal policy will best suit this colony of Victoria. Not what will best suit its bankers, its merchants, or its gentry, but what will best advance the material prosperity of all not forgetting the hard working sons of toil, whose interests are ofttimes forgotten or else totally ignored.

Graham Berry, Letter to the Editor of the *Age*[1]

Shuffle forth spear-holders to centre stage and take the bow and hear the applause you so richly deserve – except that the migrant cohort would hardly have shuffled anywhere. They would move centre stage with a bold step in their stride and cheeky grins on their faces. In the first chaotic weeks of my research I came upon this quote: 'We did not come all this way to tug forelocks.' I lost it and have never since been able to track it down to cite its source – hence it has not made its way into this account until now.

It would seem, however, that the cohort came from sectors of the Lancashire working class for whom 'tugging' or 'touching' forelocks was a long outdated or forgotten concept. Whether Liverpool's free labourers, the industrialising Mancunian working class with their new skillsets or Anna Clark's heroic young women factory workers, these people came from socioeconomic backgrounds that were hot beds for the many radical ideas and programs then flowering in southern Lancashire, including Chartism in all its richness.

The most significant factor in the decision to migrate and the settlement patterns that followed in Victoria was that the great majority of the cohort were ambitious risk-takers. Their collective profile fits Davison's description of a 'mobile, ambitious … but uneasy stratum of the British working class' to a tee. It is probable that most of the cohort would not have taken up the opportunity of an assisted passage to Victoria if it were not for the very rich gold discoveries in the colony. However, it is equally probable that many of the cohort instead would have joined the flood of English migrating in the second half of the 19th century, probably to the US or the Canadian provinces.

These were people not content with a life of the same in England. They wished to push through whatever ceilings, glass or otherwise, prevented them advancing further. With ambition comes a propensity for risk-taking. For many in the cohort the risk paid off, as they became creators of an urban and suburban society in which they had personal and political stakes as property owners and voters.

Connecting the local Lancashire communities of the migrants to their settlement of Victoria was significant in bringing this cohort to centre stage as players rather than pawns commanded by the empire builders, colonial elites and other drivers of the anglophone colonies. These Lancashire migrants were not pawns to be shifted on the chessboard of the British Empire by its elites. They were ambitious and energetic men, women and children who came from the better-off industrial working classes, and had grown up and made their way among those communities who were already pushing back against the English elites and power structures.

They were part of working-class communities that had been formulating ideas and policies on governance and social change. Most importantly, many of these ideas, beliefs and platforms were based around the concept of self-help and an informal economy based on the rituals of mutuality, family obligation and cooperative consumerism acquired in the Lancastrian communities from which the migrant cohort were drawn. These ideas and beliefs, along with the industrial and entrepreneurial skillsets the migrants brought with them, were essential in the transformation of Victoria from a pastoral economy dominated by a narrow colonial elite to a vibrant industrial, commercial and agricultural economy dominated by men and women like themselves – who became known as the goldfields generation.

The romantic, free-wheeling, independent and young single male diggers working with pan and spade frequently outside the constraints of the prevalent social mores of the time is the enduring image of the gold rush era. Both Bate and Serle can be contradictory in their accounts of the time, upholding it as a heroic period in Victoria's and Australia's history, and yet acknowledging that other forces were at work on the goldfields, which rapidly transformed chaotic tented mining camps into settled urban communities in which industrial and commercial skillsets were paramount and organised cooperative digging on a large scale was essential to long-term success. Fahey, Grimshaw, Mayne and Wright, among others, have argued that women and children on the goldfields cannot be ignored. In their view, family and community formation are essential to understanding settlement on the goldfields.

Because the bulk of the migrant cohort were family groups, this book has focused on the role of families in the gold rush migration and the ensuing settlement of Victoria by the gold rush generation. The role family played in the community building that quickly transformed the gold rush districts into settled urban and agricultural communities, and in turn shaped the development of Melbourne. Importantly, we can see how the determination to own property, whether in town or country; to operate their own small businesses; and to have access to good outcomes in health and education shaped these communities.

Though I do not claim that the migrant cohort were representative of the bulk of goldfield migrants, I suspect that the industrial skillsets they brought to Victoria were the norm among the migrants who persevered at the diggings and made gold extraction an industrial and cooperative occupation that was a far cry from the free-spirited, independent young male digger of myth. The cohort, regardless of whether they went to the goldfields, were on the whole pragmatic realists.

They may have held a romantic attachment to the idea of land ownership, whether of a small farm or a quarter-acre section in suburbia, but they did not let such attachments get in the way of a hard-headed attitude towards managing their lives, businesses, farms and urban communities. When the colonial elites failed to fund through private finance the infrastructure so badly needed, the migrants elected politicians from their own communities who were willing to break with prevailing liberal ideologies and build these essential utilities out of public funds. Victoria, including Melbourne, developed a unique artisanal property-owning culture that was to last well into the 20th century.

The cohort made up just a little over 1% of the government-assisted migrants who arrived in Victoria in that same year, and questions have been raised about how representative the Lancashire migrant cohort was of all the Assisted Migrants that landed in 1852 and 1853. My aim was not to find a representative sample, but to explore the effectiveness of the 'systems approach', which connects migration patterns in the society of departure at the local, regional and state levels to the patterns of migrant settlement in the societies and cultures receiving them. I chose the southern Lancashire cohort because Richard Seddon was a profound influence on my family's settlement of Australia and New Zealand, and because my father's family came from Bolton, Lancashire, and were early textile factory hands.

Richards claims that the most important method by which we have rescued the spear-holders from invisibility has been through the study of letters, journals and diaries. Fitzpatrick provides a particularly important example of this; but his Irish migrants are scattered across a century or more.[2] However, the letters and diaries of lower-middle-class and working-class migrants, where they have survived, are mainly fragmentary, making them unreliable testaments to the political and social thinking of any one group of migrants. Richards argues that it is likely that the roots of English migration will be found in 'the back lanes and villages', yet he over-emphasises the rural origins of the English migration.[3] I strongly suggest that these roots are located instead in the 'streets and towns', as the English migrant of the second half of the 19th century was overwhelmingly urban in origin.

The critical contribution of this work is its ability to connect the migrants from the cohort to specific streets or places with neighbours and to explore the socioeconomic influences prevalent in these neighbourhoods. Then it is possible to explore fully Bate's idea of cultural transmission – that is, the transfer to Australia of old-world institutions and ideas as part of the life experience of the migrants. What did they import with them, what did they discard, and what did they adapt to the lands and cultures they were settling? This approach allows us to observe and dissect waves or clusters of migrants in detail, wherever their origins.

Stone's argument that prosopography may be most useful in identifying revolutions of rising expectations and exploring the resultant popular movements of social, cultural, political or economic change is highly relevant to this research. This book is about a revolution of rising expectations and how that played into the migration to and settlement of Victoria in the gold rush era.

> *My answer to Messrs Merchant, Lawyer, and Banker, is this – because the bootmaker, the cabinet maker, and the paper manufacturer, are your customers, out of your pockets come your profits, fees and dividends, and lumping ones too… But why multiply reasons when it is evident that nothing but the selfishness of the non-producing portion of the community stands in the way of the alteration of our laws.*
>
> Graham Berry, Letter to the Editor of the *Age*[4]

NOTES

Chapter 1: The Best of Our Population

1. PROV, *Land 'Selection' Files*, Public Records Office of Victoria, Melbourne. VPRS 625/P0/353/24567.
2. Quoted in Stuart Macintyre, *A Colonial Liberalism: The Lost World of Three Victorian Visionaries* (Oxford: Oxford University Press, 1991), 17.
3. Keith Sinclair, *A History of New Zealand* (Auckland: Penguin Books, 1980), 187.
4. Paul Pickering, 'From rifle club to reading room: Sydney's democratic vistas, 1848–1856', *Labour History Review*, 78/1 (2013), 87–112, 87–9; see also Paul Pickering, 'A lesson lost?: Chartism and Australian democracy', *Agora*, 46/4 (2011), 4–10.
5. Richard Brown, *Chartism*, Perspectives in History (Cambridge: Cambridge University Press, 1998); Malcolm Chase, *Chartism: A New History* (Manchester: Manchester University Press, 2007); Paul A. Pickering, *Chartism and the Chartists in Manchester and Salford* (New York: St Martin, 1995).
6. Henry Gyles Turner, *A History of the Colony of Victoria* (Melbourne: Longmans, Green, 1904), Vol. 1, 299–302.
7. *Geelong Advertiser* (Geelong, Vic). Monday 7 July 1851, 2.
8. Geoffrey Serle, *The Golden Age* (Melbourne: Melbourne University Press, 1963), Ch 1 and 2.
9. Geoffrey Serle, *The Golden Age*, 7.
10. J.D. Mereweather, *Diary of a Working Clergyman, in Australia and Tasmania 1850–1853* (London, 1859), 214.
11. PROV, *Register of Assisted British Immigrants, Part VPRS 7310*, Public Records Office of Victoria, Melbourne, 1839–1871.
12. R.J. Schultz, 'The Assisted Immigrants, 1837–1850', PhD thesis (Australian National University, 1971), 18.
13. W.D. Borrie, *The European Peopling of Australasia: A Demographic History, 1788–1988* (Canberra: Demography Program, Research School of Social Sciences, Australian National University, 1994), 71.
14. Geoffrey Serle, *The Golden Age*, 9–65.
15. Graeme Davison, *Lost Relations* (Crows Nest, Sydney: Allen & Unwin, 2015), 47–52; A. James Hammerton, *Emigrant Gentlewomen: Genteel Poverty and Female Emigration, 1830–1914* (London & Totowa, NJ: Croom Helm; Rowman and Littlefield, 1979), 53–70 & 94–6; A.J. Hammerton, '"Without natural protectors': female immigration to Australia, 1832–36', *Historical Studies*, 16/65 (1975), 539–66, 539–45; Robin F. Haines, *Emigration and the Labouring Poor: Australian Recruitment in Britain and Ireland, 1831–60* (New York: St Martin's Press, 1997), 5–6 and 82–3.
16. Weston Bate, *Victorian Gold Rushes* (Fitzroy, Victoria: McPhee Gribble/Penguin, 1988), 4–5 & 25–30; Geoffrey Blainey, *A History of Victoria* (Melbourne: Cambridge University Press, 2nd edn, 2013), 43–4; Richard Broome, *Arriving: The Victorians* (McMahons Point, NSW: Fairfax, Syme & Weldon Associates, 1984), 72–4; Geoffrey Serle, *The Golden Age*, 51–6.
17. Graeme Davison, *Lost Relations*; David Fitzpatrick, *Oceans of consolation: personal accounts of Irish migration to Australia* (Carlton, Victoria: Melbourne University Press, 1995); Robin F. Haines, *Emigration and the Labouring Poor*; Eric Richards, 'British emigrants and the making of the Anglosphere', *History*, 103/355 (2018), 286–306.
18. Robin F. Haines, *Emigration and the Labouring Poor*, 250–60.
19. Eric Richards, 'British emigrants and the making of the Anglosphere', 286.
20. Weston Bate, *Victorian Gold Rushes*, 4–5.
21. Graeme Davison, 'Australia: The First Suburban Nation?', *Journal of Urban History*, 22/1 (1995), 40–74, 53.
22. The National Archives, *Colonial Office: Land & Emigration Commission, etc.*, Land & Emigration Commission, London, 1840–1855. CO 386/69 120–4.
23. Geoffrey Blainey, *A History of Victoria*, 35.

24 PROV, *Register of Assisted British Immigrants*. 9/57-67.
25 Christiane Harzig, Dirk Hoerder and Donna R. Gabaccia, *What Is Migration History?* (Cambridge: Polity, 2009), Ch 4.
26 These figures were derived from the appendices in Dudley Baines and Economic History Society, *Emigration from Europe, 1815–1930*, New studies in economic and social history (1st edn, Cambridge, New York: Cambridge University Press, 1995).
27 Christiane Harzig, Dirk Hoerder and Donna R. Gabaccia, *What Is Migration History?*, 53–4.
28 Dudley Baines and Economic History Society, *Emigration from Europe*, 6–7.
29 Dudley Baines and Economic History Society, *Emigration from Europe*, 7.
30 Charlotte Erickson, *Leaving England: Essays on British Emigration in the Nineteenth Century* (Ithaca, NY: Cornell University Press, 1994), Intro and Ch 6.
31 These are for the annual average rate per 1000 for the years 1851–1890 from Table 4 in Dudley Baines and Economic History Society, *Emigration from Europe*.
32 Charlotte Erickson, *Leaving England*, 13–14 and Ch 13.
33 Charlotte Erickson, *Leaving England*, 9–10.
34 Eric Richards, 'British emigrants and the making of the Anglosphere', 287.
35 Dudley Baines, *Migration in a Mature Economy: Emigration and Internal Migration in England and Wales, 1861–1900*, Cambridge studies in population, economy and society in past time 3 (Pbk edn, Cambridge: Cambridge University Press, 2002), 4.
36 Outward passenger lists from Britain are seriously deficient. Baines therefore turned to the published census returns to determine emigrants by county of birth. For his methodology see Dudley Baines, *Migration in a Mature Economy*, 5–6; Erickson provides a good summary of the possible deficiencies of Baines' estimates as well as their importance in Charlotte Erickson, *Leaving England*, 212–13.
37 Charlotte Erickson, *Leaving England*, 87–125.
38 Charlotte Erickson, *Leaving England*, 34-59.
39 Dudley Baines, *Migration in a Mature Economy*, Appendix 1.
40 S. Colin Holt, 'Family, kinship, community and friendship ties in assisted emigration from Cambridgeshire to Port Phillip District and Victoria, 1840–67' (PhD thesis, La Trobe University, 1987).
41 S. Colin Holt, 'Family, kinship, community and friendship ties', 172.
42 Paul Hudson and Dennis Mills, 'English emigration, kinship and the recruitment process: migration from Melbourn in Cambridgeshire to Melbourne in Victoria in the mid-nineteenth century', *Rural History*, 10/01 (1999), 55–74, 66.
43 Dudley Baines and Economic History Society, *Emigration from Europe*, 9.
44 Paul Hudson and Dennis Mills, 'English emigration, kinship and the recruitment process', 66.
45 Such as James Belich, *Replenishing the Earth: The Settler Revolution and the Rise of the Anglo-World, 1783–1939* (Oxford: Oxford University Press, 2009); Duncan Bell, *The Idea of Greater Britain: Empire and the Future of World Order, 1860–1900* (Princeton: Princeton University Press, 2007); Lisa Chilton, *Agents of Empire: British Female Migration to Canada and Australia, 1860s–1930* (Toronto: University of Toronto Press, 2007); John Darwin, *The Empire Project: The Rise and Fall of the British World-System, 1830–1970* (Cambridge: Cambridge University Press, 2011); Marjory Harper and Stephen Constantine, *Migration and Empire* (Oxford: Oxford University Press, 2010); John C. Weaver, *The Great Land Rush and the Making of the Modern World, 1650–1900* (Montreal, Ithaca: McGill-Queen's University Press, 2003).
46 Christiane Harzig, Dirk Hoerder and Donna R. Gabaccia, *What Is Migration History?*, 3.
47 Lawrence Stone, 'Prosopography', *Daedalus*, 100/1 (1971), 46–79, 67–9.
48 Richard E. Reid, *Farewell My Children: Irish Assisted Emigration to Australia 1848–1870* (Spit Junction NSW: Anchor Books Australia, 2011).
49 Weston Bate, *Victorian Gold Rushes*, 4–5.
50 Weston Bate, *Victorian Gold Rushes*, 5.
51 Robin Haines, *Life and Death in the Age of Sail: The Passage to Australia* (Sydney: UNSW Press, 2003).

Chapter 2: Populating the Biography

1. The National Archives, *Colonial Office: Land & Emigration Commission*, etc. CO 386/71/230.
2. Eric Richards, 'British emigrants and the making of the Anglosphere', 286–7.
3. Dudley Baines and Economic History Society, *Emigration from Europe*, 9.
4. Eric Richards, 'British emigrants and the making of the Anglosphere', 288.
5. Charlotte Erickson, *Leaving England*, 14.
6. Hereafter referred to as the '1851 English Census'; and likewise for the 1841 Census.
7. PROV, *Inward Overseas Passenger Lists (British Ports), Part VPRS 7666*, Public Records Office of Victoria, Melbourne. 34/8.
8. Richard Hall, 'The diary of Richard Hall of Bury, Lancashire, England: voyage to Australia in the ship Kate', 1852–54, Vaughan Evans Library, Australian Maritime Museum; PRO, *Census Returns of England and Wales, 1851, Part HO 107*, National Archives of the UK, London, 1851. 2216/108/2/5.
9. None of the major genealogical sites allow you to search for this information for the 1841 or 1831 Census Returns, probably because of the manner in which it was recorded in these early census returns.
10. PROV, *Register of Assisted British Immigrants*. 6/144/273–5.
11. See, for example, Valerie Burton (ed.), *Liverpool Shipping, Trade and Industry: Essays on Maritime History* (Merseyside: National Museums and Galleries on Merseyside, 1989); Alan Kidd, *Manchester: A History* (Lancaster: Carnegie Publishing Limited, 2006); Michael Stammers, *Liverpool: The Port and Its Ships* (Phoenix Mill [England], Wolfeboro Falls, NH: Phoenix Mill England, Wolfeboro Falls, NH: A Sutton, 1991).
12. Victoria was one of the slowest of the Australian colonies to grant women the right to vote. Women finally received this right six years after Federation in 1908.
13. SLV, *Victorian Electoral Roll 1856–57*, Library Council of Victoria and State Library of Victoria, Melbourne, 1987. Collingwood, Fitzroy Division, 49.
14. Richard Turner, 'The Apprenticeship of Richard Seddon', *Victorian Historical Journal*, 85/1 (2014), 97–118, 107.
15. Geoffrey Serle, *The Golden Age*, 18–19.
16. Stuart Macintyre, *A Colonial Liberalism*, 66–112.
17. Geoffrey Blainey, *A History of Victoria*, 118–19.
18. *Census of Victoria for the year 1891: Part III. Religions of the people: population enumerated on the 5th April, 1891*, Robt. S. Bain, Government Printing Office, Melbourne, 1892.
19. Graeme Davison, *Lost Relations*, 166–8.

Chapter 3: A Quite Unprecedented Achievement

1. The National Archives, *Colonial Office: Emigration Entry Books*, War and Colonial Department and Colonial Office, London, 1840–1855. CO 385/25/388-389.
2. *Bathurst Free Press* (Bathurst, NSW). Saturday 17 May 1851, 4.
3. *Argus* (Melbourne, Vic.). Friday 5 September 1851, 3.
4. *Argus*, Friday 12 September 1851, 1.
5. 'The Colonial Land and Emigration Commissioners' in the NSW State Archives, *State Records Archives Investigator*, NSW Government, NSW, 2014. http://investigator.records.nsw.gov.au/Entity.aspx?Path=%%CAgency55C3050.
6. The National Archives, *Colonial Office: Emigration Entry Books*. CO 385/326/208–9.
7. E.G. Wakefield, *A Letter from Sydney* (London: Joseph Cross, 1829).
8. David Feldman and M. Page Baldwin, 'Emigration and the British state, CA. 1815–1925' in Francois Weil and Nancy L. Green (ed.), *Citizenship and Those Who Leave: The Politics of Emigration and Expatriation* (Urbana and Chicago: University of Illinois Press, 2007), 141.
9. BPP, *Thirteenth General Report of the Colonial Land and Emigration Commissioners with Appendix 1852–1853* (London: Houses of Parliament, 1853), 5.
10. The National Archives, *Colonial Office: Land & Emigration Commission*, etc. CO 386/69/331–7.
11. The National Archives, *Colonial Office: Land & Emigration Commission*, etc. CO 386/69/331–7.

Notes

12 I The National Archives, *Colonial Office: Land & Emigration Commission, etc.* CO 386/69/261–5.
13 VPP, *Census of Victoria for the year 1851*, John Ferres, Government Printing Office, Melbourne, 1852, 211.
14 Geoffrey Serle, *The Golden Age*, 44–57. See also Geoffrey Blainey, *A History of Victoria*; Richard Broome, *Arriving*; David Hill, *The Gold Rush: The Fever That Forever Changed Australia* (North Sydney, NSW: William Heinemann, 2011), among others.
15 Geoffrey Serle, *The Golden Age*, 44.
16 The National Archives, *Colonial Office: Land & Emigration Commission, etc.* CO 386/70/399–401.
17 The National Archives, *Colonial Office: Land & Emigration Commission, etc.* CO 386/69-71; The National Archives, *Colonial Office: Emigration Entry Books.* CO 385/25–6.
18 Geoffrey Serle, *The Golden Age*, 47.
19 The National Archives, *Colonial Office: Land & Emigration Commission, etc.* CO 386/70/391–5.
20 The National Archives, *Colonial Office: Land & Emigration Commission, etc.* CO 386/70/394–5.
21 A draconian *Masters and Servants Act 1823* (amended 1844) based on the British law existed in NSW and became part of Victorian law when the colony was separated from NSW, but it could never be effectively enforced. See Richard Broome, *Arriving*, 61.
22 BPP, *Seventh Annual Report of the Poor Law Board* (London: Houses of Parliament, 1854), 8.
23 Geoffrey Blainey, *A History of Victoria*, 35–7.
24 The National Archives, *Colonial Office: Emigration Entry Books.* CO 386/69/331–7.
25 BPP, *Thirteenth General Report of the Colonial Land and Emigration Commissioners with Appendix 1852–1853*, 15–16.
26 BPP, *Thirteenth General Report of the Colonial Land and Emigration Commissioners with Appendix 1852–1853*, 16.
27 *Argus*, Wednesday 3 August 1853, 4; Wednesday 7 September 1853, 7.
28 BPP, *Thirteenth General Report of the Colonial Land and Emigration Commissioners with Appendix 1852–1853*, 16.
29 BPP, *Thirteenth General Report of the Colonial Land and Emigration Commissioners with Appendix 1852–1853*, 16–17.
30 Dudley Baines and Economic History Society, *Emigration from Europe*, 39–40.
31 The National Archives, *Colonial Office: Land & Emigration Commission, etc.* CO 386/69/120–4.
32 The National Archives, *Colonial Office: Land & Emigration Commission, etc.* CO 386/265–7.
33 Colonial Land and Emigration Commission (CLEC), *Colonization Circular* (2nd edn, London: Colonial Land and Emigration Commission, 1852), 4, 9 and 11–12.
34 The English include the Welsh. However, the number of Welsh applying for or being accepted into the government-assisted program was tiny – barely 1% of the total.
35 Children 14 years and over travelling with their parents were recorded as single adults.
36 All percentages were compiled by PROV, Register of Assisted British Immigrants 1839-1871, VPRS 7310. Books 6–10. See Appendices 1–2.
37 The National Archives, *Colonial Office: Land & Emigration Commission, etc.* CO 386/69/261–5.
38 PROV, *Register of Assisted British Immigrants*. Books 6–10.
39 CLEC, *Colonization Circular*, 23.
40 *Manchester Examiner and Times* (Manchester). Saturday 19 June 1852, 6.
41 'Richmond & Chandler' in *Grace's Guide to British Industrial History*, Grace's Guide Ltd, UK, http://www.gracesguide.co.uk/Richmond_and_Chandler.
42 CLEC, *Colonization Circular*, 24.
43 Keith Pescod, *Good Food, Bright Fires & Civility: British Emigrant Depots of the 19th Century* (Kew, Vic.: Australian Scholarly Publishing, 2001), 122–3.
44 Robin F. Haines, *Emigration and the Labouring Poor*, 114.
45 The National Archives, *Colonial Office: Land & Emigration Commission, etc.* CO 386/71/1-31.
46 Robin F. Haines, *Emigration and the Labouring Poor*, 111–24.
47 BPP, *The Sixth Annual Report of the Poor Law Board* (London: House of Commons, 1853), 6–7.
48 Keith Pescod, *Good Food, Bright Fires & Civility*, 1–5.

49 BPP, *Thirteenth General Report of the Colonial Land and Emigration Commissioners with Appendix 1852–1853*, 18.
50 Richard Preston, 'Undated Letter', *Letters 1852–1854*, Liverpool Maritime Museum, SAS/3/1/12 (e).
51 Richard Hall, 'The diary of Richard Hall of Bury, Lancashire, England: voyage to Australia in the ship Kate', 1852–54, Vaughan Evans Library, Australian Maritime Museum, MS KAT (198459).
52 Richard Hall, 'The diary of Richard Hall'.
53 Edward Dash, 'Journal of a voyage by the ship Ann Dashwood from Liverpool to Australia 1853', Vaughan Evans Library, Australian Maritime Museum, 1853, MS ANN (151359).
54 The National Archives, *Colonial Office: Emigration Entry Books*. CO 386/71/222–3.
55 Keith Pescod, *Good Food, Bright Fires & Civility*, 60–5.
56 Oliver MacDonagh, 'Emigration and the state, 1833–55: an essay in administrative history', *Transactions of the Royal Historical Society*, 5 (1955), 133–59, 133.

Chapter 4: Made in Lancashire

1 *Bendigo Advertiser*, Thursday 7 June 1906, 5.
2 Tom Brooking, *King of God's Own* (Auckland: Penguin Books, 2014).
3 PROV, *Register of Assisted British Immigrants*. 9/58–68.
4 Weston Bate, *Lucky City: The First Generation at Ballarat 1851–1901* (Melbourne: Melbourne University Press, 1978), 41; Weston Bate, *Victorian Gold Rushes*, 4–5.
5 Cornish and Welsh migrants were grouped by the CLEC under English. In both cases the numbers of Cornish and Welsh migrants in this period were even smaller than the migrant numbers from Lancaster.
6 All percentages were compiled from PROV, *Register of Assisted British Immigrants*, bk 6–10.
7 The National Archives, *Colonial Office: Emigration Entry Books*. CO 386/71/222–3.
8 PRO, *Census Returns of England and Wales, 1851*. 2241/702/37/123 and 2241/386/9/36.
9 PRO, *Census Returns of England and Wales, 1841, Part HO 107*, National Archives of the UK, London, 1841. 519/1/10 and 495/14/20.
10 PRO, *Census Returns of England and Wales, 1851*. 2250/402/25/92.
11 PRO, *Census Returns of England and Wales, 1851*. 2192/1096/44/156, 2191/190/60/190 and 2164/834/4/12.
12 PRO, *Census Returns of England and Wales, 1851*. 2275/327/6/19, 2275/326/4/11, 2270/30/1/5 and 2196/331/20/60.
13 M. Winstanley, 'Industrialization and the small farm: family and household economy in nineteenth-century Lancashire', *Past & Present* 152 (1996), 157–95.
14 Reid claims that the CLEC was allowing the Irish Poor Law Unions to contribute quotas of girls from their workhouses, although he admits that was not in compliance with the CLEC's regulations. Additionally, he admits that the numbers were limited, and that this only occurred prior to 1852. He also only studied assisted migrants to NSW. Richard E. Reid, *Farewell My Children*, 100–2.
15 PROV, *Register of Assisted British Immigrants*. 6/94/302 and 9/67/383.
16 Deborah Valenze, *The First Industrial Woman* (New York: Oxford University Press, 1995), 86–99.
17 Anna Clark, *The Struggle for the Breeches: Gender and the Making of the British Working Class* (Berkeley, Los Angeles, London: University of California, 1997), 62 and 209–37.
18 Alan Kidd, *Manchester: A History*, 17.
19 Anna Clark, *The Struggle for the Breeches*, 1–25.
20 L. Davidof and C. Hall, *Family Fortunes* (London and New York: Routledge, 2002), 149–92; Nigel Goose (ed.), *Women's Work in Industrial England*, Local Population Studies (Hatfield, Hertfordshire: Department of Humanities, University of Hertfordshire, 2007), 1–7.
21 Anna Clark, *The Struggle for the Breeches*, 5, 36 and 208.
22 Duncan Bythell, *The Handloom Weavers: A Study in the English Cotton Industry during the Industrial Revolution* (Cambridge: Cambridge University Press, 1969), 34–9; see also Anna Clark, *The Struggle for the Breeches*, 23–4.

23 Preston for this study includes Broughton on it northern border, which by 1850 was a rapidly industrialising extension of Preston.
24 Liverpool for this study includes the Birkenhead dock suburbs and the urban suburbs in West Derby. Greater Manchester includes the closely connected cotton towns such as Bury, Oldham and Rochdale that are now part of the county of Greater Manchester.
25 Michael Stammers, *Liverpool: The Port and Its Ships*, 7.
26 Valerie Burton, *Liverpool Shipping, Trade and Industry*, 8.
27 Valerie Burton, *Liverpool Shipping, Trade and Industry*, 104.
28 Michael Stammers, *Liverpool: The Port and Its Ships*, 30–2.
29 At some point as Bootle cum Linacre became a dockside suburb, the 'cum Linacre' was dropped and it was simply referred to as Bootle.
30 John Belchem (ed.), *Popular Politics, Riot and Labour: Essays in Liverpool History 1790* (Liverpool: Liverpool University Press, 1992), 15–16.
31 John Belchem (ed.), *Popular Politics, Riot and Labour*, 28.
32 John Belchem (ed.), *Popular Politics, Riot and Labour*, 2–6.
33 Michael Stammers, *Liverpool: The Port and Its Ships*, 41.
34 John Belchem (ed.), *Popular Politics, Riot and Labour*, 6–7.
35 PRO, *Census Returns of England and Wales, 1841*. 26/9/6/7.
36 PRO, *Census Returns of England and Wales, 1851*. 2175/577/17/63.
37 PROV, *Register of Assisted British Immigrants*. 9/60-61/170–6.

Chapter 5: Cooperatives and Building Society Shares

1 Thomas Cooper, *The Life of Thomas Cooper: Written by Himself* (London: Hodder and Stoughton, 1872), 392–3.
2 Malcolm Chase, *Chartism: A New History*, 312–26.
3 Trygve Tholfsen, *Working-Class Radicalism in Mid-Victorian England* (London: Crom Helm, 1976), 11.
4 Alan Kidd, *Manchester: A History*, 96–8.
5 Martin Hewitt, *The Emergence of Stability in the Industrial City: Manchester, 1832–67* (Aldershot, Hants: Scolar Press, 1996), 193–229.
6 Alan J. Kidd and K.W. Roberts (ed.), *City, Class and Culture: Studies of Social Policy and Cultural Production in Victorian Manchester* (Manchester: Manchester University Press, 1985), 1–73.
7 PROV, *Register of Assisted British Immigrants*. 9/56–68.
8 PRO, *Census Returns of England and Wales, 1841*. 571/1/9.
9 Manchester City Archives, *Manchester Rate Books 1706-1900*, Manchester City Council, Manchester. 1841/341/1833.
10 PRO, *Census Returns of England and Wales, 1841*. 571/1/9.
11 Alan Kidd, *Manchester: A History*, 36–7.
12 Manchester City Archives, *Manchester Rate Books 1706–1900*. 1839–1856.
13 Friedrich Engels, *The Condition of the Working-Class in England in 1844*, Social science series (London: Allen and Unwin, 1950), 90.
14 BPP, *Report of the General Board of Health on the epidemic cholera of 1848 & 1849*, House of Commons, London, 1850. Appendix A, 93–4.
15 GRO, *England and Wales Civil Registration Indexes*, General Register Office, London, England. Death Index 1852/Oct-Dec/Vol 8d/141.
16 Friedrich Engels, *The Condition of the Working-Class in England in 1844*, 90–1.
17 Nigel Goose, *Women's Work in Industrial England*, 5–6.
18 BPP, *Submission from Manchester's Factory Children Committee to the House of Commons*, House of Commons, London, 1838. Session 1837–38, Series 3, Vol 44, 381.
19 Alan Kidd, *Manchester: A History*, 96.
20 Richard Brown, *Chartism*, various; Malcolm Chase, *Chartism: A New History*, various; Paul A. Pickering, *Chartism and the Chartists in Manchester and Salford*, 59–72.
21 GRO, *England and Wales Civil Registration Indexes*. Marriage Certificate IXF264946.
22 PRO, *Census Returns of England and Wales, 1851*. 2220/95/28/84.
23 Nigel Goose, *Women's Work in Industrial England*, 11.
24 PRO, *Census Returns of England and Wales, 1851*. 2220/95/28/84.

25 Alan Kidd, *Manchester: A History*, 33.
26 Pigot and co., *Pigot's Manchester & Salford Directory 1833* (Manchester: Pigot and co., 1833), 595.
27 Pigot and co., *Pigot's Manchester and Salford Directory, 1838* (Manchester: Pigot and co., 1838), 328.
28 Manchester City Archives, *Manchester Rate Books 1706–1900*. Township of Ardwick 1842, 92/2853.
29 Manchester City Archives, *Manchester Rate Books 1706–1900*. Township of Ardwick 1842, 46/1403–9.
30 Manchester City Archives, *Manchester Rate Books 1706–1900*. Township of Ardwick 1848, 66/1077–1191 and 1849, 46-47/1394–1483. By 1850, two-thirds of the houses built by Mellor & Greenhalgh had passed into the hands of Duffield, Lofthouse, Whitfield, in Manchester City Archives, *Manchester Rate Books 1706–1900*. Township of Ardwick 1846–1850.
31 Norman McCord, *The Anti-Corn Law League* (London: Unwin University Books, 1975), 175.
32 Alan Kidd, *Manchester: A History*, 33.
33 Les Sutton, 'Mainly about Ardwick', *Manchester City Collection*, f942.733915 Su1, Manchester Archives and Local Studies, 1975, 7–9.
34 Quoted in Malcolm Chase, *Chartism: A New History*, 344.
35 Malcolm Chase, *Chartism: A New History*, various; Martin Hewitt, *The Emergence of Stability in the Industrial City*, 230–61; Alan Kidd, *Manchester: A History*, various.
36 Paul A. Pickering, *Chartism and the Chartists in Manchester and Salford*, 29.
37 Alan Kidd, *Manchester: A History*, 97.
38 Martin Hewitt, *The Emergence of Stability in the Industrial City*, 226.
39 Malcolm Chase, *Chartism: A New History*, 331.
40 The National Archives, *Registry of Friendly Societies*, Registry of Friendly Societies, London, 1832–1912. FS 6/104/340LANC.
41 BPP, *Select Committee on Votes of Electors*, House of Commons, London, 1846. 1846, Appendix part 1, 312–15.
42 Martin Hewitt, *The Emergence of Stability in the Industrial City*, 204–5; Alan Kidd, *Manchester: A History*, 98.
43 Manchester City Archives, *Manchester Rate Books 1706–1900*. Township of Ardwick, 1850, 3/63.
44 Weston Bate, *Victorian Gold Rushes*, 4-7.

Chapter 6: Australy for Ever

1 *Nottinghamshire Guardian* (London). Thursday 12 February 1852, 2.
2 Keith Pescod, *Good Food, Bright Fires & Civility*, 5.
3 PROV, *Register of Assisted British Immigrants*. 9/121/245.
4 PRO, *Census Returns of England and Wales, 1851*. 2175/155/13/40.
5 PROV, *Register of Assisted British Immigrants*. 9/132/288 and 289.
6 *Argus*, Saturday 4 December 1852, 4, and Friday 11 February 1853, 4.
7 Geoffrey Blainey, *A History of Victoria*, 43–5.
8 Weston Bate, *Victorian Gold Rushes*, 5 & 52-53.
9 Shirley Ward, *Destiny of Gold* (Victoria: Shirley Ward, 1987), 87–95, 157–63 and 200–4.
10 PROV, *Teachers Record Books, Part VPRS 13719/P1*, Public Records Office of Victoria, Melbourne, 1863–1959. 397.
11 SLV, *Victorian Electoral Roll 1856–57*. Maldon, The Loddon, 22.
12 Geoffrey Blainey, *A History of Victoria*, 58–61.
13 PROV, *Castlemaine Rate Books, Part VPRS 409*, Public Records Office of Victoria, Melbourne. P0 Unit 1, 1856–57, Forest Creek, 1011.
14 Geoffrey Blainey, *A History of Victoria*, 49–63.
15 PROV, *Register of Assisted British Immigrants*. 10/108/368; BDM VIC, *Deaths*, The Victorian Registry of Births, Deaths and Marriages, Victoria. 1854/4508.
16 PROV, *Register of Assisted British Immigrants*. 10/20/360.
17 'Ancestry.com' in, Ancestry.com Operations Inc, Provo, UT, US, http://trees.ancestry.com.au/tree/52723941/person/13547231658?ssrc=.

Notes

18 Weston Bate, *Victorian Gold Rushes*, 42.
19 Weston Bate, *Victorian Gold Rushes*, 4–5.
20 Weston Bate, *Victorian Gold Rushes*, 12-13.
21 Peter FitzSimons, *Eureka: The Unfinished Revolution* (North Sydney, NSW: William Heinemann Australia, 2012), 163–5.
22 Geoffrey Blainey, *A History of Victoria*, 48.
23 Geoffrey Blainey, *A History of Victoria*, 50.
24 Peter FitzSimons, *Eureka: The Unfinished Revolution*, 164–5; Geoffrey Serle, *The Golden Age*, 193–9.
25 H. Anderson, 'Fawkner, John Pascoe (1792–1869)' in *Australian Dictionary of Biography*, National Centre of Biography, Australian National University, Canberra, http://adb.anu.edu.au/biography/fawkner-john-pascoe-2037.
26 Weston Bate, *Victorian Gold Rushes*, 11–20.
27 October 1853; *The Cambridge History of the British Empire*, 7 pt 1, s.v. 'Australia', 255.
28 B.A. Knox, 'Hotham, Sir Charles (1806–1855)' in *Australian Dictionary of Biography*, http://adb.anu.edu.au/biography/hotham-sir-charles-3803; *Australia*, 254–5; Peter FitzSimons, *Eureka: The Unfinished Revolution*, 213–15; Geoffrey Serle, *The Golden Age*, 203.
29 Peter FitzSimons, *Eureka: The Unfinished Revolution*, 240–1.
30 State Library of Victoria, MS 7662. Box 74/3, no. 501.
31 Ronald McNicoll, 'Nickle, Sir Robert (1786–1855)' in *Australian Dictionary of Biography*, http://adb.anu.edu.au/biography/nickle-sir-robert-4301.
32 William Craig, *My Adventures on the Australian Goldfields* (London & Melbourne: Cassell and Company, 1903), 273–4.
33 BPP, *Further Papers Relative to Discovery of Gold in Australia*, House of Commons, London, 1856, 57.
34 Geoffrey Blainey, *A History of Victoria*, 48–52; Geoffrey Serle, *The Golden Age*, 200–3.
35 George William Rusden, *History of Australia* (Melbourne: Melville, Mullen & Slade, 1897) V.2, 633 and V.3, 140–61; *Sydney Morning Herald* (Sydney) Friday 4 January 1856, 4.
36 W.B. Withers, *History of Ballarat and Some Ballarat Reminiscences* (Ballarat: Ballarat Heritage Services, 1999), 92.
37 W.B. Withers, *History of Ballarat and Some Ballarat Reminiscences*, 92
38 Peter FitzSimons, *Eureka: The Unfinished Revolution*, 332–8; W.B. Withers, *History of Ballarat and Some Ballarat Reminiscences*, 93–5.
39 VPP, *Gold Fields' Commission of Enquiry: Report of the Commission Appointed to Enquire into the Condition of the Gold Fields of Victoria, &c. &c*, Parliamentary paper (Victorian Parliament) John Ferres, Government Printer, Melbourne, 1855, http://www.parliament.vic.gov.au/papers/govpub/VPARL1854-55NoA76p[i]-lxxii.pdf;
http://www.parliament.vic.gov.au/papers/govpub/VPARL1854-55NoA76p1-180.pdf;
http://www.parliament.vic.gov.au/papers/govpub/VPARL1854-55NoA76p181-365.pdf, 29 March 1855.
40 BPP, *Further Papers Relative to Discovery of Gold in Australia*, 26.
41 Peter Cook, 'Nicholson, William (1816–1865)' in *Australian Dictionary of Biography*, http://adb.anu.edu.au/biography/nicholson-william-4300.
42 Graeme Davison, 'Australia: The First Suburban Nation?', 54–9.
43 Geoffrey Bartlett, 'Berry, Sir Graham (1822–1904)' in *Australian Dictionary of Biography*, http://adb.anu.edu.au/biography/berry-sir-graham-2984/text4355.
44 Stuart Macintyre, *A Colonial Liberalism*, 114.
45 Geoffrey Serle, *The Golden Age*, 85–94.
46 Geoffrey Serle, *The Golden Age*, 239–43.
47 Charles Fahey and Alan Mayne (eds), *Gold Tailings: Forgotten Histories of Family and Community on the Central Victorian Goldfields* (North Melbourne: Australian Scholarly Publishing, 2010), 7–8.
48 Charles Fahey and Alan Mayne (eds), *Gold Tailings*, 6–7.
49 *Bendigo Advertiser*, Tuesday 7 June 1906, 6.
50 Donald Denoon, *Settler Capitalism: The Dynamics of Dependent Development in the Southern Hemisphere* (Oxford: Oxford University Press, 1983), 104.

Chapter 7: The Golden Lands

1. *Bendigo Independent* (Bendigo) Friday 24 September 1875, 3.
2. Weston Bate, *Victorian Gold Rushes*, 5.
3. Weston Bate, *Victorian Gold Rushes*, 4–5 and 26–7.
4. Clare Wright, *The Forgotten Rebels of Eureka* (Melbourne: Text Publishing Company, 2013).
5. Victoria Registrar General, *Census of Victoria* (Melbourne: J. Ferris, Government Publisher), 1854, 1857, 1861 and 1871; Geoffrey Serle, *The Golden Age*, 388.
6. G.V. Portus, 'The Gold Discoveries 1850–1860' in *Australia*, 357.
7. Geoffrey Serle, *The Golden Age*, 216–29.
8. Geoffrey Serle, *The Golden Age*, 217.
9. SLV, *Victorian Electoral Roll 1856-57*. Portland, 4; BDM VIC, *Births*, Victorian Registry of Births, Deaths and Marriages, Victoria. 1856/13442.
10. SLV, *Victorian Electoral Roll 1856-57*, Ashby, 41; BDM VIC, *Births*. 1853/23101 and 1858/12147.
11. BDM VIC, *Births*. 1860/14517, 1862/20701, 1864/22039, 1866/24325 and 1871/12511.
12. Mining Department, *Surveyors' Reports for January 1863* (Melbourne: Victorian Government, 1863), 8.
13. Mining Department, *Surveyors Reports for June 1863* (Melbourne: Victorian Government, 1863), 6–7.
14. Geoffrey Serle, *The Golden Age*, 218-219.
15. Weston Bate, *Lucky City*, 11–12.
16. Critchley Parker, *Victoria and Its Mining Resources* (London: Australian Mining Standard under the authority of Victorian Mines Department, 1908), 11–12.
17. Geoffrey Serle, *The Golden Age*, 240–1 and 388.
18. Henry Brown, *Victoria As I Found It, During Five Years of Adventure* (London: T. Cautley Newby, 1862), 269–73.
19. Geoffrey Serle, *The Golden Age*, 218–22.
20. *Bendigo Advertiser*, Tuesday 18 December 1855, 2.
21. VPP, *Gold Fields' Commission of Enquiry: Report of the Commission Appointed to Enquire into the Condition of the Gold Fields of Victoria*, &c. &c, 20.
22. VPP, *Mining Resources of the Colony of Victoria: Second Progress Report of the Commissioners Appointed to Enquire into the Mining Resources of the Colony, Parliamentary paper (Victorian Parliament)*, John Ferres, Government Printer, Melbourne, 1857, http://www.parliament.vic.gov.au/papers/govpub/VPARL1856-57No84.pdf, 200.
23. Geoffrey Serle, *The Golden Age*, 220–1.
24. Geoffrey Serle, *The Golden Age*, 222.
25. Marion McAdie, *Mining Shareholders Index 1857–1886* (Marion McAdie, 2006).
26. *Bendigo Advertiser,* Saturday 20 October 1855, 2.
27. *Bendigo Advertiser,* Saturday 15 September 1855, 2.
28. Henry Brown, *Victoria As I Found It*, 266–8.
29. Geoffrey Serle, *The Golden Age*, 223.
30. *Bendigo Advertiser,* 23 March 1865, 4.
31. Geoffrey Serle, *The Golden Age*, 225–6.
32. Martha Clendinning, *Recollections of Ballarat: A Lady's Life at the Diggings Fifty Years Ago*, Australian Manuscripts Collection, MS 10102/1 (Melbourne: State Library of Victoria, 1892).
33. Clare Wright, *The Forgotten Rebels of Eureka*, 129–30.
34. Weston Bate, *Victorian Gold Rushes*, 37.
35. Anna Clark, *The Struggle for the Breeches*, 208–9.
36. Weston Bate, *Victorian Gold Rushes*, 135–7.
37. Clare Wright, *The Forgotten Rebels of Eureka*, 149–50.
38. *Bendigo Advertiser,* Saturday 7 June 1856, 3.
39. *Bendigo Advertiser,* various 1856–1862.
40. *Ancestry.com*, http://person.ancestry.com.au/tree/8716077/person/656732619/story.
41. BDM VIC, *Births*. 1860/14683 and 1862/2260.
42. *Ancestry.com*, https://www.ancestry.com/institution/family-tree/person/tree/30491223/person/26211557183/story.

43 Weston Bate, *Victorian Gold Rushes*, 5.
44 Paul Pickering, 'From rifle club to reading room', 87.
45 Charles Fahey and Alan Mayne, *Gold Tailings*.

Chapter 8: Lives from the Diggings

1 Mary Ann Tyler, *The Adventurous Memoirs of a Gold Diggeress* (Wellington, NSW: Kate Gibbs, 1985), 36.
2 Keir Reeves and David Nichol (eds.), *Deeper Leads: New Approaches to Victorian Goldfields History* (Ballarat, Vic.: Ballarat Heritage Services, 2007); also quoted in Clare Wright, *The Forgotten Rebels of Eureka*, 138.
3 *Ballarat Star* (Ballarat, Vic.) Saturday 19 December 1896, 1.
4 PROV, *Register of Assisted British Immigrants*. 9/57/59-61.
5 BDM VIC, *Deaths*. 1853/28996.
6 Geoffrey Blainey, *A History of Victoria*, 40-41.
7 BDM VIC, *Deaths*. 1854/18559.
8 BDM VIC, *Births*. 1855/11670.
9 *Bendigo Advertiser*, Saturday 5 April 1856, 2.
10 *Bendigo Advertiser*, Tuesday 3 March 1857, 2.
11 *Bendigo Advertiser*, Saturday 12 September 1837, 3.
12 *Bendigo Advertiser*, Wednesday 13 January 1858, 2.
13 *Bendigo Advertiser*, Monday 4 July 1859, 3.
14 *Bendigo Advertiser*, Monday 22 December 1862, 3.
15 *Bendigo Advertiser*, Wednesday 21 January 1863, 2.
16 *Bendigo Advertiser*, Saturday 24 January 1863, 2.
17 PROV, *Outward Passengers to Interstate, UK, NZ and Foreign Ports 1852-1923, Part VPRS 3506*, Public Records Office of Victoria, Victoria. 1863/Jan/3.
18 BDM VIC, *Deaths*. 1863/4359.
19 BDM VIC, *Marriages*, Victorian Registry of Births, Deaths and Marriages, Victoria. 1865/2722.
20 PROV, *Register of Assisted British Immigrants*. 11/322/515.
21 PRO, *Census Returns of England and Wales, 1851*. 2211/518/38.
22 *Bendigo Advertiser*, Saturday 12 May 1866, 4.
23 *Bendigo Advertiser*, Thursday 23 March 1865, 4.
24 *Bendigo Advertiser*, Saturday 18 April 1868, 2.
25 PROV, *Probate and Administration Files, Part VPRS 28*, Public Records Office of Victoria, Melbourne. P2/162/27/484.
26 *Bendigo Advertiser*, Thursday 5 January 1862, 2.
27 Weston Bate, *Victorian Gold Rushes*, 5.
28 PRO, *Census Returns of England and Wales, 1851*. 2241/702/37/123.
29 PROV, *Register of Assisted British Immigrants*. 6/20/370–4.
30 See Diana's Death certficate in BDM VIC, *Deaths*. 1936/19343.
31 BDM VIC, *Births*. 1857/5979, 1860/7576 and 1863/6054.
32 BDM VIC, *Deaths*. 1868/7863.
33 PRO, *Census Returns of England and Wales, 1851*. 2275/326/4/11.
34 M. Winstanley, 'Industrialization and the small farm', 157–95.
35 PROV, *Register of Assisted British Immigrants*. 6/88/100–5 and 6/94/302.
36 BDM VIC, *Births*. 1853/23099.
37 BDM VIC, *Marriages*. 1855/2467.
38 PROV, *Register of Assisted British Immigrants*. 9/158/94-95.
39 SLV, *Victorian Electoral Roll 1856–57*. Fryerstown, 45.
40 SLV, *Victorian Electoral Roll 1856–57*. Moliagul, 14.
41 BDM VIC, *Births*. 1859/7161.
42 BDM VIC, *Marriages*. 1862/2392.
43 BDM VIC, *Births*. 1858/1204, 1861/2595, 1864/21258, 1867/7657, 1868/15605, 1869/14997, 1872/1037, 1874/21361 and 1876/14261.
44 BDM VIC, *Deaths*. 1887/1418 and 1893/5667.

45 PROV, *Register of Assisted British Immigrants*. 6/131/227–30 and 6/134/330.
46 SLV, *Victorian Electoral Roll 1856–57*. Talbot, 29.
47 Philip Mennell, 'Wheeler, Hon. James Henry' in *The Dictionary of Australasian Biography*, 504.
48 PROV, *Probate and Administration Files*. P2/249.
49 BDM VIC, *Marriages*. 1875/2539.
50 PROV, *Register of Assisted British Immigrants*. 6/144/273-275.
51 There is no birth certificate for Elizabeth, but her birth date was noted as 1853 in BDM VIC, *Deaths*. 1900/7900; BDM VIC, *Births*. 1856/23101 and 1858/12147.
52 SLV, *Victorian Electoral Roll 1856–57*. Ashby, 41.
53 BDM VIC, *Births*. 1860/14517, 1862/20701, 1864/22039, 1866/24325 and 1871/12511.
54 Geoffrey Serle, *The Golden Age*, 324–5.
55 PROV, *Register of Assisted British Immigrants*. 6/25/509 and 525.
56 M. Winstanley, 'Industrialization and the small farm'.
57 PRO, *Census Returns of England and Wales, 1851*. 2275/327/6/19.
58 PRO, *Census Returns of England and Wales, 1851*. 2275/325/3/9.
59 PROV, *Register of Assisted British Immigrants*. 6/28/621–3.
60 BDM VIC, *Deaths*. 1883/4740.
61 SLV, *Victorian Electoral Roll 1856–57*. Geelong, 11.
62 BDM VIC, *Births*. 1856/8238, 1860/14095, 1862/20208.
63 BDM VIC, *Deaths*. 1886/32466; , *Creswick & Clunes Advertiser* (Creswick). Friday 7 May 1886, 3.
64 Anna Clark, *The Struggle for the Breeches*, 24–5 and 46–7.
65 PROV, *Register of Assisted British Immigrants*. 10/94/366.
66 BDM VIC, *Marriages*. 1854/119.
67 BDM VIC, *Births*. 1855/1763, 1857/5126, 1860/1407 and 1863/6077.
68 PROV, *Ballarat Rate Valuation Books, Part VPRS 7265 and 7299*, Ballarat Archives Centre, Ballarat. P1 and P2, 1865-1891.
69 PROV, *Register of Assisted British Immigrants*. 6/162/214.
70 BDM VIC, *Births*. 1853/297.
71 BDM VIC, *Marriages*. 1853/2917.
72 PROV, *Register of Assisted British Immigrants*. 5/29/20 and 21.
73 BDM VIC, *Births*. 1855/1966, 1860/13726, and 1863/5821.
74 BDM VIC, *Deaths*. 1868/5611.
75 BDM VIC, *Deaths*. 1926/12544 and 1930/18006.
76 PROV, *Register of Assisted British Immigrants*. 8/140/348.
77 BDM VIC, *Marriages*. 1853/31668.
78 BDM VIC, *Births*. 1856/9636.
79 BDM VIC, *Births*. 1858/19707.
80 BDM VIC, *Deaths*. 1877/6706.
81 BDM VIC, *Deaths*. 1900/5865.
82 *Ancestry.com*. http://person.ancestry.com.au/tree/8716077/person/656732619/story.
83 *Ancestry.com*. http://person.ancestry.com.au/tree/8716077/person/656732619/story.
84 BDM VIC, *Births*. 1855/7423, 1858/7456 and 1860/13545.
85 PROV, *Outward Passengers to Interstate, UK, NZ and Foreign Ports 1852–1923*. 1862/March/5.
86 BDM VIC, *Births*. 1860/14683 and 1862/2260.
87 *Ancestry.com*. https://www.ancestry.institution.com/family-tree/person/tree/30491223/person/26211557183/story.
88 Austin McCallum, 'Morey, Edward (1832–1907)' in *Australian Dictionary of Biography*. http://adb.anu.edu.au/biography/morey-edward-4243.
89 PRO, *Census Returns of England and Wales, 1851*. 2249/393/27/98.
90 PROV, *Register of Assisted British Immigrants*. 9/61/190-191 and 9/67/380.
91 Austin McCallum, 'Morey, Edward (1832–1907)'.
92 BDM VIC, *Marriages*. 1855/945.
93 BDM VIC, *Deaths*. 1864/7792.
94 VPP, *Victorian Government Gazette*, Melbourne. G/G 1550, 1812 and G/G 2722, 2592.
95 BDM VIC, *Deaths*. 1877/8546.
96 BDM VIC, *Deaths*. 1898/10556.

97   PROV, *Probate and Administration Files*. P0/901 and P2/507.
98   PROV, *Bill of Sales Filed, Part VPRS 8350*, Public Records Office of Victoria, Melbourne. P2/299.
99   VPP, *Victorian Government Gazette*. G/G 2722, 2592; Critchley Parker, *Victoria and Its Mining Resources*, 51.
100 Austin McCallum, 'Morey, Edward (1832–1907)'.
101 PROV, *Probate and Administration Files*. P2/823.
102 Ellen Clacy, *A Lady's Visit to the Gold Diggings of Australia in 1852–53* (London: Hirst and Blackett, 1853), various; William H. Hall, *Practical Experience at the Diggings of the Goldfields of Victoria* (London: Effingham Wilson, 1852), 18 and 54.
103 Thursday 11 Sep 1856, 5; Thursday 19 May 1859, 7; Tuesday 2 Aug 1859, 5. See also Geoffrey Blainey, *A History of Victoria*, 61; Richard Broome, *Arriving*, 76; David Hill, *The Gold Rush*, 74 and 155.
104 Shirley Ward, *Destiny of Gold*, 35.
105 PRO, *Census Returns of England and Wales, 1851*. 2177/146/43/111.
106 BDM VIC, *Births*. 1853/4322, 1855/16502, 1857/8733 and 1859/22697.
107 BDM VIC, *Deaths*. 1867/3122.
108 BDM VIC, *Deaths*. 1888/13651.
109 Shirley Ward, *Destiny of Gold*, 64–6.
110 Shirley Ward, *Destiny of Gold*, 49–72, 87–95, 157–63 and 200–4.
111 Weston Bate, *Victorian Gold Rushes*, 5.
112 *Age* (Melbourne). Wednesday 22 October 1879, 3–4.

Chapter 9: Free Selection and Free Grass

1   *Age*, Thursday 16 July 1857, 5.
2   There were five Land Acts (1860, 1862, 1865, 1869 and 1878), the primary intention of which was to open up land for selection by the small or 'yeoman' farmer. They are frequently referred to as the 'selection acts'. The most important of these is the *Land Act 1869*.
3   J.M. Powell, *The Public Lands of Australia Felix* (Melbourne: Oxford University Press, 1970), 59.
4   J.M. Powell, *The Public Lands of Australia Felix*, 63.
5   Charles Fahey, 'The free selector's landscape: Moulding the Victorian farming districts, 1870–1915', *Studies in the History of Gardens & Designed Landscapes*, 31/2 (2011), 97–108, 97.
6   Charles Fahey, 'The free selector's landscape', 99.
7   PROV, *Register of Assisted British Immigrants*. 6/41/238.
8   PRO, *Census Returns of England and Wales, 1851*. 2177/143/35/140.
9   PROV, *Register of Assisted British Immigrants*. 6/41/238-240.
10 SLV, *Victorian Electoral Roll 1856–57*. Geelong, 36.
11 PROV, *Parish & Town Plans, Part VPRS 16171/P1*, Public Records Office of Victoria, Melbourne. Duneed/2561/12K.
12 AEC, *Australian Electoral Rolls*, Australian Electoral Commission, Victoria. 1903, Corio, 9.
13 BDM VIC, *Deaths*. 1893/1968.
14 PROV, *Probate and Administration Files*. P2/361.
15 BDM VIC, *Deaths*. 1904/9953.
16 PROV, *Wills, Part VPRS 7591*, Public Records Office of Victoria, Melbourne. P2/368.
17 J.M. Powell, *The Public Lands of Australia Felix*, 65.
18 Geoffrey Serle, *The Golden Age*, 267–73.
19 Council of the Convention, *Proceedings, and Documents of the Victorian Convention*, Victorian Convention, Melbourne, 3–7.
20 J.M. Powell, *The Public Lands of Australia Felix*, 66.
21 J.M. Powell, *The Public Lands of Australia Felix*, 81–2.
22 PROV, *Probate and Administration Files*. P2/198.
23 *Creswick and Clunes Advertiser* (Creswick), Friday 7 May 1886, 3.
24 PROV, *Probate and Administration Files*. P3/3686.
25 BDM VIC, *Deaths*. 1877/943.
26 PROV, *Probate and Administration Files*. P2/163 and 249; PROV, Parish & Town Plans. Wombat, 3857.

27 J.M. Powell, *The Public Lands of Australia Felix*, 82–4.
28 Shirley Ward, *Destiny of Gold*, 45–82.
29 Geoffrey Bartlett, 'Grant, James Macpherson (1822–1855)' in *Australian Dictionary of Biography*. http://adb.anu.edu.au/biography/grant-james-macpherson-3652/text5691.
30 E.O.G. Shann, 'Economic & Political Development' in *Australia*, 300–2.
31 Ron Falla, 'Land selection in the Wimmera [ased on an address to the Royal Historical Society of Victoria. State Conference (1999).]', *Victorian Historical Journal*, 71/2 (2000), 94–101, 99–100.
32 Shirley Ward, *Destiny of Gold*, 87–95, 157–63 and 200–4.
33 BDM VIC, *Marriages*. 1871/3812.
34 BDM VIC, *Deaths*. 1926/3226.
35 PROV, *Probate and Administration Files*. P3/1633.
36 PROV, *Wills*. P2/731.
37 *Age*, Monday 1 March 1926, 5 and 18.
38 Shirley Ward, *Destiny of Gold*, 94–5.
39 PROV, *Land 'Selection' Files*. VPRS 626/P0/2420/9553.
40 PROV, *Land 'Selection' Files*. VPRS 626/P0/2280/4998.
41 Charles Fahey in Phillippa Nelson (ed.), *Lands Guide: A Guide to Finding Records of Crown Land at Public Record Office Victoria* (Melbourne: Public Record Office Victoria in association with Gould Genealogy and History, 2009), 32–3.
42 BDM VIC, *Deaths*. 1918/4732.
43 PROV, *Probate and Administration Files*. P3/858.
44 PROV, *Land 'Selection' Files*. VPRS 626/P0/2420/9553.
45 Shirley Ward, *Destiny of Gold*, 200–203.
46 PROV, *Probate and Administration Files*. P2/394.
47 PROV, *Wills*. P2/228.
48 AEC, *Australian Electoral Rolls*. 1903, Laaneecoorie, 6, and 1909, Ballarat, 10.
49 BDM VIC, *Deaths*. 1912/8335.
50 PROV, *Probate and Administration Files*. P2/763.
51 PROV, *Probate and Administration Files*. P2/702.
52 PROV, *Land 'Selection' Files*. VPRS 625/P0/122/6649.
53 PROV, *Land 'Selection' Files*. VPRS 625/P0/122/6649.
54 BDM VIC, *Deaths*. 1896/2014.
55 PROV, Probate and Administration Files. P2/434.
56 PROV, *Wills*. P2/249.
57 BDM VIC, *Births*. 1893/4202.
58 BDM VIC, *Marriages*. 1873/3.
59 AEC, *Australian Electoral Rolls*. 1909, 1914 and 1924, Yea, 1.
60 BDM VIC, *Deaths*. 1928/8225.
61 Charles Fahey, 'The free selector's landscape', 98.
62 AEC, *Australian Electoral Rolls*. 1903, Gippsland, 1.
63 AEC, *Australian Electoral Rolls*. 1917, Gippsland, 20.
64 BDM VIC, *Deaths*. 1971/24914.
65 BDM VIC, *Deaths*. 1877/6706.
66 BDM VIC, *Deaths*. 1900/7272.
67 PROV, *Probate and Administration Files*. P3/1622.
68 PROV, *Parish & Town Plans*. Narracan South, Allots 1, 2 and 3.
69 PROV, *Probate and Administration Files*. P3/1379 and 2062.
70 PROV, *Land 'Selection' Files*. VPRS 629/P0/30/5389.
71 *Bendigo Advertiser*, Saturday 18 April 1868, 2.
72 PROV, *Land 'Selection' Files*. VPRS 625/P0/200/12423-12424 and 353/24567.
73 PROV, *Correspondence regarding selections of Mr John Ettershank, Part VPRS 1016*, Public Records Office of Victoria, Melbourne, 1872–1896. P0/02.
74 *Age*, Saturday 4 October 1873, 4.
75 *Age*, Saturday 4 October, 1873, 4.
76 PROV, *Inward Overseas Passenger Lists (British Ports)*. Fiche 022, 2.

77 Ettershank, John (1832–1912) in 'Obituaries Australia', National Centre of Biography, Australian National University, Canberra http://oa.anu.edu.au/obituary/ettershank-john-355; Ian Itter, *John Ettershank: The Red Brick Woolshed* (Swan Hill, Victoria: Ian Itter, 2013).
78 'Albert Graving Dock' in Victoria Heritage Database, Heritage Council Victoria, Melbourne. Place ID 1231, https://vhd.heritagecouncil.vic.gov.au/places/1231/download-report .
79 Ettershank, John (1832–1912) in *Obituaries Australia* http://oa.anu.edu.au/obituary/ettershank-john-355; Ian Itter, *John Ettershank: The Red Brick Woolshed*, 20–8.
80 PROV, *Correspondence regarding selections of Mr John Ettershank*. P0/02.
81 Edmund F. Moore, *The Law Reports 1875* (Reprint, London: Forgotten Books, 2013), 360–5.
82 PROV, Correspondence regarding selections of Mr John Ettershank. P0/02.
83 PROV, *Land 'Selection' Files*. VPRS 625/P0/12424.
84 PRO, *Census Returns of England and Wales, 1841*. 571/1/8/9.
85 Geoffrey Blainey, *A History of Victoria*, 58–9.
86 PROV, *Land 'Selection' Files*. VPRS 625/P0/200/12423-12424 and /353/24567.
87 BDM VIC, *Deaths*. 1882/2090.
88 *Bendigo Advertiser*, Tuesday 20 September 1881, 2.
89 *Bendigo Advertiser*, various 1884–1912.
90 Ian Itter, *John Ettershank: The Red Brick Woolshed*; PROV, *Probate and Administration Files*. P2/4880210.
91 Donald Horne, *The Lucky Country* (2nd rev. edn, Ringwood, Vic.: Penguin, 1998), 15–19.

Chapter 10: An Advancing Civilisation

1 *Age*, Wednesday 22 October 1879, 3–4.
2 Graeme Davison, *The Rise and Fall of Marvellous Melbourne* (Carlton, Victoria: Melbourne University Press, 2004), 7.
3 James Belich, *Replenishing the Earth*, 79–99.
4 John Darwin, *After Tamerlane: The Global History of Empire Since 1405* (New York: Bloomsbury, 2008), 253–4.
5 Graeme Davison, *Marvellous Melbourne*, 7.
6 BDM VIC, *Deaths*. 1939/7701.
7 PROV, *Wills*. P2/1081.
8 AEC, *Australian Electoral Rolls*. 1914, 1919, 1924 and 1936, Footscray.
9 *Mount Alexander Mail* (Castlemaine). Thursday 16 October 1861, 2.
10 Graeme Davison, *Lost Relations*, 124.
11 Alan Birch, 'Economists and railways in colonial Australia: a note', *The Journal of Transport History*, 7/3 (1966), 180–3.
12 Geoffrey Serle, *The Golden Age*, 237.
13 *Mount Alexander Mail*, Thursday 16 October 1861, 2.
14 Graeme Davison, *Lost Relations*, 124–5.
15 *Mount Alexander Mail*, Tuesday 20 October 1885, 3; Saturday 12 May, 1883, 2.
16 PROV, *Register of Assisted British Immigrants*. 6/35/4–9.
17 PRO, *Census Returns of England and Wales, 1851*. 2193/145/48 and 42–54.
18 PROV, *Register of Assisted British Immigrants*. 6/35/4–9.
19 BDM VIC, *Births*. 1854/960 and 1858/290.
20 BDM VIC, *Births*. 1861/5262; BDM VIC, *Deaths*. 1863/6250.
21 The Terang Dairy Coop is still a substantial dairy producer in Terang and the surrounding region and occupies the premise of one of the original dairy factories in the township.
22 PROV, *Parish & Town Plans*. Terang Township, 5778.
23 PROV, *Probate and Administration Files*. P0/923 and P2/522.
24 PROV, *Register of Assisted British Immigrants*. 8/142/54–7.
25 PRO, *Census Returns of England and Wales*, 1851. 2180/96/12.
26 SLV, *Victorian Electoral Roll 1856–57*. Portland, 4.
27 PROV, *Probate and Administration Files*. P0/264.
28 BDM VIC, *Births*. 1856/13442.
29 BDM VIC, *Births*. 1858/7757, 1859/14610, 1861/8694, 1863/5632, 1865/129 and 1866/5946.
30 BDM VIC, *Deaths*. 1877/50.

31 PROV, *Probate and Administration Files*. P0/264.
32 PROV, *Wills*. P2/67.
33 PROV, *Probate and Administration Files*. P0/264.
34 BDM VIC, *Deaths*. 1893/12649.
35 BDM VIC, *Deaths*. 1877/41.
36 PROV, *Probate and Administration Files*. P0/69 and P2/379.
37 BDM VIC, Deaths. 1942/24706; PROV, *Wills*. P2/1174/333/132; PROV, *Probate and Administration Files*. P3/1034/171/104.
38 *Ancestry.com*. https://www.ancestryinstitution.com/family-tree/person/tree/114723749/4101334420726/story.
39 BDM VIC, *Deaths*. 1898/10556.
40 *Ballarat Star*, Wednesday 27 July 1898, 2; Saturday 30 July 1898, 2.
41 PROV, *Probate and Administration Files*. P2/507.
42 *Ballarat Star*, Friday 17 May 1895, 3.
43 *Ballarat Star*, various articles from 1880–1898.
44 Shirley Ward, *Destiny of Gold*, 87–95, 157–63 and 200–4.
45 PROV, *Probate and Administration Files*. P2/389.
46 PROV, *Wills*. P2/225.
47 PROV, *Probate and Administration Files*. P3/292.
48 Graeme Davison, *Marvellous Melbourne*, 7.
49 Richard Broome, *Arriving*, 76.
50 PROV, *Teachers Record Books*. 3651.
51 BDM VIC, *Marriages*. 1881/3052.
52 PROV, *Teachers Record Books, Part VPRS 13654/P2*, Public Records Office of Victoria, Melbourne. 618.
53 PROV, *Teachers Record Books*. 3651.
54 PROV, *Teachers Record Books*. 618.
55 PROV, *Teachers Record Books*. 3651.
56 AEC, *Australian Electoral Rolls*. 1909, Corio, 23.
57 BDM VIC, *Deaths*. 1940/19523.
58 PROV, *Probate and Administration Files*. P3/3432.
59 PROV, *Wills*. P2/1121.
60 *Geelong Advertiser*, Wednesday 18 September 1940, 4.
61 Richard Trembath and Donna Hellier, *All Care and Responsibility: A History of Nursing in Victoria 1850–1934* (Melbourne: Florence Nightingale Committee Australia, 1986), 7–9.
62 Richard Trembath and Donna Hellier, *All Care and Responsibility*, 7–9 and 20.
63 Quoted in Richard Trembath and Donna Hellier, *All Care and Responsibility*, 10–11.
64 Richard Trembath and Donna Hellier, *All Care and Responsibility*, 32–8.
65 Various quotes by different individuals in Richard Trembath and Donna Hellier, *All Care and Responsibility*, 24.
66 BDM VIC, *Deaths*. 1887/353 and 1925/3908.
67 Richard Trembath and Donna Hellier, *All Care and Responsibility*, 27–8.
68 BDM VIC, *Marriages*. 1858/3939.
69 BDM VIC, *Births*. 1858/13473.
70 BDM VIC, *Births*. 1879/18313.
71 AEC, *Australian Electoral Rolls*. 1903, Ballarat, 8.
72 BDM VIC, *Marriages*. 1887/1573.
73 PROV, *Register of Assisted British Immigrants*. 6/131/1230.
74 PRO, *Census Returns of England and Wales, 1851*. 2212/367/22/80.
75 Michelle M. Knehans, 'The archaeology and history of pharmacy in Victoria', *Australasian Historical Archaeology*, 23 (2005), 41–6.
76 Michelle M. Knehans, 'The archaeology and history of pharmacy in Victoria', 42.
77 PROV, *Probate and Administration Files*. P2/322.
78 BDM VIC, *Marriages*. 1875/2539.
79 'Wheeler, Hon. James Henry' in *The Dictionary of Australasian Biography*.
80 PROV, *Probate and Administration Files*. P2/249.
81 BDM VIC, *Births*. 1876/15532, 1880/14995, 1883/22923, 1891/2560 and 1893/30905.

82 AEC, *Australian Electoral Rolls.* 1903-1919, Footscray.
83 PROV, *Probate and Administration Files.* P2/677.
84 BDM VIC, *Deaths.* 1919/18647.
85 PROV, *Probate and Administration Files.* P3/3351.

Chapter 11: Marvellous Melbourne

1   *Age*, Saturday 8 August 1885, 5.
2   Graeme Davison, 'Marvellous Melbourne' in *The Encyclopedia of Melbourne*, School of Historical Studies, Department of History, University of Melbourne, Melbourne http://www.emelbourne.net.au/biogs/EM00906b.htm.
3   *Age*, Saturday 8 August 1885, 5.
4   Graeme Davison, 'Marvellous Melbourne' in *The Encyclopedia of Melbourne*.
5   *Age, Saturday* 8 August 1885, 5.
6   Graeme Davison, *Marvellous Melbourne*, 1–28.
7   Donald Horne, *The Lucky Country*, 15–19.
8   Kenneth T. Jackson, *Crabgrass Frontier* (New York & Oxford: Oxford University Press, 1985), 3–11 and 304–5.
9   Graeme Davison, 'Australia: The First Suburban Nation?', 41.
10 Graeme Davison, 'Australia: The First Suburban Nation?', 54–9.
11 Graeme Davison, 'Australia: The First Suburban Nation?', 58.
12 BDM VIC, *Deaths.* 1852/21428.
13 PROV, *Register of Assisted British Immigrants.* 7/72/136-141 and 7/78/343.
14 SLV, *Victorian Electoral Roll 1856–57.* Jolimont, 28.
15 PRO, *Census Returns of England and Wales, 1851.* 2191/190/60/190.
16 SLV, *Victorian Electoral Roll 1856–57.* Collingwood, 36.
17 SLV, *Victorian Electoral Roll 1856–57.* Collingwood, 49.
18 SLV, *Victorian Electoral Roll 1856–57.* Fitzroy, 48.
19 Church of England, *Marriage Registers*, Melbourne, 1848–1955, 1937.
20 BDM VIC, *Deaths.* 1877/4804 and 1881/5526.
21 Sands & McDougall, *Melbourne and Suburban Directory* (Melbourne: Sands and McDougall, 1862–1880). 1865, 123. John and David moved into Hoddle Street in 1863 but did not start operating their businesses respectively until 1864 and 1865.
22 Sands & McDougall, *Melbourne and Suburban Directory*, 1865, 94.
23 Sands & McDougall, *Melbourne and Suburban Directory*, 1865, 230.
24 Anna Clark, *The Struggle for the Breeches*, various.
25 Graeme Davison, *Marvellous Melbourne*, 101–6.
26 Sands & McDougall, *Melbourne and Suburban Directory.* 1863, 117–18.
27 Sands & McDougall, *Melbourne and Suburban Directory.* 1872, 120–1.
28 PROV, *Collingwood Rate Books, Part VPRS 377*, Public Records Office of Melbourne, Melbourne. 1872/37.
29 PROV, *Fitzroy Rate Books, Part VPRS 4301*, Public Records Office of Victoria, Melbourne. 1867/146/2899.
30 Sands & McDougall, *Melbourne and Suburban Directory.* 1871, 463.
31 PROV, *Collingwood Rate Books, Part VPRS 2340*, Public Record Office of Victoria, Melbourne. 1885/192/7495.
32 PROV, *Collingwood Rate Books.* 1876/39–40/1485–8.
33 BDM VIC, *Deaths.* 1877/8364.
34 BDM VIC, *Marriages.* 1868/4090.
35 PROV, *Collingwood Rate Books.* 1878/40/1485–8.
36 PROV, *Fitzroy Rate Books.* 1861–1864/2600–1.
37 PROV, *Fitzroy Rate Books.* 1871/107/56.
38 Peter Stanley and Lyndsay Cox, *The Remote Garrison: The British Army in Australia 1788–1870* (Kenthurst, NSW: Kangaroo Press, 1986), 127–8.
39 *Collingwood Observer* (Collingwood). Friday 12 March 1886, 1.
40 Graeme Davison, *Marvellous Melbourne*, 184–5.
41 *Argus*, Saturday 30 August 1884, 13.

42 PROV, *Probate and Administration Files*. P3/114.
43 PROV, *Fitzroy Rate Books*. 1878–1879/280/4–5 and 1889–1890/299/2–3.
44 PROV, *Fitzroy Rate Books*. 1889–1890/340–2.
45 PROV, *Fitzroy Rate Books*. 1890/280–2.
46 AEC, *Australian Electoral Rolls*. 1903, North Melbourne, 18.
47 BDM VIC, *Deaths*. 1890/6416.
48 James Ballantyne, *Homes and Homesteads in the Land of Plenty* (Melbourne: Mason, Firth & McCutcheon, 1871), 115–17.
49 SLV, *Victorian Electoral Roll 1856–57*. Abbotsford, 7.
50 BDM VIC, *Births*. 1855/3145, 1856/10734, 1858/428, and 1859/10838.
51 PROV, *Outward Passengers to Interstate, UK, NZ and Foreign Ports 1852–1923*. 1860/Apr/2.
52 PRO, *Census Returns of England and Wales, 1861*, National Archives of the UK, London, 1861. RG9/2720/101/16/74.
53 PROV, *Inward Overseas Passenger Lists (British Ports)*. 1888/April/496/3.
54 SLV, *Victorian Electoral Roll 1856–57*. Collingwood, 9.
55 VPP, *Victorian Government Gazette*. G/G792/1023-4 and G/G3317/2047.
56 Sands & McDougall, *Melbourne and Suburban Directory*. 1880, 640; PROV, *Probate and Administration Files*. P3/873; BDM VIC, *Deaths*. 1876/2343.
57 BDM VIC, *Deaths*. 1871/8082.
58 PROV, *Probate and Administration Files*. P3/873.
59 PROV, *Register of Assisted British Immigrants*. 7/49/333.
60 PRO, *Census Returns of England and Wales, 1851*. 2188/417/17/62.
61 BDM VIC, *Marriages*. 1855/106.
62 PRO, *Census Returns of England and Wales, 1841*. 559/26/1.
63 PRO, *Census Returns of England and Wales, 1851*. 2188/417/17/62.
64 Church of England, *Marriage Registers*. 1855/496.
65 PROV, *Outward Passengers to Interstate, UK, NZ and Foreign Ports 1852–1923*. 1856/Nov/2.
66 SLV, *Victorian Electoral Roll 1856–57*. Melbourne, 72 and Richmond, 13.
67 Sands & Kenny, *Commercial and General Melbourne Directory* (Melbourne: Sands, Kenny and Co, 1857–1861); Sands & McDougall, *Melbourne and Suburban Directory*.
68 Graeme Davison, *Marvellous Melbourne*, 22–8.
69 PROV, *Caulfield Shire Rate Books, Part VPRS 2334*, Public Records Office of Victoria, Melbourne. 1878–1894.
70 BDM VIC, *Deaths*. 1895/14995.
71 PROV, *Probate and Administration Files*. P2/423; PROV, Wills. P2/244.
72 BDM VIC, *Deaths*. 1898/18166; PROV, Probate and Administration Files. P2/501.
73 PROV, *Wills*. P2/284.
74 Anna Clark, *The Struggle for the Breeches*, 1–25.
75 PROV, *Register of Assisted British Immigrants*. 7/50/363-364.
76 PRO, *Census Returns of England and Wales, 1851*. 2257/134/13/53.
77 PRO, *Census Returns of England and Wales, 1841*. 507/16/6.
78 PROV, *Rate Books of North and South Melbourne, Part VPRS 2332*, Public Records Office of Victoria, Melbourne. 1859/20/620 and 1866/41/1276.
79 BDM VIC, *Births*. 1854/1372.
80 BDM VIC, *Births*. 1855/101466, 1857/5246, 1861/2561, 1863/10278, 1865/11006, 1867/10456, 1869/18018, 1872/25651, and 1874/18440.
81 Sands & Kenny, *Commercial and General Melbourne Directory*. 1859, 137.
82 Sands & McDougall, *Melbourne and Suburban Directory*. 1865, 234 and 351.
83 Vicki Peel, Hawthorn in *The Encyclopedia of Melbourne*. http://www.emelbourne.net.au/biogs/EM00693b.htm.
84 PROV, *Hawthorn Rate Books, Part VPRS 2339*, Public Records Office of Victoria, Melbourne. 1889–1899.
85 PRO, *Census Returns of England and Wales, 1851*. 2185/118/14/38.
86 PROV, *Register of Assisted British Immigrants*. 9/64/266.
87 BDM VIC, *Marriages*. 1855/2573.
88 BDM VIC, *Births*. 1856/9156 and 1858/12768.
89 AEC, *Australian Electoral Rolls*. 1903, North Melbourne, 34.

90 PROV, *Kew Rate Books, Part VPRS 2338*, Public Record Office of Victoria, Melbourne. 1891, P0, 3 and 1896, P01, 4.
91 BDM VIC, *Deaths*. 1908/7186.
92 AEC, *Australian Electoral Rolls*. 1903, North Melbourne, 34.
93 Graeme Davison, *Marvellous Melbourne*, 54.
94 AEC, *Australian Electoral Rolls*. 1917, Northcote, 4.
95 Graeme Davison, *Marvellous Melbourne*, 101–6.
96 Geoffrey Blainey, *A History of Victoria*, 147.
97 Geoffrey Blainey, *A History of Victoria*, 148.
98 Geoffrey Blainey, *A History of Victoria*, 149–51; Graeme Davison, *Marvellous Melbourne*, 243–50.
99 PROV, *Fitzroy Rate Books*. 1889/274–9 and 1900/280–5.

Chapter 12: We Did Not Come All This Way to Tug Forelocks

1 *Age*, Tuesday 7 June 1859, 4.
2 David Fitzpatrick, *Oceans of consolation*.
3 Eric Richards, 'British emigrants and the making of the anglosphere', 305.
4 *Age*, Tuesday 7 June 1859, 4.

BIBLIOGRAPHY

Primary Sources

Archives

AEC, *Australian Electoral Rolls*, Australian Electoral Commission, Victoria.

Colonial Land and Emigration Commission, *Colonization Circular* (2nd edn, London: Colonial Land and Emigration Commission, 1852).

GRO, *England and Wales Civil Registration Indexes*, General Register Office, London, England.

Manchester City Archives, *Manchester Rate Books 1706–1900*, Manchester City Council, Manchester.

Mining Department, *Surveyors' Reports for June 1863* (Melbourne: Victorian Government, 1863).

—, *Surveyors' Reports for January 1863* (Melbourne: Victorian Government, 1863).

PRO, *Census Returns of England and Wales, 1841, Part HO 107*, National Archives of the UK, London, 1841.

—, *Census Returns of England and Wales, 1851, Part HO 107*, National Archives of the UK, London, 1851.

—, *Census Returns of England and Wales, 1861*, National Archives of the UK, London, 1861.

PROV, *Ballarat Rate Valuation Books, Part VPRS 7265 and 7299*, Ballarat Archives Centre, Ballarat.

—, *Bill of Sales Filed, Part VPRS 8350*, Public Records Office of Victoria, Melbourne.

—, *Castlemaine Rate Books, Part VPRS 409*, Public Records Office of Victoria, Melbourne.

—, *Caulfield Shire Rate Books, Part VPRS 2334*, Public Records Office of Victoria, Melbourne.

—, *Collingwood Rate Books, Part VPRS 377*, Public Records Office of Melbourne, Melbourne.

—, *Collingwood Rate Books, Part VPRS 2340*, Public Records Office of Victoria, Melbourne.

—, *Fitzroy Rate Books, Part VPRS 4301*, Public Records Office of Victoria, Melbourne.

—, *Hawthorn Rate Books, Part VPRS 2339*, Public Records Office of Victoria, Melbourne.

—, *Inward Overseas Passenger Lists (British Ports), Part VPRS 7666*, Public Records Office of Victoria, Melbourne.

—, *Kew Rate Books, Part VPRS 2338*, Public Records Office of Victoria, Melbourne.

—, *Land 'Selection' Files*, Public Records Office of Victoria, Melbourne.

—, *Outward Passengers to Interstate, UK, NZ and Foreign Ports 1852–1923, Part VPRS 3506*, Public Records Office of Victoria, Victoria.

—, *Parish & Town Plans, Part VPRS 16171/P1*, Public Records Office of Victoria, Melbourne.

—, *Probate and Administration Files, Part VPRS 28*, Public Records Office of Victoria, Melbourne.

—, *Rate Books of North and South Melbourne, Part VPRS 2332*, Public Records Office of Victoria, Melbourne.

—, *Teachers Record Books, Part VPRS 13654/P2*, Public Records Office of Victoria, Melbourne.

—, *Wills, Part VPRS 7591*, Public Records Office of Victoria, Melbourne.

—, *Register of Assisted British Immigrants, Part VPRS 7310*, Public Records Office of Victoria, Melbourne, 1839–1871.

—, *Teachers Record Books, Part VPRS 13719/P1*, Public Records Office of Victoria, Melbourne, 1863–1959.

—, *Correspondence Regarding Selections of Mr John Ettershank, Part VPRS 1016*, Public Records Office of Victoria, Melbourne, 1872–1896.

The National Archives, *Registry of Friendly Societies*, Registry of Friendly Societies, London, 1832–1912.

—, *Colonial Office: Emigration Entry Books*, War and Colonial Department and Colonial Office, London, 1840–1855.

—, *Colonial Office: Land & Emigration Commission, etc.*, Land & Emigration Commission, London, 1840–1855.

Births, Deaths and Marriages

BDM VIC, *Births*, The Victorian Registry of Births, Deaths and Marriages, Victoria.
—, *Deaths*, The Victorian Registry of Births, Deaths and Marriages, Victoria.
—, *Marriages*, The Victorian Registry of Births, Deaths and Marriages, Victoria.
Church of England, *Marriage Registers*, Melbourne, 1848–1955.

Parliamentary Papers

BPP, *Submission from Manchester's Factory Children Committee to the House of Commons*, House of Commons, London, 1838.
—, *Select Committee on Votes of Electors*, House of Commons, London, 1846.
—, *Report of the General Board of Health on the Epidemic Cholera of 1848 & 1849*, House of Commons, London, 1850.
—, *The Sixth Annual Report of the Poor Law Board* (London: House of Commons, 1853).
—, *Thirteenth General Report of the Colonial Land and Emigration Commissioners with Appendix 1852–1853* (London: Houses of Parliament, 1853).
—, *Seventh Annual Report of the Poor Law Board* (London: Houses of Parliament, 1854).
—, *Further Papers Relative to Discovery of Gold in Australia*, House of Commons, London, 1856.
Registrar General, Victoria, *Census of Victoria* (Melbourne: J. Ferris, Government Publisher).
SLV, *Victorian Electoral Roll 1856–57*, Library Council of Victoria and State Library of Victoria, Melbourne, 1987.
VPP, *Victorian Government Gazette*, Melbourne.
—, *Census of Victoria for the Year 1851*, John Ferres, Government Printing Office, Melbourne, 1852.
—, *Census of Victoria for the Year 1891: Part III. Religions of the People: Population Enumerated on the 5th April, 1891*, Robt. S. Bain, Government Printing Office, Melbourne, 1892.
—, *Gold Fields' Commission of Enquiry: Report of the Commission Appointed to Enquire into the Condition of the Gold Fields of Victoria, &c. &c, Parliamentary Paper (Victorian Parliament)*, John Ferres, Government Printer, Melbourne, 1855, <http://www.parliament.vic.gov.au/papers/govpub/VPARL1854-55NoA76p[i]-lxxii.pdf
http://www.parliament.vic.gov.au/papers/govpub/VPARL1854-55NoA76p1-180.pdf
http://www.parliament.vic.gov.au/papers/govpub/VPARL1854-55NoA76p181-365.pdf>
—, *Mining Resources of the Colony of Victoria: Second Progress Report of the Commissioners Appointed to Enquire into the Mining Resources of the Colony, Parliamentary paper (Victorian Parliament)*, John Ferres, Government Printer, Melbourne, 1857, <http://www.parliament.vic.gov.au/papers/govpub/VPARL1856-57No84.pdf>.

Encyclopedias, Dictionaries, Directories

The Dictionary of Australasian Biography.
Pigot and co., *Pigot's Manchester & Salford Directory 1833* (Manchester: Pigot and Co., 1833).
—, *Pigot's Manchester and Salford Directory, 1838* (Manchester: Pigot and Co., 1838).
Sands & Kenny, *Commercial and General Melbourne Directory* (Melbourne: Sands, Kenny and Co, 1857–1861).
Sands & McDougall, *Melbourne and Suburban Directory* (Melbourne: Sands and McDougall, 1862–1880).

Manuscripts

Clendinning, Martha, *Recollections of Ballarat: A Lady's Life at the Diggings Fifty Years Ago*, Australian Manuscripts Collection, MS 10102/1 (Melbourne: State Library of Victoria, 1892).
Council of the Convention, 'Proceedings, and Documents of the Victorian Convention', Victorian Convention, Melbourne.
Dash, Edward, 'Journal of a voyage by the ship Ann Dashwood from Liverpool to Australia 1853', Vaughan Evans Library, Australian Maritime Museum, MS ANN 151359.
Hall, Richard, 'The diary of Richard Hall of Bury, Lancashire, England: voyage to Australia in the ship Kate', 1852–54, Vaughan Evans Library, Australian Maritime Museum, MS KAT 198459.
La Trobe, Charles Joseph, Papers of Charles Joseph La Trobe (Melbourne).
Preston, Richard, 'Undated Letter', *Letters 1852–1854*, Liverpool Maritime Museum, SAS/3/1/12(c).

Newspapers

Age (Melbourne).
Argus (Melbourne, Vic.).
Ballarat Star (Ballarat, Vic.).
Bathurst Free Press (Bathurst, NSW).
Bendigo Advertiser (Bendigo).
Bendigo Independent (Bendigo).
Collingwood Observer (Collingwood).
Creswick & Clunes Advertiser (Creswick).
Geelong Advertiser (Geelong, Vic.).
Manchester Examiner and Times (Manchester).
Mount Alexander Mail (Castlemaine).
Nottinghamshire Guardian (London).
Sydney Morning Herald (Sydney).

Books

Ballantyne, James, *Homes and Homesteads in the Land of Plenty* (Melbourne: Mason, Firth & McCutcheon, 1871).
Brown, Henry, *Victoria As I Found It, during Five Years of Adventure* (London: T. Cautley Newby, 1862).
Clacy, Ellen, *A Lady's Visit to the Gold Diggings of Australia in 1852–53* (London: Hirst and Blackett, 1853).
Cooper, Thomas, *The Life of Thomas Cooper: Written by Himself* (London: Hodder and Stoughton, 1872).
Craig, William, *My Adventures on the Australian Goldfields* (London & Melbourne: Cassell and Company, 1903).
Hall, William H., *Practical Experience at the Diggings of the Goldfields of Victoria* (London: Effingham Wilson, 1852).
Mereweather, J.D., *Diary of a Working Clergyman, in Australia and Tasmania 1850–1853* (London, 1859).
Parker, Critchley, *Victoria and Its Mining Resources* (London: Australian Mining Standard under the authority of Victorian Mines Department, 1908).
Rusden, George William, *History of Australia* (Melbourne: Melville, Mullen & Slade, 1897).
Turner, Henry Gyles, *A History of the Colony of Victoria* (Melbourne: Longmans, Green, 1904).
Tyler, Mary Ann, *The Adventurous Memoirs of a Gold Diggeress* (Wellington, NSW: Kate Gibbs, 1985).
Wakefield, E.G., *A Letter from Sydney* (London: Joseph Cross, 1829).
Withers, W.B., *History of Ballarat and Some Ballarat Reminiscences* (Ballarat: Ballarat Heritage Services, 1999).

Secondary Sources

Encyclopedias and Databases

Ancestry.com (Provo, UT, US: Ancestry.com Operations Inc).
Australian Dictionary of Biography (Canberra: National Centre of Biography, Australian National University).
The Encyclopedia of Melbourne (Melbourne: School of Historical Studies, Department of History, University of Melbourne <http://www.emelbourne.net.au>).
Grace's Guide to British Industrial History (UK: Grace's Guide Ltd http://www.gracesguide.co.uk).
Obituaries Australia (Canberra: National Centre of Biography, Australian National University).
Victoria Heritage Database (Melbourne: Heritage Council Victoria).
The Cambridge History of the British Empire, vol. 7 pt. 1, s.v. 'Australia'.
Jupp, James, *The Australian People: An Encyclopedia of the Nation, Its People and their Origins* (Melbourne: Cambridge University Press, 2001).
McAdie, Marion, *Mining Shareholders Index 1857–1886* (Marion McAdie, 2006).
The NSW State Archives, *State Records Archives Investigator* (NSW Government, New South Wales, 2014).

Bibliography

Books

Baines, Dudley, *Migration in a Mature Economy: Emigration and Internal Migration in England and Wales, 1861–1900*, Cambridge studies in population, economy and society in past time 3 ([Pbk edn, Cambridge: Cambridge University Press, 2002).

Baines, Dudley, and Economic History Society, *Emigration from Europe, 1815-1930*, New studies in economic and social history (1st Cambridge University Press edn, Cambridge; New York: Cambridge University Press, 1995).

Bate, Weston, *Lucky City: The First Generation at Ballarat 1851–1901* (Melbourne: Melbourne University Press, 1978).

—, *Victorian Gold Rushes* (Fitzroy, Victoria: McPhee Gribble/Penguin, 1988).

Belchem, John (ed.), *Popular Politics, Riot and Labour: Essays in Liverpool History 1790* (Liverpool: Liverpool University Press, 1992).

Belich, James, *Replenishing the Earth: The Settler Revolution and the Rise of the Anglo-World, 1783–1939* (Oxford: Oxford University Press, 2009).

Bell, Duncan, *The Idea of Greater Britain: Empire and the Future of World Order, 1860–1900* (Princeton: Princeton University Press, 2007).

Blainey, Geoffrey, *A History of Victoria* (2nd edn, Melbourne: Cambridge University Press, 2013).

Borrie, W. D., *The European Peopling of Australasia: A Demographic History, 1788–1988* (Canberra: Demography Program, Research School of Social Sciences, Australian National University, 1994).

Brooking, Tom, *King of God's Own* (Auckland: Penguin Books, 2014).

Broome, Richard, *Arriving, The Victorians* (McMahons Point, NSW: Fairfax, Syme & Weldon Associates, 1984).

Brown, Richard, *Chartism*, Perspectives in History (Cambridge: Cambridge University Press, 1998).

Burton, Valerie (ed.), *Liverpool Shipping, Trade and Industry: Essays on Maritime History* (Merseyside: National Museums and Galleries on Merseyside, 1989).

Bythell, Duncan, *The Handloom Weavers: A Study in the English Cotton Industry during the Industrial Revolution* (Cambridge: Cambridge University Press, 1969).

Chase, Malcolm, *Chartism: A New History* (Manchester: Manchester University Press, 2007).

Chilton, Lisa, *Agents of Empire: British Female Migration to Canada and Australia, 1860s–1930* (Toronto: University of Toronto Press, 2007).

Clark, Anna, *The Struggle for the Breeches: Gender and the Making of the British Working Class* (Berkeley, Los Angeles, London: University of California, 1997).

Darwin, John, *After Tamerlane: The Global History of Empire Since 1405* (New York: Bloomsbury, 2008).

—, *The Empire Project: The Rise and Fall of the British World-System, 1830–1970* (Cambridge: Cambridge University Press, 2011).

Davidof, L., and Hall C., *Family Fortunes* (London and New York: Routledge, 2002).

Davison, Graeme, *The Rise and Fall of Marvellous Melbourne* (Carlton, Victoria: Melbourne University Press, 2004).

—, *Lost Relations* (Crows Nest, Sydney: Allen & Unwin, 2015).

Denoon, Donald, *Settler Capitalism: The Dynamics of Dependent Development in the Southern Hemisphere* (Oxford: Oxford University Press, 1983).

Engels, Friedrich, *The Condition of the Working-class in England in 1844*, Social science series (London: Allen and Unwin, 1950).

Erickson, Charlotte, *Leaving England: Essays on British Emigration in the Nineteenth Century* (Ithaca, NY: Cornell University Press, 1994).

Fahey, Charles, and Mayne, Alan (eds), *Gold Tailings: Forgotten Histories of Family and Community on the Central Victorian Goldfields* (North Melbourne: Australian Scholarly Publishing, 2010).

Feldman, David, and Baldwin, M. Page, 'Emigration and the British state, CA. 1815–1925' in Francois Weil and Nancy L. Green (ed.), *Citizenship and Those Who Leave: The Politics of Emigration and Expatriation* (Urbana and Chicago: University of Illinois Press, 2007), 135–55.

Fitzpatrick, David, *Oceans of Consolation: Personal Accounts of Irish Migration to Australia* (Carlton, Victoria: Melbourne University Press, 1995).

FitzSimons, Peter, *Eureka: The Unfinished Revolution* (North Sydney, NSW: William Heinemann Australia, 2012).

Goose, Nigel (ed.), *Women's Work in Industrial England*, Local Population Studies (Hatfield, Hertfordshire: Department of Humanities, University of Hertfordshire, 2007).
Haines, Robin, *Life and Death in the Age of Sail: The Passage to Australia* (Sydney: UNSW Press, 2003).
Haines, Robin F., *Emigration and the Labouring Poor: Australian Recruitment in Britain and Ireland, 1831–60* (New York: St Martin's Press, 1997).
Hammerton, A. James, *Emigrant Gentlewomen: Genteel Poverty and Female Emigration, 1830–1914* (London & Totowa, NJ: Croom Helm; Rowman and Littlefield, 1979).
Harper, Marjory, and Constantine, Stephen, *Migration and Empire* (Oxford: Oxford University Press, 2010).
Harzig, Christiane, Hoerder, Dirk, and Gabaccia, Donna R., *What Is Migration History?* (Cambridge: Polity, 2009).
Hewitt, Martin, *The Emergence of Stability in the Industrial City: Manchester, 1832–67* (Aldershot, Hants: Scolar Press, 1996).
Hill, David, *The Gold Rush: The Fever That Forever Changed Australia* (North Sydney, NSW: William Heinemann, 2011).
Horne, Donald, *The Lucky Country* (2nd rev. edn, Ringwood, Vic.: Penguin, 1998).
Itter, Ian, *John Ettershank: The Red Brick Woolshed* (Swan Hill, Victoria: Ian Itter, 2013).
Jackson, Kenneth T., *Crabgrass Frontier* (New York & Oxford: Oxford University Press, 1985).
Jupp, James, *The English in Australia* (Cambridge, England: Cambridge University Press, 2004).
Kidd, Alan, *Manchester: A History* (Lancaster: Carnegie Publishing Limited, 2006).
Macintyre, Stuart, *A Colonial Liberalism: The Lost World of Three Victorian Visionaries* (Oxford: Oxford University Press, 1991).
McCord, Norman, *The Anti-Corn Law League* (London: Unwin University Books, 1975).
Moore, Edmund F., *The Law Reports 1875* (Reprint, London: Forgotten Books, 2013).
Nelson, Phillippa (ed.), *Lands Guide: A Guide to Finding Records of Crown Land at Public Record Office Victoria* (Melbourne: Public Record Office Victoria in association with Gould Genealogy and History, 2009).
Pescod, Keith, *Good Food, Bright Fires & Civility: British Emigrant Depots of the 19th Century* (Kew, Vic.: Australian Scholarly Publishing, 2001).
Pickering, Paul A., *Chartism and the Chartists in Manchester and Salford* (New York: St. Martin, 1995).
Powell, J.M., *The Public Lands of Australia Felix* (Melbourne: Oxford University Press, 1970).
Reeves, Keir, and Nichol, David (eds), *Deeper Leads: New Approaches to Victorian Goldfields History* (Ballarat, Vic.: Ballarat Heritage Services, 2007).
Reid, Richard E, *Farewell My Children: Irish Assisted Emigration to Australia 1848-1870* (Spit Junction NSW: Anchor Books Australia, 2011).
Richard Trembath and Donna Hellier, *All care and responsibility: a history of nursing in Victoria 1850-1934* (Melbourne: Florence Nightingale Committee Australia, 1986).
Roberts, Alan J. Kidd and K. W. (ed.), *City, class and culture: Studies of social policy and cultural production in Victorian Manchester* (Manchester: Manchester University Press, 1985).
Serle, Geoffrey, *The Golden Age* (Melbourne: Melbourne University Press, 1963).
Sinclair, Keith, *A History of New Zealand* (Auckland: Penguin Books, 1980).
Stammers, Michael, *Liverpool: the port and its ships* (Phoenix Mill [England], Wolfeboro Falls, NH: Phoenix Mill England, Wolfeboro Falls, NH: A Sutton, 1991).
Stanley, Peter, and Cox, Lyndsay, *The Remote Garrison: The British Army in Australia 1788–1870* (Kenthurst, NSW: Kangaroo Press, 1986).
Tholfsen, Trygve, *Working-Class Radicalism in Mid-Victorian England* (London: Crom Helm, 1976).
Valenze, Deborah, *The First Industrial Woman* (New York: Oxford University Press, 1995).
Ward, Shirley, *Destiny of Gold* (Victoria: Shirley Ward, 1987).
Weaver, John C., *The Great Land Rush and the Making of the Modern World, 1650–1900* (Montreal, Ithaca: McGill-Queen's University Press, 2003).
Wright, Clare, *The Forgotten Rebels of Eureka* (Melbourne: The Text Publishing Company, 2013).

Journal Articles

Birch, Alan, 'Economists and railways in colonial Australia: A Note', *The Journal of Transport History*, 7/3 (1966), 180–3.

Davison, Graeme, 'Australia: the first suburban nation?', *Journal of Urban History*, 22/1 (1995), 40–74.

Fahey, Charles, 'The free selector's landscape: moulding the Victorian farming districts, 1870–1915', *Studies in the History of Gardens & Designed Landscapes*, 31/2 (2011), 97–108.

Falla, Ron, 'Land selection in the Wimmera [Based on an address to the Royal Historical Society of Victoria. State Conference (1999)]', *Victorian Historical Journal*, 71/2 (2000), 94–101.

Hammerton, A.J., '"Without natural protectors": female immigration to Australia, 1832–36', *Historical Studies*, 16/65 (1975), 539–66.

Hudson, Paul, and Mills, Dennis, 'English emigration, kinship and the recruitment process: migration from Melbourn in Cambridgeshire to Melbourne in Victoria in the mid-nineteenth century', *Rural History*, 10/01 (1999), 55–74.

Knehans, Michelle M., 'The archaeology and history of pharmacy in Victoria', *Australasian Historical Archaeology*, 23 (2005), 41–6.

MacDonagh, Oliver, 'Emigration and the state, 1833–55: an essay in administrative history', *Transactions of the Royal Historical Society*, 5 (1955), 133–59.

Pickering, Paul, 'A lesson lost?: Chartism and Australian democracy', *Agora*, 46/4 (2011), 4–10.

—, 'From rifle club to reading room: Sydney's democratic vistas, 1848–1856', *Labour History Review*, 78/1 (2013), 87–112.

Richards, Eric, 'British emigrants and the making of the Anglosphere', *History*, 103/355 (2018), 286–306.

Stone, Lawrence, 'Prosopography', *Daedalus*, 100/1 (1971), 46–79.

Turner, Richard, 'The apprenticeship of Richard Seddon', *Victorian Historical Journal*, 85/1 (2014), 97–118.

Winstanley, M., 'Industrialization and the small farm: family and household economy in nineteenth-century Lancashire', *Past & Present* 152 (1996), 157–95.

Theses and Unpublished Material

Holt, S. Colin, 'Family, kinship, community and friendship ties in assisted emigration from Cambridgeshire to Port Phillip District and Victoria, 1840–67' (PhD thesis, La Trobe University, 1987).

Schultz, R.J., 'The Assisted Immigrants, 1837–1850', PhD thesis (Australian National University, 1971).

Sutton, Les, 'Mainly about Ardwick', *Manchester City Collection*, f942.733915 Su1, Manchester Archives and Local Studies, 1975.

INDEX

This index is divided into the following groupings:

- The Migrants and Their Families
- Ships
- Lancashire Cities, Towns and Villages
- Victorian Counties, Parishes, Cities, Towns and Villages
- Goldfields, Mines and Mining Companies
- Other

The Migrants and Their Families

Aldous
   Thomas, 161
   Martha (née Lancaster) *see* Lancaster, Martha
Ashcroft
   Hannah, 24, 111, 124, 138
Ashworth
   William, 65
Atkinson
   William, 65, 96, 111, 137, 154
Bailey
   Elizabeth, 174, 175
   Margaret, 174
   Martha, 174
   Mary, 174
   Robert, 174, 175
   Thomas, 23, 92, 174–176
   Bailey family, 92, 174–177
Barker
   Alice Mary (née Rainford) *see* Rainford, Alice Mary
Barry
   Jane (née Lancaster) *see* Lancaster, Jane
   Stephen, 186
Bennett
   Charles, 61, 65, 95
Booth
   John, 96
Bowden
   James Bowden, 83
   Lucy *see* Doody, Lucy
Brewster
   Jane, 137
Burton
   Annie Elizabeth, 204
   Thomas, 203–207
Butler
   Anne *see* Proctor, Ann
   James, 65, 125–126, 143–146, 155
   John *see* Proctor, John
   Mary, 95, 109, 125, 143–145
   Thomas *see* Proctor, Thomas
   Butler family, 70, 94
Cornthwaite
   George, 162
   Isaac, 140, 162
   Jane (née Wiseman), 126
   John, 26, 29, 126, 139, 140, 162
   John Jnr, 162
   William, 140, 162
Cross
   Mary Jemima, 157
Dahl
   Fredrick Christian, 126, 140
Davis
   Frances (née Harley) *see* Harley, Frances
Dickinson
   Thomas, 96, 137, 154
Doody
   Ann, 80
   Catherine, 80
   Denis, 80–81
   Fanny (*née* Jameson), 132
   John, 80
   John Jnr, 80
   John Snr, 80
   Joseph, 2, 14, 21, 29, 79–83, 87, 88, 103, 111, 115, 121, 121–135, 142, 163–171
   Lucy (née Bowden), 2, 14, 21, 79, 83, 87–88, 125, 130–132
   Doody, Mary, 80–83
   William, 1, 2, 14, 25, 28, 79, 83, 130–133, 163–168
   Doody family, 2, 8, 14, 22, 28, 79, 88, 110, 126, 126–133, 163–169, 182
Ferris
   William Henry, 202–204, 207
   Ferris family, 207
Foley
   Mary, 66–67
   Sarah, 66, 91

238

Index

Foy
  Foy, Ann, 24, 111, 138–140
Francis
  John, 94– 95, 110, 137
Fraser
  Jane, 96
Guy
  Bridget, 177,–179
  Henry, 179
  James, 26, 113, 126, 172–179
  James Jnr, 179
  John, 136, 140, 159, 177
  John Jnr, 177
  Mary, 179
  Guy family, 111, 177
Halliday
  Elizabeth (née Lancaster) *see* Lancaster, Elizabeth
Harley
  Ellen Marion, 204
  Frances (née Davis), 186, 204, 207
  Frances Jnr, 204
  John, 204
  John Jnr, 204
  Millicent Francis, 204
  Harley family, 206–207
Holden
  Robert, 65
Holt
  Alice, 198
  Bella, 198
  David, 73, 194–197
  Edward, 73, 194–199
  Edward Jnr, 194–199
  George, 198
  Harriet, 73, 193–198
  Jane, 197–199
  John, 24, 27, 61, 65, 73, 95–199, 208
  Nellie, 198
  Richard, 193–197
  Samuel, 73, 193
  Holt family, 193, 199, 207, 208
Hugo
  Emma Louise, 24, 201–204
  Emma Snr, 201
  John, 202
  John Jnr, 202
Jameson
  Fanny *see* Doody, Fanny
Kearney
  Margaret, 67
Lancaster
  Edward, 162
  Elizabeth, 160
  Gordon William, 161
  Jane, 135, 186
  Joseph, 115, 135, 161
  Martha, 160
  Mary, 61, 66, 135, 160
  MaryAnn, 135
  Susannah, 135, 185–187
  Thomas, 135, 160–162
  William, 65–66, 115, 126, 135, 160–161
  Lancaster family, 186
Mack
  James, 200
  John, 200
  Thomas, 200
  William, 199–200
  William Jnr, 200
  Mack family, 31, 199
Marchant
  Jane *see* Proctor, Jane
Martin
  Henry, 135
Massey
  James, 65
Mayne
  Francis, 139
  John, 139
  John Jnr, 139
  Thomas, 139
Mercer
  Ann Circassia (née Wheeler), 188
  Maria, 135
  Parysatis, 14
  Smith, 61, 65, 96, 115, 135, 188
  William, 103, 115, 135, 154, 188
  William Jnr, 126, 134–136, 181, 187–190
  William III, 188
  Mercer family, 135
Morell
  Thomas, 195–197
Morey
  Edward, 29, 103, 111, 120–126, 140–143, 179
  Mary Ann (née Trickett), 26, 29, 120–126, 142–143, 177, 180, *see also* Trickett, Mary Ann
  Morey family, 115
Munday
  Henry, 138
Murray
  Jane, 126, 140
Oriel
  William, 186
  Jane *see* Lancaster, Jane
Padley
  Anna Maria, 196
Proctor
  Ann, 25–26, 144, 175, 181–182
  Anne, 94
  Francis, 158
  Henry, 158

Jane, 25, 158–159
John, 25, 145, 155–159
Thomas, 33, 143–144, 156–159
Proctor family, 29, 126, 146
Rainford
  Alice Mary (née Barker), 183–184
  Elizabeth, 150–151
  James, 1150–151
  James Jnr, 151
  John, 151
  Joseph, 150–151
  Thomas, 33, 150–151, 182–184
  Rainford family, 150
Reynolds
  Alice, 134
  Diana, 160
  James, 160, 172
  John, 134, 159–160
  Nancy, 160
  Thomas, 64, 126, 134, 159
  Thomas Jnr, 134
Rigby
  Anna Gertrude, 140
  Charlotte, 109, 111, 126, 140
  Charlotte Christina, 140
Seddon, 14, 58, 74, 111–114, 174, 185, 200
  Agnes, 74
  James, 8, 58, 74, 103, 200
  James Jnr, 73, 200–201
  John, 173–174, 200
  Joseph, 173–174, 200
  Robert, 74, 200
  Ruth, 58, 74, 200–201
  Ruth (jnr), 74
  Thomas, 200
  William, 74, 200, 208
  Seddon family, 8, 12, 29, 74, 174, 200–201
Shillington
  Samuel, 160
Slater
  Henry, 160
Smith
  Elizabeth, 67, 204
  Elizabeth A., 204–208
  James, 204
  Mary, 204
Sowcroft
  James, 64
Tait
  John Anderson, 126, 140
Trickett
  Alexander, 24–26, 120–125, 141–142
  Mary, 109
  Mary Ann, 61, 66–67, 103, 109, 127, *see also* Morey, Mary Ann
  Trickett family, 110–111, 115, 127, 140–141

Wheeler
  Ann Circassia *see* Mercer, Ann Circassia
Williams
  Richard, 186–187
Wiseman
  Jane *see* Cornthwaite, Jane
Wood
  Elizabeth, 20, 125, 136
  James, 20, 72, 136, 140, 154, 163
Woods
  James, 26, 65, 72, 92, 136, 154
  John, 113, 154
  Peter, 154
  William, 136, 154
  Woods family, 110, 113, 150

Ships

Ann Thompson, 140
Araminta, 55, 175
Blue Jacket, 140
Borneuf, 90, 137
British Queen, 91
Confiance, 138
Derry Castle, 135
Eagle, 199
Garland, 139
Hope, 121, 201, 204
Kate, 18
Kohinoor, 120
London, 97
Marco Polo, 90
Morning Light, 202
Red Jacket, 132
Royal George, 139
Thames, 2, 8, 14, 58
Ticonderoga, 90
Wanata, 16, 144, 157

Lancashire Cities, Towns and Villages

Blackburn, 69, 204
Bolton, 58, 75, 132, 212
Broughton, 65–67, 96, 111, 135–137
Bury, 18, 52, 64, 69
Clayton-le-Moors, 204
Liverpool, 8, 16–31, 38, 55–75, 91, 95, 125, 140–143, 150, 174–179, 192, 200–202
  Accrington, 65, 204
  Birkenhead, 55, 74
  Bootle, 65–73, 193
  Crosshall Street, 177
  Fairview Place, 201
  Garstang, 66
  Haslingden, 66
  Kirkdale, 31, 72–73, 192, 200
  Mersey River, 71

Mersey Street, 193
Merseyside, 21, 55, 71–74, 89
Morpeth Docks, 74
Regent Street, 193
Saint Anne Street, 202
Seaforth, 193
Toxteth Park, 202
West Derby, 69
West Everton, 72
Manchester, 2, 14, 21–22, 48, 57–88, 103, 125, 133, 164–168
  Ancoats, 85
  Ardwick, 2, 14, 21, 83–88
  Chapelfield Road, 83
  Granby Place, 80
  Granby Row, 80–83
  London Road district, 14, 81–83, 103
  Mellor Street, 83
  River Street, 84
  Salford, 47–48
Oldham, 58, 64, 69, 75, 134
  Soho Forge Square, 64, 134
Pilling, 65
Prescott, 74, 92, 174
Preston, 58, 65–66, 70, 137

Victorian Counties, Parishes, Cities, Towns and Villages

Ararat, 112, 113, 144, 178, 179
Ballarat, 4, 28, 59, 96, 98, 101–103, 111–114, 120–123, 127, 134–144, 159–160, 165, 171–172, 179, 185–189, 200
  Ballarat Base Hospital, 185
  Ballarat, West, 159
  Ballarat Woollen and Worsted Mill, 142–143, 172, 180
  Bridge Street, 138
  Lyons Street, 142
  Phoenix Foundry, 143, 172
  Wendouree, 160
Bealiba, 158
Bears Lagoon, 1, 14, 28, 33, 78, 133–134, 155, 163–169, 172
Beaufort, 113
Bendigo, 2, 4, 31, 57, 79, 96–98, 103–106, 111–115, 121–122, 127, 130–132, 163–165, 171–174, 182, 186, 189, 200, *see also* Sandhurst
  Bendigo Iron Works, 172
  Pall Mall, 126
  Central School or Camp Hill School, 182
Castlemaine, 15, 36, 95–96, 112–114, 127, 170–174, 181, 200
  Castlemaine Railway Station, 177
Creswick, 96, 111, 135–137, 154
Darlington, 175

Daylesford, 135, 155, 171, 187–188
East Janiember, 166, *see also* Janiember
Echuca, 184
Elephant Bridge, 177
Geelong, 19, 24, 30, 35, 60, 89, 90, 91, 92, 94, 95, 110, 112, 133, 134, 135, 136, 137, 138, 144, 148, 149, 150, 159, 160, 173, 174, 177, 183, 199, 203
  Geelong and Western District Protestant Orphanage, 184–185
  Geelong District Kitchener Memorial Hospital, 184–185
Gippsland, 112, 161–162
Harcourt, 173
Hobson's Bay, 51
Indentured Head, 141
Inglewood, 132, 163, 168
Janiember, 163, *see also* East Janiember
Linton, 142
  Linton Park, 142
Loddon River, 165
Maldon, 173
Maryborough, 112, 140
Melbourne, 2, 5, 7, 11, 25, 30–31, 36, 43, 51–52, 61–65, 73, 79, 90–93, 95–103, 111, 113, 130, 140–143, 149–151, 155, 161, 165, 169–181, 188–211
  Abbotsford, 199
  Bridge Road, 205
  Burwood Road, 205–208
  Carlton, 194, 204
  Caulfield, 203
  Cecil Street, 193–194
  Chapel Street, 188
  Collingwood, 27, 193–199, 207
  Collins Street, 194
  Courtney street, 204
  Cremorne Street, 203
  Cubitt Street, 203
  East Malvern, 188
  Elizabeth Street, 194
  Fitzroy, 194–199, 207
  Fitzroy Bluestone Quarry, 196
  Flinders Street, 203
  Flinders Street West, 202
  Footscray, 172
  Hawthorn, 106, 205–207
  Hoddle Street, 194–200, 208
  Kew, 26
  Kew Asylum, 168
  La Trobe Street, 205
  Little Lonsdale Street, 194
  Liverpool Street, 198
  Martin Street, 206
  Melbourne University, 172
  Moore Street, 172
  North Fitzroy, 96, 196–198

North Melbourne, 205
Northcote, 205–207
O'Shanassy Street, 205–206
Park Street, 204
Richmond, 179, 202–205
Royal Melbourne Hospital, 186, 204, 205
Smith Street, 27, 193
South Yarra, 103, 188
Watkins Street, 198–199
Westgarth Street, 197
Williamstown, 160, 165, 172
Williamstown Railway Workshops, 160
Yarra River, 141, 143, 199
Molesworth, 160
Moondarra, 161–162
Moorabool, 150
Murray River, 145, 165
Murray River Railway, 173
Newstead, 173
Port Phillip, 3, 5, 141
Port Phillip District, 45–46, 55, 99
Portland, 135, 177–178, 201
Sandhurst, 2, 4, 112, 121–122, 163–167, 185, *see also* Bendigo
Sandhurst (Bendigo) hospital, 185
Seymour, 172, 179
Serpentine Creek, 163, 165
St Arnaud, 144, 157–158, 181
St Arnaud Hospital, 157
St Arnaud Manchester Unity Lodge, 157
Victoria Hotel, 181
Ulverstone, 70, 157
Talbot, 113, 154
Terang, 24, 92, 174–176
Thorpdale, 162
Steiglitz, 26, 93, 113, 134, 154
Warragul, 162
Wimmera, 161
Wombat Parish, 154
Yarck, 160–161

Goldfields, Mines and Mining Companies

Adelaide Lead, 136
Alma, 140, 162
Amherst, 136
Anglesey, 160
Barkers Creek, 95
Bealiba Reef, 145
Beechworth, 112
Berry Lead, 142
Bonshaw Co., 143
Break O Day, 126, 140
Campbells Creek, 95
Carisbrook, 142
Cathcart, 178

Chalk Junction Gold Mining Company, 142
Clunes, 4, 114
Dunolly, 113, 144
Eureka, 98–105
  Eureka Stockade, 98, 102, 141, 155
Forest Creek, 14, 33–36, 94
  Forest Creek National School, 94
Frenchmen's Lead, 140
Great Extended Eagle Company, 133
Happy Valley, 141
Jewellers' Shop, 143
Last Chance Co., 143
Long Gully, 122, 130–131
Madame Berry, 142–143
Magpie and Frenchman's Mining Company, 142
Magpie Creek, 140
Maxwell Reef, 133
Mount Alexander, 4, 29, 36, 94, 98, 103, 114, 135, 200
Mount Ararat, 178
New Australian Mining Co, 143
New Koh-i-Noor Co., 143
Northern Start Co, 144
Peter's Diggings, 145
Pleasant Creek, 144
Prince Albert Mining Company, 142
Prince of Wales Mining Co., 143
Queen's Birthday Reef, 145
Queen's Jubilee Co, 143
Red Bank, 144
Riddle's Paddock, 151
Specimen Hill, 131, 141
Stawell, 113
Wellington Company, 122, 132–133

Other

Anti-Corn Law League (ACLL), 84, 87
Backhaus, Father, 182
Bailey, William, 142
Baker, 'Captain', 145
Ballantyne, Reverend James, 199
Barkly, Sir Henry, 173
Batman, John, 99
Bear, John, 165
Belfast, UK, 38
Berry, Graham, 15, 80, 103–105, 209, 212
Bonwick, James, 182
Brisbane, Qld., 126
Briscoe & Co, 194–196
Brown Brothers, 122
Brown, Henry, 119–122
Brown, William, 121
Cavanagh brothers, 114
CLEC, 7, 16–22, 26, 33–55, 61–66, 72, 75, 90–91, 95, 102, 203

Index

Clendinning, George, 123
Clendinning, Martha, 123
Cobden, Richard, 84
Cooper, Thomas, 78
Cork, UK, 38
Craig, William, 101
Dash, Edward, 53
Deakin, Alfred, 4
Dublin, UK, 38
Duffield, Charles, 86
Duffield, Lofthouse, Whitfield, 78, 83, 86
Eaglestone, William, 165
Esmond, James, 114
Ettershank, Christina, 165
Ettershank, Edward, 165
Ettershank, John, 1, 2, 79, 155, 163, 164, 165, 166–172
Fawkner, John Pascoe, 99, 102
Foster, John, 97–102
Foulds & Holt, 195–196
Galway, UK, 38
Glasgow, UK, 38
Grant, James McPherson, 14, 155, 167
Greenhalgh, Thomas, 83
Greenock, UK, 38
Grey, George, 14
Hall, Richard, 18, 52–53
Hobart, Tasmania, 96
Horan, Margaret, 166
Hotham, Sir Charles, 98–105
HRH Prince Albert, 43
James, Mayor J.A., 174
La Trobe, Charles, 7, 3–, 40–46, 64, 97–102
Limerick, UK, 38
Lloyd, Sarah, 123
Lloyd, Tom, 123
Lofthouse, James, 86
Londonderry, UK, 38
Longmore, Francis, 167

Loughlin, Martin, 142
Madras, India, 44
Melborn, Cambridgeshire, UK, 11
Mellor & Greenhalgh, 83–84
Mellor, George, 83–87
Mereweather, Reverend, 5
Merrivale, Herman, 35–41, 50
Newcastle, Duke of, 37
Nicholson, William, 103
Nickle, Sir Robert, 101
Norfolk, Duke of, 11, 100–101
Otago, NZ, 126, 132, 140
Pakington, Sir John, 98
Parkes, Henry, 15
Plymouth, UK, 38
Poor Law Board, 22, 42, 50, 66
Poor Law guardians, 45, 49–50, 66
Preston, Richard, 51
Richmond and Chandler, 47–50
Rishton, Charles, 193–194
Sala, George Augustus, 190–191
Seddon, Richard, 3, 14, 31, 57, 103–106, 113, 140, 212
Sligo, UK, 38
South Lancashire Permanent Building Society, 86–87
Stawell, William, 97–101
Sydney, NSW, 51, 101, 155, 165, 192
Syme, David, 30, 146, 170–171
Tea Tree, Tasmania, 96
Tyler, Mary Ann, 129
Wakefield, Edward Gibbon, 37, 45, 148
Walcott, S., 22, 47
Waterford, UK, 38
Wentworth, William, 99
Wheeler, James Henry, 103, 135, 188
Whitfield, George, 84–86
Whitfield, Joseph, 84
Withers, William Bramwell, 101–102

ABOUT THE AUTHOR

Richard Turner graduated as Doctor of Philosophy in History at La Trobe University in September 2019. He was also awarded the Nancy Millis Medal for producing a thesis of exceptional merit. Turner previously had a significant career as a filmmaker, with 21 credits to his name as a director, producer and writer. In the 1980s he was also an important contributor to the gay publications industry in Australia as a journalist, editor and publisher, for *Campaign Magazine*, *Sydney Star*, *Star Observer* and *Outrage*, and as a director of the Gay Publications Cooperative. He also contributed regularly to the *Sydney Morning Herald*, SBS TV, TVNZ, Network Ten and ABC TV.

Lightning Source UK Ltd.
Milton Keynes UK
UKHW040709270521
384461UK00004B/129